THEORIZING
DIGITAL
CULTURES

Sara Miller McCune founded SAGE Publishing in 1965 to support the dissemination of usable knowledge and educate a global community. SAGE publishes more than 1000 journals and over 800 new books each year, spanning a wide range of subject areas. Our growing selection of library products includes archives, data, case studies and video. SAGE remains majority owned by our founder and after her lifetime will become owned by a charitable trust that secures the company's continued independence.

Los Angeles | London | New Delhi | Singapore | Washington DC | Melbourne

THEORIZING
DIGITAL
CULTURES

GRANT BOLLMER

Los Angeles | London | New Delhi
Singapore | Washington DC | Melbourne

Los Angeles | London | New Delhi
Singapore | Washington DC | Melbourne

SAGE Publications Ltd
1 Oliver's Yard
55 City Road
London EC1Y 1SP

SAGE Publications Inc.
2455 Teller Road
Thousand Oaks, California 91320

SAGE Publications India Pvt Ltd
B 1/I 1 Mohan Cooperative Industrial Area
Mathura Road
New Delhi 110 044

SAGE Publications Asia-Pacific Pte Ltd
3 Church Street
#10-04 Samsung Hub
Singapore 049483

Editor: Michael Ainsley
Assistant editor: John Nightingale
Production editor: Imogen Roome
Copyeditor: Sarah Bury
Proofreader: Brian McDowell
Indexer: Elske Janssen
Marketing manager: Lucia Sweet
Cover design: Lisa Harper-Wells
Typeset by: C&M Digitals (P) Ltd, Chennai, India
Printed in the UK

Library of Congress Control Number: 2018935288

British Library Cataloguing in Publication data

A catalogue record for this book is available from the
British Library.

ISBN 978-1-4739-6692-5

ISBN 978-1-4739-6693-2 (pbk)

At SAGE we take sustainability seriously. Most of our products are printed in the UK using responsibly
sourced papers and boards. When we print overseas we ensure sustainable papers are used as measured
by the PREPS grading system. We undertake an annual audit to monitor our sustainability.

CONTENTS

ABOUT THE AUTHOR

Grant Bollmer's research examines the history and theory of digital media. He is the author of the book *Inhuman Networks: Social Media and the Archaeology of Connection* (2016) and has published numerous articles and essays about digital culture. He has taught in the United States, Australia, and New Zealand, and is currently an Assistant Professor of Communication at North Carolina State University and an Honorary Associate of the Department of Media and Communications at the University of Sydney.

ACKNOWLEDGEMENTS

There are a number of people without whom this book would not exist. The initial idea came from conversations with Chris Rojek. Michael Ainsley and John Nightingale have helped shepherd it through to its completion. I thank them all, along with everyone else at SAGE for the work they have done. I began this book while a lecturer in the University of Sydney's Digital Cultures programme, and many of the themes and topics it covers came from discussions with other lecturers, professors, and graduate students in Digital Cultures and in the Media and Communications department, particularly Chris Chesher, Kathy Cleland, Gerard Goggin, Jonathon Hutchinson, César Albarrán Torres, Chris Rodley, and Kyle Moore. My colleagues at North Carolina State University also deserve mention, especially Steve Wiley, Nick Taylor, and JeongHyun Lee, along with my undergraduate students, both at Sydney and at NC State. Katherine Guinness has read through this manuscript time and again, and, above all, remains an endless source of new ideas, repeatedly expanding my intellectual world. I'd also like to acknowledge the undergraduates at NC State and the University of North Carolina at Chapel Hill who tried out drafts of some of these chapters in their classes.

INTRODUCTION

WHY THEORIZE DIGITAL CULTURES?

Theorizing Digital Cultures begins by making a case for the importance of theory for the study of digital culture. This chapter claims that theories should be linked to material infrastructures and physical practices, and also suggests that a major focus of any analysis of media and technology should be to historicize the present in order to figure out what is, in fact, new or specific about the contemporary moment.

TERMS: culture; digital; dominant; emergent; Global South; infrastructures; materiality; residual

THEORISTS: Marcel Mauss, Raymond Williams

EXAMPLES: Corning's 'A Day Made of Glass'; lighting in photography and biometrics; read receipts; virtual reality

Our daily practices have been remade and reimagined by a wide range of **digital** technologies. This refers to the many *computational* devices that exist around us – devices that operate through calculation and mathematical processing, be they smartphones, laptops, or even cars and refrigerators. When we talk of digital media, we often discuss how computers have transformed the ways we communicate, create, and relate to one another. Yet, not all computers are digital, and digital does not only refer to computers. At the same time, the effects of digital media are not just about human practices and human relations. Digital media shape a much wider ecology, one in which human beings are only one part. What does it mean to claim that digital media have transformed our world? What are these changes? How can we understand their significance? And what can we do about them?

Theorizing Digital Cultures introduces many key claims about how digital media relate to the thing we call **culture**. It explains how digital media – in providing a material, infrastructural basis for practices and interactions – affect identities, bodies, social relations, the arts, and the environment. These effects are neither neutral, nor are they inevitable. Rather, the relationship between digital media and culture is *political*. Digital media create differences and oppositions that must be negotiated. They involve power relations that shape what human bodies are and do and legitimate these relations as neutral or natural. This book is designed to provoke questions about our current technological reality, not merely to understand, but to think about how best to *change* ourselves and our technologies – hopefully for the better, in ways that encourage a more egalitarian, democratic, and just world.

It may be best to begin with a concrete example, working our way out to some of these more abstract issues. The name of glass manufacturer Corning may be familiar because of consumer kitchen products like CorningWare and Pyrex. Yet Corning has sold off these well-known brands to focus their attention elsewhere. Instead of cookware, Corning now makes glass for digital technologies – from computer and television screens, to touchscreens and fibre optic cables. Notably, Corning produces the glass touchscreens for Apple products (Apple 2017). These technologies are already ubiquitous. Yet Corning imagines that our near future will be filled with even more screens. In 2011, they released a promotional video entitled 'A Day Made of Glass'. This ad depicts a world filled with interactive glass touchscreens inserted into bathroom mirrors and desks at school. For Corning, a refrigerator is not only an appliance for the storage of food, or a place to display photos. The image reproduced here, for instance, depicts

Figure I.1 Corning's 'A Day Made of Glass'

Source: YouTube.

a kitchen counter as a digital screen, with video and weather streaming live as one prepares breakfast on the same surface (Figure I.1). A fridge, in Corning's future, is a screen for digital information, replacing magnets and paper with interactive images. The fridge, like the mirror and countertop, is a place for social networking and website browsing. Corning's goal with these videos is to emphasize glass as an interface for digital media. The slogan that appears in these videos, 'Enabling a future of communication, collaboration, and connectivity', suggests that Corning's glass – which can conduct electricity and detect human touch – is an essential mediator linking physical space and a seemingly immaterial, computational world of digital data.

Often, the goal of interface design is to make technologies invisible, blending into the everyday architecture of our lives. Yet we only interact with digital media based on the physical qualities of our technologies. If you crack your iPhone screen, the jagged edges you run your finger across will remind you that you're not touching information – you are touching broken glass. The ability to experience digital information depends on the material ways technologies like glass have been reinvented to sense human touch, and software has been designed to respond to tactile interactions. At the same time, our practices, gestures, and bodies adjust depending on how we interact with digital media, especially as new technologies gradually vanish from our conscious awareness.

Many of the innovations depicted in 'A Day Made of Glass' are variations on digital media we already use. It does not depict a radically different future. It shows us how our lives have already been shaped by digital interfaces.

Who we are, how we come to understand our identities and bodies, and how we relate to others are all influenced by digital media. These relations are a product of the physicality of technology. Our technological surfaces – be they an interactive glass countertop or an iPad – obscure a large number of complex processes, in which technologies are designed to respond and communicate throughout the planet, collecting, storing, analyzing, and transmitting information at a speed that seems instantaneous, all while withdrawing into the background of our world and remaining an imperceptible part of the environment.

Think about the most basic aspects of your life, from communication between friends and family, to shopping, to work, to exercise, to relaxing and enjoying entertainment. Digital media have transformed each of these practices. It's difficult to find something that, in some way, hasn't been affected by digital media. Our lives have been shaped by the physical capacities of digital technologies to record and analyze the data our bodies generate in daily life. Data are used to suggest ideal or optimal ways of acting, guiding our conduct in the name of efficiency. The ability to successfully navigate work and personal life depends on effortlessly using digital media. Maintaining friendships and relationships often requires the management of information. Getting – and keeping – a job may depend on one's ability to use social media and create an individual brand that has value, in and of itself (Gregg 2011; Marwick 2013). Even sleep is modified by technologies that manage time and the pace of our body's internal clock (Crary 2014; Sharma 2014). This extends from wearable devices that quantify our movements (and track when we wake and when we fall asleep), to apps that analyze how well we sleep throughout the night. Sleep Cycle, an example of one of these apps available as I write, has you place your phone on your bed next to your pillow. Using motion data recorded by an iPhone, the app analyzes how well you sleep based on your movements in the night, determining an optimum time for you to wake up. Another, SleepBot, in addition to motion data, uses sound recording to note if you're having breathing problems, or if noises in the night happen to be disturbing your rest.

At the same time, social media corporations assume you have, to paraphrase Facebook CEO Mark Zuckerberg, one 'authentic' identity, which can be understood and managed through uploaded data. The data you generate from the mere use of digital media commodifies your body and identity. Your online activities are tracked through 'cookies' – small pieces of data that are sent to your computer while you browse the internet, designed to record your actions and choices – and other innovative methods for capturing and knowing interests and tastes, often without your awareness.

These technologies are used to create databases of consumer data, which are analyzed and interpreted (usually though computational data analytics software) to predict and control future behaviour (Andrejevic 2013; Turow 2011). The 'big social data' produced through digital media (Coté 2014) are assumed to represent you and your abilities, to such an extent that your Facebook account could eventually play a role in calculating your credit score, determining whether or not you qualify for a credit card, loan, or mortgage (Taylor & Sadowski 2015).

But we can neither limit the impact of digital media to personal identities or individualized actions, nor can we restrict digital culture to the interactions we have over social media. Digital technologies have fundamentally changed how we approach 'old' media. Reading has proliferated with digital media, if in ways that are vastly different from printed books (Hayles 2012). Netflix and other online streaming services have changed how film and television are distributed, consumed, and produced, reinventing how we share and talk about the shows we watch, along with the industrial context of media production and media ownership (Lotz 2014). Even more broadly, creative expression often employs a 'postdigital' style that reflects on the limits and potentials of digital technology (Berry & Dieter 2015), reliant on software packages like Autodesk Maya, Ableton Live, and Adobe Photoshop, which are often distributed through informal, piracy-based economies via peer to peer digital sharing, as are many songs, books, and videos made today (cf. Borschke 2017). Software plays a massive role in shaping culture, transforming almost all previous forms of media and technology, and yet is rarely thought about at all (Manovich 2013).

The enduring legacy of digital media is to imagine what we see on the screen of a computer as an 'immaterial' space permeated by the free flow of information and communication, untethered from the 'real', physical world, enabling all sorts of 'virtual' possibilities. The internet, we have been led to believe, is a network that spans the totality of the globe, transcending distance and accelerating time to perpetual instantaneity. The perfectly reasonable question, 'Where is the internet?', has often been mocked as something only the most technically illiterate could possibly ask. The claim that the internet is 'a series of tubes', a phrase coined in 1996 by United States Senator Ted Stevens, a Republican from Alaska, has routinely been ridiculed, even though, in many ways, the internet *can* be described as a series of tubes (Blum 2012).

We often understand the internet as a placeless, ephemeral 'thing', best embodied by the popularity of the 'cloud' metaphor to describe data storage.

But these beliefs are seriously misguided. In spite of these popular claims about virtuality and 'clouds', the above changes are all an effect of the **materiality** of digital media. They result from what digital media do at an infrastructural level. Material **infrastructures** – the screens, wires, servers, protocols, and software of digital media – guide the global circulation of capital, communication, and transportation, underwritten by algorithms that sort, control, and manage bodies and commodities.

Our lives rely on these digital infrastructures. Our cities and houses are becoming 'smart', just as our phones already have, by adding sensors and software into buildings, streets, and public spaces. Our environment is permeated with cameras and computers that are on and connected, gathering data and responding to changes in real time. Our appliances, from our refrigerators to our cars, increasingly depend on software updates managed through wireless connectivity, becoming part of 'the internet of things' – a connected network of everyday objects linked to the internet that enables the management and transfer of data by things like lightbulbs, thermostats, and ovens. This global system of consumer devices requires the proliferation of routers and relays, connected to distant server farms that are themselves connected through a surprisingly small number of undersea cables (Starosielski 2015).

Digital media consume a massive amount of energy, create an ever-expanding amount of toxic waste, devour a staggering quantity of the world's raw materials, produce a class of labourers whose livelihoods depend on scavenging waste in the **Global South**, and rely on supply chains that exploit workers to produce massively expensive yet ultimately disposable technological devices (Maxwell & Miller 2012; Parikka 2015). Digital media influence a wide range of social and cultural relations, from daily interactions to the reshaping of the environment and labour throughout the world. So how can we possibly understand these changes? How might we have an impact in doing something about them?

'THEORY' FOR DIGITAL CULTURES

Digital media infrastructures require theory to explain their significance and their politics. There are many explanations for the changing relationship between the digital and the 'whole way of life' we refer to as culture (Williams 1983a: xvi). This book is an introduction to some of the arguments about these changes. It approaches theory as a set of tools we can use to understand ordinary practices and beliefs, with the specific intent of intervening in or changing the everyday world around us (cf. Nealon & Giroux 2012). This book attempts to think theoretically about a series of issues and problems provoked by digital media. Different problems, after all, require different theoretical approaches. This book is designed to give you the materials for thinking about and transforming your own daily life, and hopefully the lives of others, especially as the most fundamental, basic facts of your existence are permeated by digital media. In this book, theory is not something divorced from practical reality. Theory is not an intellectual activity that has little relevance beyond the walls of a university. Instead, *theory is a way to understand the world and intervene in it.*

In many ways, you are already engaged in the practice of doing theory. Everyone does theory in some way or another. You have a number of ideas about how the world works, of how people think, of what's right or wrong, of what's good or bad. These beliefs are all theories about your world and how you relate to others. Your beliefs are tied to how you behave and act, although they may also contradict how you act. Often, many of these beliefs are not things you recognize consciously but are what you understand as common sense. Even more subtly, they are built into the actions you perform when you train your body to do something, regardless of any conscious awareness of this 'theory'. This way of defining theory may seem strange, because it emphasizes how thought cannot be distinct from a set of practices.

A way of framing this can be seen with how, in French, there's a distinction between two kinds of knowledge: *savoir* and *connaissance*. *Connaissance* refers to 'knowledge of', as in 'I know about you' or 'I know about philosophy'. Most of the time, in English, this is what we mean by theory or knowledge, and is what we mean when we talk about beliefs or thoughts. *Savoir*, on the other hand, refers to knowledgeable practice, of knowing 'how to'. *Savoir* is still knowledge, and still about theory, even if it may not clearly be about 'thought'. And, while it's important to differentiate between these kinds of knowledge, they are often linked. 'Knowledge of' and 'how-to' are associated when we think of what theory is and does.

If you're an athlete or a musician, for instance, you've long practised a specific way of performing a sport or playing a musical instrument. This is done with the assumption that there is a best way to perform a specific act. I may 'know of' many different strategies for playing a game, for instance. But these strategies only work if I also know 'how to' actually perform them. These different strategies are theories, and they aren't always things you consciously contemplate. You practise so you can perform without thinking about your actions. But specific techniques change over time, even if significant changes may not be noticeable in one's own lifetime.

Many advances in the history of sport or music come from people challenging assumptions, asking why we accept a specific practice or technique as best. Why do we think of one way of running as better than another? Why do we assume that a specific way of performing music sounds good whereas another way sounds bad? The great anthropologist Marcel Mauss once talked of how he learned to swim in the early twentieth century: 'In my day, swimmers thought of themselves as a kind of steamboat', in that they'd swallow water and then spit it out again (1992: 456). Clearly, we no longer swim like this. A different theory now informs how we swim, which results in different practices. When a new, improved way of swimming began to be taught in Mauss's own lifetime, he found it difficult, if not impossible to forget the way of swimming he had learned in his youth. Today, the influence of technology on competitive swimming is fairly obvious. Many Olympic records have been broken in recent years, in part because of specific swimwear fabrics designed to reduce drag in the water. In 2016, Olympic swimmers like Michael Phelps engaged in the traditional Chinese medicine therapy called 'cupping', which involves suctioning glass cups onto one's skin for several minutes for its supposed therapeutic and competitive benefits, although cupping has been around for millennia and is regarded by many as pseudoscience. The theory has changed, but that theory never exists completely outside a performed, material act. What we think and what we do are linked, even if they may contradict each other as well. We may know that a different technique may be more efficient or safer, and yet we may still act differently.

This is not to imply a kind of radical relativism, in which value depends merely on individual judgement. Sometimes there are clear ways of making judgements. One way of performing a specific sport can be judged according to who wins and who loses a competition – and in terms of the physical effects on human bodies. A method for running that consistently results in victories but permanently damages a runner's legs isn't very good, although this would involve ethical and moral questions about the value of a human body in relation to competition. Mauss's old method for breathing underwater would result in much slower swimming, along with the unpleasant potential of accidentally inhaling water. Our practices change, along with the theories that inform our practices. The ways we have of evaluating these practices and theories also change over time. In understanding our present, we should think historically, questioning where our theories came from, and what assumptions we're making if we take them as natural.

Things are rarely clear when we turn to judging politics and the arts. What differentiates 'high culture' from 'low culture'? Is it about specific kinds of technical mastery? Is 'good art' a result of the skill of the artist, their command of the paintbrush or camera? Or is 'good art' about creative originality? About how a specific idea has never been expressed before? Or is it about popularity? Is 'good art' merely what's the most popular? Is it simply about the tastes rich people happen to have, when compared to the tastes other people happen to have? Where did these ideas about high and low culture, or good and bad art come from? The way we judge art often relates to abstract ideas we have about what 'good' art is and what it is supposed to do. What do these judgements do in terms of shaping practices and politics today? What if a different way of understanding the social and political function of art was better, or merely different?

We can think about our practices with digital media in a similar way. Theories inform how we interact online, even if we may not consciously recognize them. For instance, if you send a message with Facebook's Messenger app, it will tell you if and when it is seen by the recipient. This is called a 'read receipt', and most forms of digital messaging, from email to Snapchat, have the capability to generate read receipts even if few do this in practice. What does it mean if a recipient doesn't respond immediately, even if Facebook tells you that they've seen your message? Your assumptions are informed by theory, in that they are guided by abstract beliefs about how people use Facebook to communicate, and what it means when people use Messenger in a specific way. This theory may also affect how you respond to incoming messages over Facebook. Maybe you stop looking at Messenger until you're ready to respond, because you know full well that in looking at a message, the other person will then know that you've seen it and may make assumptions about why you haven't responded immediately.

Our practices, be they playing a sport or using Facebook, are all bound together with theories, which are themselves bound together with techniques and technologies that mediate relations. Practices are ways of acting that express larger, abstract beliefs about the world. This means that theory is not just something you have in your mind. Theory is a model for action, of how to understand and make sense of the world in which you live. To change these practices – to question reality, to invent new techniques, to merely create something different – means looking towards theory with the goal of *doing* and *changing* things. So, to give a concise definition, in this book *theory is a process*. It is *an abstraction that informs habits and practices*. And, most importantly, *theory changes based on context*. Critically evaluating theory enables us to modify our old habits and practices, or even produce new ones.

This does not mean that we can think of ourselves as autonomous individuals, where our interventions end at a mere change of personal behaviour, or that personal beliefs about the world are good enough to explain and intervene in what's actually happening around us. Theories should attempt to explain and intervene in larger contexts. They are based on *evidence* that can generalize beyond a single person's experience. They have an explanatory force that differentiates them from beliefs. The power of a good theory is found in how it explains and provides a new way of thinking about a range of everyday practices, often with the political intent of reinventing those practices. Theory is neither a description nor a subjective judgement. Theory comes from an examination of a broader context, and attempts to invent a way of reframing how we understand and act within that context.

Today, this means directly engaging with a context defined by technology. As the philosopher Avital Ronell once remarked, 'There is no off switch to the technological' (1989: xv). The influence of digital media does not disappear if we happen to turn off our smartphone and place it in a drawer, out of sight. Infrastructure may mostly be invisible, but just because we don't see it doesn't mean it's not there. The internet does not stop shaping how we think of ourselves and others whenever we may be 'disconnected'. There is no 'digital detox' that comes from taking a break from our devices. Our technologies still shape the larger context in which this break may occur. Unless we're willing to go completely 'off the grid' and live a truly alternative lifestyle detached from the rest of society (which is always a possibility, I might add, if one that requires the maintenance of specific boundaries that may not be clearly marked), we inevitably return to a world shaped and defined by digital media. Even then, planetary transformations associated with global warming are directly intertwined with our use of digital media, the energy it uses, and the waste it produces. The air around us is filled with radio waves and wireless signals, even if we never use a mobile phone or Wi-Fi.

Once we get to a scale that moves beyond individual behaviour and awareness, there is no complete escape from digital media. Thus, we must turn to theory to understand the specific influence of digital media on our lives today beyond a simplistic view that treats technologies as objects humans use, subject to human will. We must move beyond a narrow perspective that treats our own individual efforts in controlling and managing the influence of technology as good enough to mitigate against the effects of technology throughout society. The world is much larger than what we observe and know from individual experience, and any intervention must occur at a scale beyond that of the individual – and any attempt at theorizing must move beyond individual behaviours, beliefs, and feelings.

This book claims that theorizing digital cultures is a necessary task in understanding both the specific and general effects of digital media. To theorize is to look out at our world, at what appears to be empirically given and true, and ask: How did this world come to be? What assumptions am I making when I accept something as common sense? To theorize is to understand the historical processes that created our world, the implicit understandings that guide what appears as normal or natural, and to demand: How could this world be different? What would need to happen to make it different? Theory is a necessary detour in asking these questions, a detour through abstraction that is directed towards understanding the concrete reality of the world and how to change it (cf. Hall 2003).

This means understanding technologies not as neutral objects, but as sites of political power. It means examining how technologies treat different bodies differently, positioning some in authority and some to be controlled and managed. This is the case for even the most seemingly neutral aspects of media and technology. You might not think that lighting in photography and film, for instance, has any political valence. Yet lighting has long privileged white bodies over black ones, a bias that emerges from the physical quality of film stock, the techniques used in cinematography, and assumptions that then guide practices devoted to realism in photography and cinema. As Richard Dyer has elaborated: 'The photographic media and, *a fortiori*, movie lighting assume, privilege and construct whiteness. The apparatus was developed with white people in mind and habitual use and instruction continue in the same vein, so much so that photographing non-white people is typically construed as a problem' (1997: 89). Practices in photography and cinema are a combination of the *material, physical qualities of media* (film stock, lighting, the physical reflectance of skin, the way the medium stores light, etc.) and *beliefs* that inform the way media is employed (typically, racist beliefs that position white bodies as more significant than black ones, where, consequentially, the medium obscures black bodies through the use of lighting in photography and film).

These biases continue in the development of digital biometric identification technologies used in both airport security and social media, which likewise privilege some bodies over others in how technologies are designed. They are designed to recognize white faces, while the faces of those who are not white may not be clearly identified. Given how systems are programmed, this may mark a non-white body as 'risky' simply because the technologies in use cannot properly identify the features of that body (Gates 2011; Magnet 2011).

This is not limited to race, or even traditional understandings of surveillance and control. For instance, software designed to detect pornographic images (usually to automate censorship on social media) is programmed with a specific model of what pornography is in the first place, which tends to reproduce the beliefs and desires of those designing the software. 'Computer scientists, an overwhelmingly straight male population, are creating algorithms to identify a narrow, conservative, straight male conception of pornography' (Gehl, Moyer-Horner & Yeo 2017: 531). The way that software and hardware are designed records bodies differently based on a combination of the physical properties of media and culturally normative values perpetuated and enforced by media.

Technologies emphasize some acts, behaviours, and bodies while discouraging or punishing others. Digital media destroy the environment while suggesting our data are somewhere in the cloud and our devices must be shiny, new, and cool to be of value. And, too often, the inevitability of technological progress is assumed to be so natural that there is no alternative to more devices, more media, and more information. To understand our current context requires a serious look at how technologies enable or prohibit specific acts, how they transform identities and bodies, how they reshape creative expression. Where did these practices come from? What do they do? How can we change them, without making the incorrect assumption that technologies are neutral?

THE IMPORTANCE OF DATED EXAMPLES

The concepts in this book are explained through examples, many of which are either recent or are only a few years old at the time I write this. Some of these examples may strike you as dated. Even if they do not now, in just a few years they will be. This is inevitable whenever we talk about digital media. What seems to be significant now will become something obscure in mere months. So why should we be concerned with dated examples?

Dated things give us an historical perspective on current events. As the renowned literary critic Fredric Jameson once proposed, 'Always historicize!' should be an imperative for any attempt at cultural analysis (1981: 9). Understanding our present requires thinking about the past, which allows us to better discern what's new about our current moment. What might be genuinely new may not appear to be very flashy or interesting, and thus may be difficult to notice as our attention is drawn towards something that appears particularly strange but is in fact quite common in the history of media and culture.

For instance, the fact that there are people who have died and have active Facebook accounts currently seems weird and new. Yet, one of the uses of recording technologies going back to the nineteenth century has been to record and communicate with the deceased (see Bollmer 2016: 115–133; also see Andriopolous 2013; Peters 1999; Sconce 2000). Throughout the history of technology, one function of media has been to make someone who died reappear. There's a longstanding link between media, ghosts, and theological beliefs about the afterlife (most obviously seen in how a medium is also someone who can communicate with spirits). The strangeness of seeing someone who has died on social media is not a particularly new feature of digital media. This example demonstrates how we have to think of digital culture as a combination of the old and the new.

One of the major figures who guided the development of cultural studies, Raymond Williams, divided culture into the categories of **dominant**, **residual**, and **emergent**. We can use these three categories to help us avoid mistaking something that may be very old as new.

Dominant refers to that which is the commonly accepted logic at any one point in time. Yet this dominant does not characterize everything (Williams 1977: 125). There are always points that escape this dominant, points that cross the old and the new – the residual and the emergent.

Residual refers to that which 'has been effectively formed in the past, but it is still active in the cultural process, not only and not at all as an element of the past, but as an effective element of the present' (Williams 1977: 122). There are two distinct kinds of history through which we can identify the continued effects of these residual elements of culture (see Jameson 1981: 9).

First, we have a history of things and objects. This aspect of our history is relatively simple. Many of the technologies we use are quite literally old. From television and telephone wires to the internet, our present is made up of infrastructures that extend back decades – if not centuries – into the past. Power grids in the United States, for instance, are regularly criticized for relying on ageing infrastructure, built as they are upon dated engineering ideas and obsolete organizational structures. And even new trends are often reliant on old media. People still fetishize vinyl records, and old typewriters seem to be interesting to some. Our present is permeated with media and objects that are 'residual' (cf. Ackland 2006).

Second, there are the narratives we tell about these media, which are also often exceptionally old. We may decry how people are distracted by their smartphones, disconnected and detached from the surrounding world. Fears of distraction, however, date back to at least the late 1800s and early

1900s (see, for instance, Crary 1999). These same fears characterized how people discussed, for instance, the kaleidoscope. The invention of the kaleidoscope coincided with fears of distraction in a world of spectacular images, in which the kaleidoscope was thought to be a rejection of reality (Farman 2015). Many of our beliefs about the value of connectivity can be linked to changes around the same time (Bollmer 2016; Otis 2001). Stories about the internet and how it transcends space and time date back to Victorian-era claims about the telegraph (Carey 1989; Standage 1998). Worries that new technologies will destroy our memory echo claims made in Ancient Greece, most notably by Socrates in the dialogue *Phaedrus*, in which Plato complains of writing destroying memory.

Digital media are made up of many very old things, both through physical infrastructures and larger belief systems. So, while we tend to celebrate the newness of anything associated with digital media, there's a lot of residual aspects that shape digital culture. Understanding technology in the present requires a view that looks towards the past, otherwise we mistake something as new when it's actually residual. It is only by looking towards the residual that we can understand what Williams refers to as the **emergent**, the 'new meanings and values, new practices, new relationships and new kinds of relationships [that] are continually being created' (Williams 1977: 123). We can only understand what's new by looking at what's old.

Also, the persistence of older technologies and narratives often transform – somewhat surprisingly – something that was once residual into a newly emergent paradigm. Until a few years ago, it was generally thought that the hype surrounding virtual reality had died. The fantasy of being in a simulated body in a simulated space, a fantasy that drove a lot of technological development in the 1990s, seemed to be a relic of that era. Yet, with the rise of the Oculus Rift, a virtual reality headset initially designed for videogames, the promises of virtual reality appear to be coming back into style. In 2014, Facebook purchased the Oculus Rift, promising at their annual F8 conference that the future of social media is intertwined with virtual reality. What once was thought to be dead and gone has returned with a surprising vengeance. It is possible that the VR hype that exists as I write this is little more than hype, however. The Oculus Rift has not been nearly as popular as anticipated, and it seems that excitement about VR may vanish yet again.

Virtual reality is not new. It is a product of a history of simulation that goes back to Victorian-era toys, the stereoscope, and the flight simulator (see Hillis 1999). Its promises repeat narratives of transcendence that have long characterized discussions of new technologies – discussions we will review in the next chapter. But to understand the persistence of virtual reality requires us to look back to both the history of technology and the history of narratives told about technology. This means that we should not dismiss any example as merely dated, but as part of our shared technological history – and looking back at that history will reveal how many of our narratives recur over and over again, often with subtle differences. Examining this history can disclose points in the past when a different future was imagined, revealing 'progress' to be not a single line that moves forward to the present, but a series of intersecting trajectories, the movement of which is marked by contingency rather than certainty – our current moment is, in many ways, based on an accumulation of accidents and errors. Embracing this view opens up new pathways and ideas in the present, and new ways to challenge the 'naturalness' of our digital culture (Parikka 2012; Zielinski 1996).

There is another, more simple reason to embrace dated examples. This book serves as a document of the moment in which it was written. As such, this is a way of recording information about the present and the beliefs and claims through which we make sense of technology. The examples chosen are not neutral but are part of the process of theorization that I am attempting to describe. So, we should always embrace these 'dated' examples because, in illustrating concepts, these examples serve to define just how our concepts make sense of the world.

This book is divided into two parts. The first reimagines what we might mean by the term 'digital cultures'. Chapter 1 looks at how 'digital culture' has been previously theorized and sketches how this book understands digital culture as the intersection of material infrastructures, historical narratives, and possibilities enacted by physical bodies. Chapter 2 defines 'culture', drawing on two different traditions, that of Raymond Williams and British cultural studies, and that of Bernhard Siegert and the German media theory of 'cultural techniques'. Chapter 3 describes what we might mean by the term 'digital', expanding it far beyond the simplistic and incorrect binary that contrasts digital with analogue.

Part II develops our definition of digital cultures to touch upon many of the key theoretical debates that are important for understanding digital media today. Chapter 4 looks back at the legacy of cybernetics and how it shapes what we imagine technologies and bodies to do, especially in terms of the problematic history of 'posthumanism' and the fascinating claims of second-order cybernetics. Chapters 5 and 6 move from this history of cybernetics to examine how digital media shape human identity and the capacities of biological bodies, both in terms of online performances of self and in terms of the augmentation and reinvention of human biology. Chapter 7 looks at the role of aesthetics, sensation, and affect in digital culture, reviewing some of the major arguments of classical aesthetic theory and how these claims have been reinvented or reimagined because of the possibilities of digital media, and Chapter 8 examines specific judgements and forms that are often used to describe digital media. Chapter 9 conceptualizes the role of infrastructure in shaping social relations, with a specific focus on how digital media transform the state, political economy, and the environment. We conclude with a brief speculation of what comes after digital culture, given recent developments in quantum computing and other changes that speak to a reinvention of 'the digital'.

Let's now turn to define in more depth 'digital cultures', along with some of the historical implications this phrase carries with it.

PART I

DEFINING DIGITAL CULTURES

1

WHAT ARE DIGITAL CULTURES?

This chapter reviews the legacy of the term 'digital culture', updating it to provide a framework for thinking about digital media and its cultural significance. This framework ties together narratives about technology and its infrastructural materiality, alongside the physical capacities of the body – human or otherwise. In providing this framework, this chapter discusses the importance of materiality in media studies, conjoined with attention to narrative.

TERMS: collective intelligence; cultural determinism; digital dualism; epiphylogenesis; liminality; materiality; metaphysics; metaphysics of presence; noosphere; print culture/oral culture; technological determinism; technological Singularity; Web 2.0

THEORISTS: Tom Boellstorff, Jacques Derrida, Milad Doueihi, Nathan Jurgenson, Pierre Lévy, Marshall McLuhan, John Durham Peters, Bernard Stiegler

Throughout this book, I'm using 'digital culture' to refer to the general context in which the changes mentioned in the introduction have taken place. This term is, however, somewhat old, and its present use does not precisely follow the claims with which it is commonly associated. Many current invocations of digital culture refer to social media and smartphones in everyday life, along with the practices performed by individuals online (e.g. Dobson 2015). This follows a version of media studies that suggests our key focus should be on investigating what *people* are doing *with media* (Couldry 2012). Given the sheer proliferation of digital media, this means that we might say that the 'digital' in digital culture is redundant. But I would advise against doing this. Concepts become less useful as they become synonyms for nearly everything, and the digital does not touch everything in the same way. The difference between digital media and culture is a difference we should maintain.

The plural 'digital cultures' is better, as there is no one, singular digital culture. Digital media are distributed unevenly across the globe, and the effects of digital media are not uniform. Even if I use the singular 'digital culture' in this book, I must stress that *there are only digital cultures* – the ways that digital media have influenced culture are different in specific places and at specific times. Given the vagueness of the term digital culture today, we're going to review how it has been defined in the past, and how that definition has changed over time. And while using 'digital culture' to refer to what people do with digital media is completely valid, there should also be more of an attempt to pin down what we mean by this phrase. In fact, we should reject many of the associations that characterized digital culture in the 1990s and early 2000s in favour of a more complex understanding of both 'digital' and 'culture'.

We'll continue with this task of defining digital and culture as separate, if linked, concepts in the next two chapters. In this chapter, I want to discuss historical associations that have characterized digital culture – associations we should question and challenge. In particular, we should refuse a theological way of thinking of digital media as a **metaphysical** perfection of the human. Technology has often been endowed with spiritual abilities, and many of the ways we talk about digital media are remnants of religious beliefs that position technology as a kind of god. Instead, I claim, we should think of digital culture as made up of three elements, *narratives* about technology, *material infrastructures* that shape communication, and the physical capacities of *bodies*, human or otherwise, in their ability to move and perform specific acts. Digital culture is found at the intersection of these three elements.

PAST WAYS OF DEFINING DIGITAL CULTURE

The Theology of Digital Culture

Throughout the 1990s and early 2000s, 'digital culture' was one of several names used to describe the cultural impact of computational technologies. It arrived alongside 'technoculture' (Penley & Ross 1991) and 'cyberculture' (Bell 2001). Digital media were (and by many, still are) thought of as 'new media' (Lister et al. 2009; Manovich 2001), representing a distinct historical and cultural break.

These terms often referred to utopian, even *theological* technological potentials. Media have regularly been imagined as technological gods that, through communication, unite people across the planet, absorbing and fusing different bodies into one. This is a **metaphysical** understanding of technology, where media perfect some human essence that may otherwise be obscured in daily life. For instance, human beings are imagined as fundamentally social and communicative. The fact that we regularly misunderstand each other, then, is a problem. The essence of the human, the theology of digital media suggests, will be revealed once we can finally understand others, directly knowing and feeling their experience – at least supposedly. We've long imagined how media will correct for the fact that we do not have access to what another person is thinking or feeling, and that we can unite different people through better technologies that have higher resolution and less noise in the transmission (see Krämer 2015; Peters 1999). This understanding of communication comes with spiritualist beliefs about using media to talk to the deceased, be it through photography to visualize spirits, or by 'resurrecting' someone from the data they left behind, having them 'live' forever as a hologram or robot.

This dream of spiritual unification through media has long influenced how we imagine new technology, be it the telegraph, telephone, or the internet. In the 1990s it took a specific form. The online world was thought to be a 'cyberspace' of infinite potential, detached from physical geography. Communities were no longer anchored by proximity, but through open and collaborative knowledge production and sharing. Authorship belonged to no single individual, but a collective body with a shared **collective intelligence**. Pierre Lévy, the French theorist who came up with the concept of collective intelligence, imagined digital culture to be a new stage in human evolution, leading to larger social transformations from how we communicate (Lévy 1997: xix–xx). Lévy saw this new moment as the invention of a **noosphere**, a space of pure information in which individual minds would become synthesized into a collective brain, to be contrasted with the 'biosphere' of biological life and the 'atmosphere' of the air around us. Where 'bios' refers to the Greek word for life, and 'atmos' to vapour or gases, 'noosphere' derives from the Greek word for mind, 'nous'. Lévy adapted this idea from the writings of Jesuit priest and paleontologist Pierre Teilhard de Chardin (1959), who saw human evolution as gradually moving away from physical matter and towards a world of ideas, in which all human minds would become synthesized with god at a time he referred to as the 'Omega Point'.

The theological vision of Teilhard de Chardin, where humans would leave their bodies behind for a noosphere of communication, permeates many common assumptions about digital technologies, which are often influenced by a desire to transcend material reality (Hillis 1999). In early discussions of digital culture, bodies seemed to vanish as social interaction migrated online. Identities were thought to be fluid and flexible, with our physical bodies replaced with self-fashioned avatars that reflected a playful and transgressive approach to embodiment and identity (e.g. Stone 1995; Turkle 1995). The means of production for creative work no longer belonged to an elitist culture industry but were placed in the hands of any fan with the desire and time to produce, consume and share online, collaborating in an online democracy of creativity (Jenkins 2006). States would disappear as the internet would replace federal governments, and national boundaries would be rewritten in the name of global flows of information (Castells 2010; cf. Dean 2009). The distinction between human and computer would wane away, and we would become posthuman cyborgs, synthesized with digital media (Hayles 1999).

These beliefs can be found in numerous examples of science fiction from the past several decades. *The Matrix* (1999) has probably been the most popular and influential depiction of these ideas, but they also inform television shows like *Chuck* (2007–2012), *Mr. Robot* (2015–), *Battlestar Galactica* (2004–2009), and the dystopian visions of *Black Mirror* (2011–), the videogame *Watch Dogs* (2014), the Johnny Depp bomb *Transcendence* (2014), and countless others. Maybe you've heard echoes of these ideas in the words of Silicon Valley elites when they speak of the promises of digital media yet to come, and how the connection and collaboration of social media will enable true democracy and justice, without the regulation of federal governments (see Morozov 2013).

Beliefs associated with the **technological Singularity** (Kurzweil 2005), which have informed both science fiction and research on artificial intelligence and robotics, are almost identical to Teilhard de Chardin's

'Omega Point'. Instead of synthesis with god, however, those awaiting the technological Singularity believe that humans and technology will converge around 2040, when it's predicted that computer processing and storage capacity will become advanced enough to simulate a human brain. As a result, 'Singulatarians' believe that we will leave our corporeal bodies and live forever in a computer simulation, or perhaps inhabiting a robot body. Beliefs associated with digital culture in the 1990s, we can see, have informed popular representations of digital media for some time.

There is a reason for this. These arguments *do* describe the promises of digital media, which are grounded in everyday uses of social media and the internet. You may have personally felt the impact of some of these effects, especially if you have ever used software to write a story or song or video and then shared it online, or if you have contributed to Wikipedia (as your authorship becomes part of a collective project of world knowledge). Many forms of participatory **Web 2.0** technologies change how we understand authorship and sharing. It's easy to imagine the internet as a collaborative space, immaterial, and detached from much of daily life. These utopian, theological beliefs combine longstanding views about the ability of technology to achieve metaphysical perfection with the everyday experiences of collaboration fostered by networked media.

We must acknowledge that these beliefs are wrong, partial, or misguided. They reflect very old ideas associated with theology and religion, not the physical or social effects of new technologies. But the theological perspective we often bring to new technologies is responsible for shaping many of our uses of digital media, and directly informs predictions about the future of humanity and technological progress. An early advocate for digital literacy in contemporary culture, Milad Doueihi, has claimed, 'digital culture is the *only* rival to religion as a universal practice ... [digital culture is] a world religion with its prophets and priesthood, its institutions and sects and believers, its dissenters and schismatics' (2011: 3).

Many of these early beliefs about digital media have little to do with what's happened in the past several decades. With social media, identities have become more rigid. You only have one identity on Facebook, at least supposedly. Even if you do perform multiple identities online, data analytics companies attempt to identify and control the 'real you' beyond your awareness and intention. There is no immaterial cyberspace but rather a proliferation of connected, material devices throughout the planet. Local community and the state, while certainly transformed by digital media, have not been remade into a single, global village. Rather, community has become fragmented, and governments are increasingly building physical walls and detention camps to control migration to reaffirm the power of state government (Brown 2010). There hasn't been an embrace of collective intelligence aside from Wikipedia and other forms of social media deliberately designed to foster collaboration (although usually with the goal of accumulating individuals' user data and commodifying it in some way). Instead, creativity in recent years can be characterized by an intense effort to use digital media to maintain control of creative properties through intellectual property and copyright law. Many of the remixing techniques that characterized hip-hop in the 1980s and 1990s, often celebrated as a major part of digital culture (cf. Deuze 2006), are now more intensely policed than ever in the name of the intellectual property (see Katz 2010; Vaidhyanathan 2001). Laws now explicitly prohibit forms of sharing and creative (mis)use we once had. In fact, with what we know about digital media today, many of the theological beliefs associated with digital media are not only false but have been damaging in terms of obscuring the material, environmental, and social impact of our technologies. Many of these effects continue to be hidden below a theological rhetoric that sees in new technology a digital, communicative saviour for the ills that currently plague the world.

Digital Culture and Print Culture

Not all historical beliefs associated with digital culture have been misguided or incorrect. Digital culture has referred to changes associated with literacy, juxtaposed with **print culture**. Since the work of the foundational media theorist Marshall McLuhan (1962, 1964; also see Ong, 2002), it has been argued that the physical qualities of a medium transform knowledge practices. McLuhan claimed that there is a difference between societies organized around speech and those organized around writing, which are themselves different from societies organized around print.[1]

What would happen if you only communicated through speech? How would your life be different? How would you relate to others? How would you know the past? With books, newspapers, and magazines, our knowledge is reproduced, distributed, circulated, and archived in specific, technologically shaped ways. It's wrong to suggest that oral cultures have no way of storing information. But the fact remains that practices of ritual and oral performance have a different relationship to objectivity, truth, and memory than written documentation. It is possible that writing transforms memory so individuals no longer possess an ability to remember that they may have once had. (For instance, do you remember any phone numbers? Or does your phone remember them for you?) But this is not to suggest that one way of remembering – or one way of communicating – is better than another, or that more technology makes us less human, a point we'll return to later. It is merely to suggest that the way we communicate, in the physical form through which information is transmitted between individuals, has a profound way of shaping how different people relate to each other and to themselves.

Print culture emerges from the technologies we have for writing and reading, producing specific senses of community and nation through the exchange of printed materials (see, for instance, Anderson 2006; Warner 2002). Just as print culture is different from **oral culture**, digital culture signifies a distinct series of changes from print culture. Digital media transform practices of literacy, of reading and writing, and changes in literacy are ultimately responsible for other transformations in 'identity, location, territory and jurisdiction, presence and location, community and individuality, ownership, archives, and so on' (Doueihi 2011: xv). These changes remake the knowledge of history and the jurisdiction of law, potentially contributing to the shaping of democracy through the distribution of knowledge (Davies & Razlogova 2013). But it's quite difficult to figure out what these changes are, to sort out what's genuinely an effect of a new technology or if something has actually characterized social relations for some time.

So, What Should We Do about These Incorrect Narratives?

The radical changes thought to be produced by digital technology in the 1990s and early 2000s never arrived. Instead, we have a history of media – in its infrastructural materiality – and another history of beliefs about what media are *imagined* to do. Many of the things people believe about new technologies are not grounded in material reality. But this does not mean that we can simply dismiss these beliefs as wrong, as if the vast majority of people are merely duped, ignorantly navigating a world they do not understand. Both narratives and materiality are important dimensions of media history.

John Durham Peters makes a similar point though an anecdote about the use of the word 'digital' in Bangladesh:

Because the state has boosted the term so much, *digital* in Bangladeshi slang has apparently come to attach itself to things that are newfangled or modern, including the disposable toilet 'Peepoo' baggies distributed in hopes of reducing the spread of disease and keeping the water clean. This felicitous coinage has discerned a crucial truth: sometimes the digital just collects the same old poop. (Peters 2015: 50)

We should be constantly vigilant about misleading narratives told about new technologies and how these narratives are often handed down from history, reflecting not the actuality of media and technology, but larger beliefs about proper human bodies, well-managed social relations, and an ideal future. They tell us not about something new but repeat the same stories people have been saying about media for decades, if not centuries. But, at the same time, we cannot dismiss these narratives as being merely incorrect, because, as wrong as they may be, they nonetheless shape how people act with and use technology, and they inform values as they are lived and felt.

A DIFFERENT WAY TO DEFINE DIGITAL CULTURES

We need a framework for theorizing digital cultures that can acknowledge three separate elements. First, we must admit that many of the narratives told about digital media are not about digital media, but nonetheless have cultural significance. They are theoretical claims and inform how people believe and act in relationship to technology. Second, we should still acknowledge that digital media, in and of themselves, *do things*. They are infrastructural and provide the grounds upon which human beings act and live. So, we must look for infrastructures, even though they may be buried underneath narratives that may actually obscure what media do. Third, we must embrace how human agency is in dialogue with and shaped by media (Bollmer 2015). Our world only happens at the intersection of narrative, infrastructure, and the capacities of the body (human or otherwise). These three elements are not stable and unchanging. Rather, they co-evolve over time. This leads us to a question that guides the approach we're going to take throughout this book: what does it mean to take a *materialist* approach to digital media?

Materiality

The past decade or so has seen numerous scholars move away from many of the traditional tools and methods of media studies – namely, the analysis of representations and the meanings people make from and with media – to focus more specifically on infrastructure and materiality. Media, after all, have their own material form and often act in ways that do not enter into human awareness. Instead of solely reading representations, to acknowledge the role of media in culture we have to stress that *technologies exist beyond the human world of meaning.* Our technologies act as foundations for human activity that may be invisible to the awareness of most individuals. To address the role of technology requires us to investigate media beyond the meanings we find in images, representations, and interpretations (cf. Hansen 2000: 4).

Why are we only making this move towards materiality now? Haven't technologies always been material? With the internet and network technology, there appears to be, on one hand, a 'dematerialization' of technological objects in favour of ephemeral, digital information. This has incorrectly led a massive number of people to imagine the internet and computers as somehow less than material (see Munster 2014). On the other hand, there has been the convergence of a vast range of different devices into one (Miller 2011: 72–94). We no longer have discrete, individualized boxes in our living rooms, each one for a different form of media – a VCR, a videogame console, a cable box, a DVD player, a Blu-Ray player, and so on. We now have computers that can run any form of media through the same abstract, digital language (Ernst 2013; Manovich 2001).[2] A Playstation 4 or Xbox One, for instance, performs all of the functions that an entire range of different devices used to do. So, we have a seemingly different relationship to the materiality of media, in part because materiality appears to be vanishing. We don't need to own physical storage media anymore, for instance, because we can just download or stream movies, music, and even videogames.

Near the beginning of his influential book *Understanding Media*, Marshall McLuhan states, 'In a culture like ours … it is sometimes a bit of a shock to be reminded that, in operational and practical fact, *the medium is the message*' (1964: 7, italics added). With this axiom, McLuhan proposes that any attempt to understand a medium – say, television – requires the examination of the physical, technological capacities of a TV rather than the content of a television programme. Instead of the meaning of a specific television show, we should examine the way a television reproduces images, the fidelity of its transmission, and how it permits people across the globe to share in watching the same event at the same time even while they are far apart from each other. If we neglect the physical role the medium itself plays, we forget the essence of media: it is the medium, in its materiality, that is the message communicated.

McLuhan defines technology as a means for extending the human body's capacities for sensation and communication. Radio enables a new way to hear others at a distance, for instance. Photography enables a new way to record images and save them over time, changing how we see the past. Similar claims can be made for each medium. Every medium extends the body in space and time, albeit in different, medium-specific ways. Each transforms the sensory capacities of human consciousness. In extending the body, every technology dramatically changes the possibilities for how we experience the self, along with how we relate to those around us, both close and distant. Following McLuhan, one of the tasks of media studies is to compare different technologies to investigate how specific forms of media result in differences in how people understand their own bodies and their interactions with others.

In his own day, McLuhan was a massively popular intellectual figure. Yet, a focus on materiality has often been on the margins of media studies. For decades, it has been scorned as a reductive **technological determinism**. There are reasons for rejections of technological determinism. Many versions of technological determinism *are* misguided and should be avoided. It is wrong to say that technology is the *sole agent* in historical change, as if our media emerge out of nowhere and have clear and guaranteed outcomes. At the same time, erroneous claims about technology's determining agency often have less to do with technology itself than they do with the narrative framing of technology's role in historical events. In making claims about materiality, analysts often conflate ideologies about progress, human nature, or democracy with technology itself, obscuring just what a technology may or may not be doing in the process.

We should never believe, for instance, that Facebook, Twitter, and blogging directly cause democratic revolutions because they inherently democratize the means of communication. This argument has characterized Western commentary on political upheaval in the Middle East, from the so-called 'Twitter Revolution' in Iran during 2009 and 2010, through the events of the 'Arab Spring' between 2010 and 2013. Arguing that these events happened because of social media leads to absurd claims that suggest Western technologies intrinsically promote freedom because of their technological capacities for circulating information and capital, as if history obeyed an equation that would read 'dictatorship + social media = democracy'. This conflates (human) narratives about freedom and democracy with the material agency of the technological. It ignores the reality of surveillance (Trottier 2012), the political economy of social media (Fuchs 2015), and the difficulty in defining 'freedom' in any universal way (Rose 1999). But there is an irony in dismissing these causal arguments as technological determinism. If one argues that the material capacities of technology cause liberal revolution, then one overlooks the materiality of technology, even when speaking in the name of its material effects. The physical capacities of the technological are ignored in the name of human narratives about freedom and information.

In rejections of technological determinism, many scholars assume that human beings are the primary, if only agents producing culture, and technologies are merely tools to enact human desire (e.g. Brunton & Coleman 2014).

The closer one looks at materiality, these authors maintain, the more one simply finds human practices and human acts. This argument, which we can term **cultural determinism**, is just as misguided as ones that locate the force of all historical change in technology, or those that assume technology to be a physical manifestation of longstanding cultural narratives about progress or freedom. One cannot understand the world as if it is entirely shaped by one kind of agency – be it technological will or human will – even though many popular arguments about the effects of technology simply vacillate between these two positions (see Williams 1974: 5–6). Our technologies *do things*, and they often do them in ways not intended by humans, with techniques invisible to human observation or beyond human control. We have to take the objects around us on their own terms, not merely as things that perpetuate human will (see Peters 2015: 88–91).

Any attempt to understand 'culture' requires an engagement with the physical means through which humans engage with each other and the world, which also means that we cannot assume technologies to be 'unnatural'. The human body and its capacities, for instance, are shaped through the technologies we use. Many of us only have 'properly functioning' bodies because we wear glasses or contact lenses, or because we use weight machines and exercise equipment. Yet we don't think of these technologies as perversions that transform our bodies into something unnatural. Why is this? How do these boundaries and limits change over time?

Additionally, technologies and objects do not necessarily need humans. While McLuhan effectively positioned the human body and sensory experience as the locus of his own understanding of media, our world seems to be increasingly run by invisible, autonomous mechanisms that have led numerous theorists to wonder if placing the human at the centre of our world is misguided, suggesting that we should take technologies and objects as independent entities with a will and agency that is far more important in shaping the world than the will and agency of the human (e.g. Bennett 2010; Bogost 2012; Morton 2010).

We still must acknowledge that language, symbols, and narrative, as 'immaterial' as they may seem, are still important and can never be forgotten in our attention to materiality. Narratives are material practices (cf. Barad 2007), and 'meaning' only happens through an intertwining of the materiality of technology and what is and can be said. The philosophers Gilles Deleuze and Félix Guattari refer to this as 'double articulation', in which physical materiality and a symbolic order are articulated at the same time (1987: 43). Like McLuhan, Deleuze and Guattari argue against any separation of meaning or symbolic content from the physical medium in which that content takes place. The medium is still, in a way, the message.

Unlike McLuhan, Deleuze and Guattari do not give complete primacy to materiality, or to human experience. Rather, the physical materiality of a medium is always articulated with a symbolic structure, and this symbolic structure is not inherently linguistic. Our machines read a 'language' that few humans are able to understand. Our body movements and gestures are a non-linguistic 'language' that shape what a body is and how it communicates (Flusser 2014; Salazar Sutil 2015). There is a language to dance, one that permits expression through the body's movements and that cannot be reduced to linguistic meaning or sense. Similarly, when using a Wii, Kinect, or other gestural interface (such as those on the iPhone and iPad), there is a 'language' that comes from how your hands physically move through space and manipulate a device. Pulling two fingers apart or pushing them together to zoom in or out on an image is not an innate way of understanding images and interfaces. It is learned, and it is part of the 'language' through which we manipulate our media today. Symbols, meaning, and materiality are all necessary parts of understanding culture, and are all articulated together. One does not precede another, with technology determining culture or culture determining technology.

Digital Dualism and the Metaphysics of Presence

This emphasis on materiality can lead to some problems. The turn to materiality often accompanies a rejection of language's capacity to order and make sense of reality. Rather than something that helps us make sense of the world around us, language is reduced to a mere side effect of the materiality of bodies, brains, and machines. We should avoid this understanding of materiality. It is a mistake to disregard language or any other symbolic form, especially in how they organize and contribute to making sense and legitimating specific behaviours and practices. Our symbols are material, and speech and language have material effects even if they may not seem to be things we can touch and hold in our hands.

One of the most well-known versions of this mistake is an argument that we can call 'the critique of **digital dualism**'. It goes like this: once we acknowledge that everything is material, we must admit that there is only one world, and the distinctions that people make with the words 'online' and 'offline' are distortions or errors. This distinction is merely symbolic; it does not reflect how the reality of our world is so thoroughly permeated by digital media that any distinction between online and offline is simply false.

This argument sounds very good. The 'online' is not somehow a false, virtual world that exists detached from the rest of our lives, to be sure.

Yet, the critique of digital dualism has many problems. To understand digital culture involves taking everything as being equally real and material but acknowledging that the categories and distinctions people make still matter in producing behaviours and relations.

The critique of digital dualism was proposed by sociologist Nathan Jurgenson. In an essay Jurgenson wrote for the popular journal *The New Inquiry*, he claims:

> we have been taught to mistakenly view *online* as meaning *not offline*. The notion of the offline as real and authentic is a recent invention, corresponding with the rise of the online. If we can fix this false separation and view the digital and physical as enmeshed, we will understand that what we do while connected is inseparable from what we do when disconnected. That is, disconnection from the smartphone and social media isn't really disconnection at all: The logic of social media follows us long after we log out. There was and is no offline. … Digital information has long been portrayed as an elsewhere, a new and different cyberspace, a tendency I have coined the term 'digital dualism' to describe: the habit of viewing the online and offline as largely distinct. The common (mis)understanding is experience is zero-sum: time spent online means less spent offline. We are either jacked into the Matrix or not; we are either looking at our devices or not. When camping, I have service or not, and when out to eat, my friend is either texting or not. The smartphone has come to be 'the perfect symbol' of leaving the here and now for something digital, some other, *cyber*, space. (Jurgenson 2012)

There's a lot here that we should agree with. Digital media are 'enmeshed' with the rest of the world, and the distinction between online and offline is not zero-sum. Yet, against Jurgenson, we must claim that the time spent online and time offline *are* different, and the way these distinctions are produced and maintained rely on a massive and intertwined set of technologies and practices. Acknowledging that both online and offline are material and real does not require the erasure of difference between the two. And just because it's difficult to separate online and offline when smartphones and information seem to follow us everywhere we go *does not mean that this distinction is a mistake to make.*

The anthropologist Tom Boellstorff, in his classic ethnography of the virtual world Second Life, gives many examples of how online, virtual spaces are real, but must be thought of as different from what is referred to as 'the real world'. 'What makes these virtual worlds real', he states, 'is that relationships, romance, economic transactions, and community take place within them' (2008: 245). These elements and experiences within virtual worlds have real effects, with real emotions and personal investments at stake. The same can be stated for social media today, or any other online space. They are real because they mobilize real emotions. They are material, in that they relate to real bodies that only exist in a physical space, even if that physical space is one that relies on networked servers throughout the world, accessed only through keyboards, screens, and software (which, of course, is itself physical, if mostly invisible to immediate experience).

At the same time, many of the people Boellstorff interviewed were quick to note distinctions between Second Life and other parts of their daily lives. There was a 'gap' between online and offline, one that was regularly transgressed or blurred, but a gap regardless. Second Life was something else, not bound by the same rules as other parts of daily life. It was differentiated, if not fully disarticulated, from other spheres of existence. This gap between Second Life and offline life was central to how users of Second Life made sense of their world and their own interactions. Boellstorff, drawing on countless examples from the history of anthropology, argues that these kinds of gaps have long been central to cultural practices, with boundaries set for any number of purposes – although these boundaries are often transgressed. In cultural anthropology, the concept **liminality** (or of the **liminal** or **liminoid**), as discussed by Victor Turner, explicitly refers to these kinds of boundaries. A liminal space is marked off as different, with a boundary. This boundary may be completely symbolic – it may be little more than a circle drawn on a floor, or a verbal statement. Yet crossing a liminal boundary effects a change in whoever ventures over it. According to Turner (1982), rituals of liminality involve a transition between two states of identity, such as rites of passage.

Today, these liminal rituals have been replaced or reinvented through games, ceremonies, and other virtual spaces. In a sense, something like a graduation ceremony or an initiation perpetuates this history of liminal spaces. We enter, and when we exit something has changed. A videogame can be thought of as a liminal space – the rules inside the game are different from those outside it (many theorists of videogames argue that games are bound by a 'magic circle', following anthropologists like Turner). We're nonetheless transformed through our participation in the game, even if we still grasp the lines that differentiate a game from 'real life'. These distinctions are essential for any collective, cultural understanding of how specific behaviours are appropriate – or inappropriate – in specific contexts. This transformation is not 'false' because the boundary is agreed upon by convention and the shared knowledge of the participants in the ritual. It is very real, but there is a distinction, and that distinction is material because it makes a difference in how people perform and relate to each other, even if it may never take a permanent form.

We must always begin by assuming that all practices are material and real. The words we use to describe things – even fictions – are also material and real because they have material and real effects. They shape practices, and they help us make sense of our world and ourselves. At the same time, the distinctions we make – online and offline, fictional and real – are not merely errors. Rather, they mark boundaries that matter. The technologies we use contribute to maintaining boundaries, or potentially challenging them. It's easy to make a distinction between a game and 'real life'. It's not as easy to make a distinction between online and offline when it comes to social media, especially since Facebook and other social media corporations clearly want us to think of the totality of our lives and identities as being on Facebook. But what isn't on Facebook? What can't you communicate over Snapchat? There are many things. There are always limitations and boundaries. To suggest that there's no real difference, and that acknowledging this difference is digital dualism, is to actually miss the very real, material effects of technology. Instead, the critique of digital dualism is a perpetuation of the ideology advanced by social media corporations – especially Facebook – in the suggestion that your Facebook profile is really you, when it is a selected and edited version of you for the consumption of others, based on the data Facebook is able to record, store, and analyze.

A better way to acknowledge the distinction between online and offline is through a concept derived from the philosopher Jacques Derrida, the **metaphysics of presence**, which also allows us to question larger distinctions between the human and technology. In his book *Of Grammatology* (1997), Derrida argues that several undercurrents characterize the entire history of Western philosophy, undercurrents that relate to the distinction between speech and writing. We have historically placed truth in the spoken word, because speech is linked to the presence of the body of the speaker. In learning to write, Western philosophy suggests, something is lost. The *presence* between speakers found in spoken dialogue is removed when people start writing things down. For Derrida, 'logocentrism' names how writing becomes thought of as a lesser 'supplement' to the full presence of speech, as something that obscures and cannot be fully real.

But, at the same time as it privileges the presence of speech, Western philosophy ironically suggests that the cultivation of writing enables the advancement of culture and civilization through literacy, while those who only speak are, supposedly, uncultured barbarians. Learning to write is thought to enable the distinction between nature and culture that suggests that only educated, literate people are no longer 'savages', even if 'savages' are closer to nature because of the 'presence' that comes from not writing. The metaphysics of presence produces this contradiction – that we are simultaneously more developed, and yet more debased, than the others we define ourselves against. And, significantly, this distinction can only be made by those who write – in thinking about human development, we often posit a mythic past that is both lesser and 'more full'.

The work of Jacques Derrida is exceptionally complex, and the metaphysics of presence refers to an entire strategy in philosophy where, in any binary opposition, one of the terms in a specific pair is privileged as more 'full' or more 'original', while the other is secondary or degraded. I'm using Derrida to make a simple point – one similar to claims made by Jurgensen about digital dualism but with quite different implications. Like those who decry a loss of presence with writing, we can only claim the online as being less than real because much of our lives are spent online. Here, Derrida and Jurgensen are making similar points. But, and here's where they differ, *it is not as if we can then say that writing and speech are literally no different, and that distinguishing between them is a mistake.* Speech and writing are different, as is online and offline. The error is to privilege one as being more present than another, as more or less real. This hierarchical distinction is a mistake, not the ability to make the distinction.

So, we must not defer to claims that online interactions are somehow less than real, that online spaces are immaterial and that behaviours on the internet do not matter because the internet isn't 'real life'. This kind of distinction is empirically and theoretically false and can be used to legitimate violence against another. After all, a regular excuse internet trolls invoke in attacking and harassing others is that the internet is less than real. But, at the same time, the differences between how interactions are mediated do, in fact, matter. Speaking is different from texting. Writing by hand is different from typing. And just because social media appear to have permeated all facets of daily life does not mean that we should accept there to be no real distinction between talking face to face and sending pictures over Snapchat. At the same time, we nevertheless need to take seriously the narratives – as wrong as they may be – that suggest that online relations 'aren't real' if we want to understand how theory informs acts and behaviours online.

This same idea can be extended to discuss technology in general. Bernard Stiegler, a philosopher influenced by Derrida, makes this point when he suggests that the human has no real 'nature' that exists outside the techniques and technologies used to order life and culture. Life is, Stiegler suggests, a 'process of exteriorization', and a 'pursuit of life by means other than life' (1998: 17). Stiegler refers to this process as **epiphylogenesis** (1998: 135). He argues that we must begin by acknowledging that human life is inherently linked to a wide range of technologies and techniques, from speech to telling time. Rejections of a technology because it perverts human nature do not make sense. We are naturally technological beings. Instead, we have to evaluate technologies on their specific functions, and how they remake social relations in specific contexts. We should remove overarching claims about human nature when we evaluate the politics and implications of any new form of media. When we turn to this 'nature', we too easily drift back towards beliefs about wholeness, suggesting that technology inevitably degrades human life.

CONCLUSION

This chapter was intended to do two things. First, to review how digital culture has been defined in the past, discussing assumptions that have long characterized discussions of digital media. We should reject many of these claims. But we should retain distinctions made between oral culture, print culture, and digital culture. Second, this chapter proposed a different model for defining digital culture, one that brings together the materiality of communication, the narratives told about media (as correct or incorrect as they may be), and the practices and actions of bodies as they use and are reimagined through new technologies. We'll continue drawing out the implications of this model in the next two chapters, as we define in more detail both 'culture' and 'digital' as key terms for understanding media today.

NOTES

1. McLuhan also believed in the theological capacities of media when he argued that television would bring about a 'global village', restoring communal aspects of oral cultures lost through print and literacy. McLuhan invented the term 'global village' and is responsible for advancing a large number of theological myths about technology.

2. Accounting for the material specificity of computers also requires understanding the differences between programming languages, operating systems, file formats, and how they relate to ways of managing information at a physical, infrastructural level (see Berry 2011; Kittler 2013: 219–229).

2

CULTURE AND TECHNIQUE

This chapter reviews definitions of *culture*, focusing specifically on the work of Raymond Williams and the concept of 'cultural techniques' in the German media theory of Bernhard Siegert. In bringing together these two traditions, it proposes a way of defining culture that can serve to help understand the influence of digital media.

TERMS: base and superstructure; cultural techniques; culture; economic determinism; structure of feeling; technique

THEORISTS: Matthew Arnold, Judith Butler, Friedrich A. Kittler, Marcel Mauss, Bernhard Siegert, E. P. Thompson, Raymond Williams

EXAMPLES: Benjamin Grosser's 'Facebook Demetricator'; Facebook's 'Like' Button

In the last chapter, I suggested that 'digital culture' was a vaguely defined term, and I attempted to propose a framework that positions digital culture at the intersection of narratives, infrastructures, and bodies. Yet, why should we refer to this as digital culture? We still haven't suggested why either **digital** or **culture** are essential terms. Digital culture often refers to little more than what people happen to be doing with digital media. While this is a perfectly acceptable way of defining digital culture, one that has led to a number of politically productive and sociologically stimulating investigations of digital media, there's a lot more to digital culture than people's use of digital media. To understand this, however, we have to go into detail defining both the word 'culture' and the word 'digital'. These words are more complex than most current discussions of digital culture suggest. This chapter focuses on 'culture'. In the next chapter, I turn to a discussion of 'digital'.

It shouldn't be surprising that the culture of digital culture is poorly defined. As Raymond Williams remarked in his book *Keywords*,

> Culture is one of the two or three most complicated words in the English language. This is so partly because of its intricate historical development, in several European languages, but mainly because it has now come to be used for important concepts in several distinct intellectual disciplines and in several distinct and incompatible systems of thought. (1983b: 87)

I am not attempting to suggest a single, definitive definition of culture in this section. Instead, I'll review two different understandings of this word, one influential for media and cultural studies in the Anglophone world – the understanding of culture proposed by Williams – along with an emerging paradigm associated with what is often referred to as 'German media theory', which thinks of culture in explicit relationship to technology through the concept of *Kulturtechniken*, or **cultural techniques**. These two traditions have often been opposed as incompatible. Regardless, I suggest that they can be brought together to addresses the specific function of technology in culture. I do not want to imply that this synthesis of these two traditions is the singular definition of culture. Rather, I'm bringing them together because they permit a way of defining culture that does not exclude the determining role of media and technology, but, at the same time, does not reduce everything to the effects of media and technology.

First, we'll review how Williams defined culture, and how this understanding has influenced contemporary media and cultural studies.

RAYMOND WILLIAMS AND CULTURE

Raymond Williams is one of the founding figures of cultural studies, along with E. P. Thompson, Richard Hoggart, and Stuart Hall. In his classic book, *Culture & Society: 1780–1950*, originally published in 1958, Williams argued that the word 'culture' only achieved its contemporary definition around the time of the Industrial Revolution, alongside transformations in other associated words: industry, democracy, class, and art (1983a: ix). But this concept had a history, one that Williams identified through three different, if interconnected, definitions: *ideal* (or agricultural), *documentary* (or artistic), and *social* (or anthropological).

The *ideal* definition of culture is related to the word's initial relation to practices of agriculture. Before the Industrial Revolution, culture referred to the 'tending of natural growth', and later, 'by analogy, a process of human training' (1983a: xvi). We can hear echoes of this understanding of culture when, in a biology class, you refer to a sample of bacteria or fungi grown in a petri dish as a culture. It is this way of defining culture that gives us the idea of 'cultivating' crops for the best or most ideal growth. It is also the understanding of culture that has given us 'being cultured' as a kind of intellectual and spiritual refinement. Eventually, culture ceased to describe a process of agricultural cultivation, but came to mean 'a general state or habit of the mind', a definition that itself was generalized to mean a 'state of intellectual development, in a society as a whole' (1983a: xvi). Culture is an ideal, and through education we are guided and shaped towards the pursuit of perfection and growth that leads to the maintenance of 'civilization'. The ideal definition of culture suggests that there are universal forms of judgement and moral value, and, as farmers tend to their crops, to culture is to tend, cultivate, and pacify minds.

Williams highlights the foundations of the ideal definition in the writings of Matthew Arnold, an English poet, critic, and school inspector. Arnold, in his book *Culture and Anarchy* (1993), first published from 1867 to 1868 as a series of articles, suggests that his goal is to:

> Recommend culture as the great help out of our present difficulties; culture being a pursuit of our total perfection by means of getting to know, on all the matters which most concern us, the best which has been thought and said in the world. ... Culture, which is the study of perfection, leads us ... to conceive of true human perfection as a *harmonious* perfection, developing all

sides of our humanity; and as a *general* perfection, developing all parts of our society. (Quoted in Williams 1983a: 115, original italics)

Culture is not merely the process of cultivation, but the achievement of a fully cultivated state. Being cultured is to achieve perfection both within the body and mind, through which an individual is perfectly located within society, which then achieves perfection as a harmonious, unified whole all through the means of knowing and learning 'the best which has been thought and said in the world', which Arnold elsewhere referred to as 'the sweetness and light of culture'.

Arnold contrasts culture with *anarchy*, which he defines as social disorder and the inability of individuals to be managed. He often sees anarchy in the working classes with their love of 'their beer, their gin, and their *fun*' (Arnold 1993: 236). For Arnold, workers are, in their drunken raucousness, certainly not cultured. Thus, culture is both a process towards perfection that will never truly be obtained *and* an absolute state essential for proper governance, achieved through the education of liberal arts and humanities. This cultivation pacifies and orders; it governs and controls through the arts. The teaching of the arts and literature is to transform anarchy into culture, guaranteeing civility and proper governance through the care of the educator.

You may have encountered these ideas before, especially in disciplines such as literature or art history. Many scholars in these fields uphold a tradition that goes back to Arnold. What you learn is deemed to be 'the best', and the reason you learn about 'the best' is because knowledge of this subject matter supposedly makes you a better person: cultivated, refined, *cultured*. Since the 1960s and 1970s the ideal definition of culture has regularly been challenged by those contesting the literary and arts canon taught in high schools, colleges, and universities. As Williams and many of those following him have pointed out, these judgements of 'the best' are often bound together with assumptions that reproduce classism, sexism, racism, homophobia, and more. The literature and art thought to be 'the best' has a noticeable bias towards specific identity categories which reflect the interests of those who get to define 'the best', often disguised by seemingly neutral value judgements such as 'beautiful'. Conversely, the judgement of 'boring' or 'ugly' often has little relation to any specific artistic quality, but because they represent identities that aren't of those in power and, thus, do not get to define what is 'beautiful' or 'the best' (Guinness n.d.; cf.

Ngai 2012). Regardless, humanities programmes still legitimate themselves with a logic that descends from Arnold and the ideal definition of culture. You learn about art and literature because it makes you a better, more well-rounded person. It allows you to become 'civilized' and a worthwhile part of Western 'civilization'. Through education in the arts, you become knowledgeable of what is 'best' and can make judgements of what is 'best'.

These ideas about culture and its link to the ideals of civilization are foundational for the history of British imperialism and continue to shape certain ideas that connect 'civilization' with cultural practices, which often legitimate discrimination in the name of 'culture'. A one-time slogan for the multinational corporation Unilever was 'Soap is civilization'. In soap advertising from the Victorian era, hygiene was something that differentiated black and white bodies, and the consumer good of soap enabled proper care and cultivation of a 'civilized' body (Figure 2.1). British soap advertising would regularly employ a trope in which soap, through its power to clean the body, would change black bodies into white ones (McClintock 1995: 207–231). Practices of hygiene were, like the educational practices taught by Arnold, thought to elevate a specific body from anarchy to culture, pacifying 'uncivilized' bodies through techniques that were designed to clean and manage, which were additionally used to legitimate British colonial power in countries like India and elsewhere.

These associations continued even into the 1990s and 2000s. In the 1990s, a series of commercials and ads in the United States for Right Guard deodorant featured professional basketball player Charles Barkley, known for his belligerent antics on and off the basketball court, dressed up as an archaeologist, or on horseback for a stereotypically British foxhunt, stating that 'anything less would be uncivilized' than the use of Right Guard deodorant. While one could argue that these commercials were clearly ironic, parodying classical associations between cleanliness and culture, a Nivia for Men ad that appeared in the September 2011 issue of *Esquire* was not so satirical. It featured a clean-cut black man preparing to throw away what appears to be the head of another black man with a beard and afro hairstyle, all positioned under the tag 'Re-Civilize Yourself'. In all of these ads certain practices – be they hygiene, education, or the enjoyment of fine arts – transform a body into a properly governed, 'cultured' individual. And, in these ads at least, this process of 'civilizing' is clearly linked with imperialism and racial discrimination.

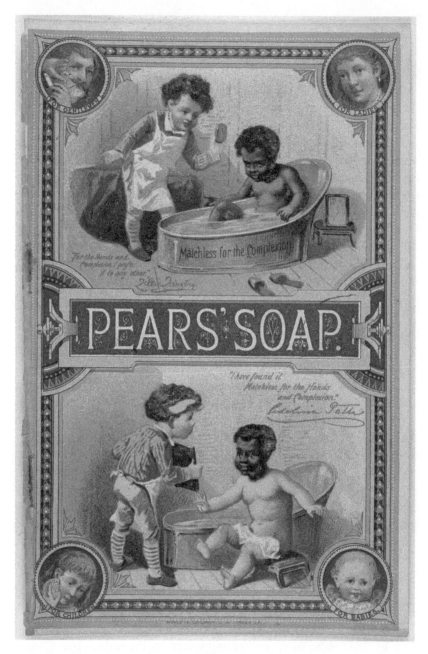

Figure 2.1 An advertisement for Pears' Soap from the 1880s.

The second definition of culture is closely related to the first. The *documentary* definition of culture refers to 'the body of intellectual and imaginative work, in which, in a detailed way, human thought and experience are variously recorded' (Williams 2001: 57), or 'the general body of the arts' (Williams 1983a: xvi). Here, culture refers not only to literature, painting, or theatre, but television, film, and popular culture. In fact, Williams treated this category broadly as referring to any practice that could be thought to produce meaning. The importance of this category does not inherently follow from the ideal definition of culture, even though the ideal definition is often reliant on the arts. The arts do not merely serve as a record of the 'best' that has been thought and said. Rather, the arts *document* 'specific evidence about the whole organization within which it was expressed' (Williams 2001: 62). Placing art and literature into context allows us to approach 'meanings and values as they are actively lived and felt', something Williams referred to as the **structure of feeling** (1977: 132). It is in the arts that the structure of feeling is 'likely to be expressed; often not consciously' (2001: 65), simply because documentation becomes the only way we know and understand our history and our place within it. Documentary culture expresses the past 'to us in direct terms, when the living witnesses are silent' (2001: 65).

Thus, anything that appears to be about shared 'meaning' can be a document about culture – not just art and literature, but popular culture more broadly, which could include comic books, folk songs, and, today, memes and other examples of user-generated content shared over social media. The analysis of culture, for Williams, ceases to be about the judgement of 'the best', but the use of documentation to understand the past, which permits us to understand and intervene in our present. This use of culture, which becomes even more overtly political in the writings of a number of Williams' followers, understands art, literature, and popular culture as forms that document a specific way people experience, know, and make sense of the world in which they live. But this definition of culture begins to strain the closer one looks at the ways people have of documenting the structure of feeling and producing culture. Is there anything that *cannot* express how it feels to live at a specific place and time? If 'we look at the whole period, we recognize that its creative activities are to be found, not only in art but, following the main lines of the society, in industry and engineering, and, questioning the society, in new kinds of social institution' (Williams 2001: 88).

Culture becomes about a vast range of human practices, of ways of documenting existence and shaping and reinventing the larger environment.

This also turns us towards technology and media, as 'culture' begins to refer to the making and usage of *things* and the creation of *institutions*, which are, according to John Durham Peters, 'the domain of media studies. We are conditioned by conditions we condition. We, the created creators, shape tools that shape us. We live by our crafts and conditions' (2015: 51). This may not involve 'meaning' in ways we tend to think of it, which is why I've been placing it in scare quotes, as the 'meaning' of a building or a device is often found in physical practices rather than the symbolic interpretation of its significance (though this is not to say that these things are not made or designed with symbolic significance – any Apple product, for instance, is loaded with a massive amount of symbolic meaning). As well, it should always be noted that documentation depends on what can be written down and stored over time. This understanding of culture points towards the material specificity of what media enable to be recorded, circulated, and accessed, which may mean that a conscious, cognitive sense of 'meaning' is secondary to the physical relationship we have to media.

Williams' third and final definition of culture is the *social*, or anthropological understanding of culture. As 'the best' leads to more general questions about the arts, reframing the arts as the general crafting of things also leads us to a more general understanding of culture. The social definition of culture refers to 'a description of a particular way of life, which expresses certain meanings and values not only in art and learning but also in institutions and ordinary behaviour' (Williams 2001: 57). Culture becomes a 'whole way of life, material, intellectual and spiritual' (1983a: xvi). Probably most clearly associated with the use of 'culture' in anthropology, this final definition is also the broadest and least specific of the three discussed by Williams. Nonetheless, it signifies an emphasis on *everyday life*, on the daily existence of people as they make, contest, and reimagine the possibilities for culture. To use the words of Stuart Hall, '"Culture" is not *a* practice; nor is it simply the descriptive sum of the "mores and folkways" of all societies – as it tended to become in certain kinds of anthropology. It is threaded through *all* social practices, and is the sum of their interrelationship' (1980: 60).

A way to clarify this final definition is through Williams' interpretation of the classical Marxist distinction between **base and superstructure**. In many versions of Marxism, there is a common belief that the 'base', or the material mode of production (capitalism, feudalism, socialism, communism, etc.) *determines* the 'superstructure', which is used to refer to 'all cultural and ideological activities' (Williams 1980: 32).[1] The economic structure of a specific society is thought to shape everything that could be thought of as culture. This is **economic determinism**, as the economic mode of production determines everything else that exists as a singular, causal force. This mentality, in which the mode of production determines all, is referred to as 'vulgar Marxism'. Williams, however, challenges this version of the base and superstructure distinction, noting that the base cannot and should not be thought of as some abstract form that goes by the name of capitalism or socialism. Rather,

> 'The base' is the real social existence of man. 'The base' is the real relations of production corresponding to a stage of development of the material productive forces. ... So we have to say that when we talk of 'the base', we are talking of a process and not a state. And we cannot ascribe to that process certain fixed properties for subsequent translation to the variable processes of the superstructure. ... We have to revalue 'superstructure' towards a related range of cultural practices, and away from a reflected, reproduced or specifically dependent context. And, crucially, we have to revalue 'the base' away from the notion of a fixed economic or technological abstraction, and *towards the specific activities of men in real social and economic relationships,* containing fundamental contradictions and variations and therefore always in a state of dynamic process. (Williams 1980: 34, italics added)

Williams, rather than accept a division that suggests culture is an immaterial reflection, determined by economics, reframes the base as *what people do.* The base becomes the acts that people perform in social and economic relationships, and the superstructure is made of specific representational and creative practices that are often about understanding, organizing, or making sense of the everyday acts that comprise the base. This defines the base as activities of human beings as they make the world in which they live, which includes the technological tools they use and the processes they perform, while the superstructure becomes the symbolic and creative methods people use to make sense of their own bodies, identities, and their place within a larger society. In emphasizing that the base is a *process,* Williams also shows us how these relations are constantly changing, and the signifying practices of culture, while they may be distinct from the base, cannot be said to be detached from (or fully determined by) these everyday acts and processes. Culture becomes the way that the everyday acts of specific people are *expressed* and made comprehensible and ordered in daily life, and how these acts become shared beyond the mind and activities of a solitary individual, which serves to organize and make sensible the everyday relations of production in which we engage. This, as well, makes culture a potential location for political struggle and social change, as culture serves to legitimate the relations that are the base.

E. P. Thompson, a Marxist historian who was also massively influential for the early development of cultural studies, was quite critical of what he saw in some of Williams' theories, and one of his criticisms is particularly important to remember. As we already mentioned, many of Williams' claims, especially as culture becomes a 'whole way of life', have a tendency to transform anything and everything into culture. Yet, as Thompson noted, Williams tended to focus on popular culture and leisure activities, which limited culture in specific ways (1961: 33). Thompson wanted Williams to stress issues of power far more than personal tastes and interests, emphasizing that culture is a field in which classes exert control over others, and in which those marginalized or exploited by dominant interests resist, confront, or challenge those in power. This would, Thompson noted, transform the analysis of culture from an examination of a 'whole way of life' to '"the study of relationships between elements in a whole way of *conflict*"' (1961: 33). I happen to agree with Thompson. We should always be sure to stress issues of power, and we should acknowledge how culture is a 'whole way of life' that emerges from struggle. We should not reduce literally everything to culture. We should not merely accept culture to be how people live and get by. We must emphasize that culture is always permeated by power, difference, and inequality – *that culture matters most when it is a field for conflict and control.*

Culture has multiple meanings, and what we mean by 'digital culture' is a blend of a number of these meanings, usually referring to some mixture of the arts and a 'whole way of life' influenced by practices surrounding digital media. I think Thompson's reframing of the social definition of culture is important. We should understand digital media as having an effect on the struggles involved over structures of inequality and power. Williams' own view of technology (1974) suggests that one must understand media as embedded in larger social formations. Technology is neither a pure cause nor a pure effect; it is neither something that fully determines all history nor something only determined by human interests. Instead, technology is a consequence of and a contributor to a larger social and historical context. It exists as part of the broader context that is 'the base'. Additionally, as media and technology participate in this space alongside human beings and their acts, they are built to legitimate specific forms of social organization as being natural and immutable. In their use, they justify specific ways of relating as fixed. As technologies exist materially, they shape social relations at a level that is somewhat independent of direct human intention and awareness, and the study of technology can then reveal much about the larger assumptions built into how social relations and culture are structured (cf. Harvey 2010: 192–193). While I believe that this way of understanding the relationship between technology and culture is present in Williams, it overtly informs the German media studies tradition of *Kulturtechniken*, or 'cultural techniques'.

GERMAN MEDIA THEORY AND CULTURAL TECHNIQUES

In Williams' history of the word 'culture', there is an association between culture and civilization. There is a different tradition associated with what's called German media theory. This name refers to a range of different authors influenced by the important media theorist Friedrich A. Kittler (1990, 1999). Kittler was not particularly interested in people working together to create a whole way of life. Rather, he examined how the material capacities of media enable specific things to be recorded and stored, which, in turn, shape what a human body does and knows about itself. For Kittler, what we consider to be human beings, the human mind, and rationality, are all products of the encounter with media. Media are prior to – a priori – that which we think of as human (1999: 109). Rather than think of media as tools used by humans, Kittler thinks of 'humans' as an effect of the technical ability of media, from spoken language to recorded sound, to enable communication and the transmission of information. Culture, following Williams, seems to be about human pursuits, be they perfection, the arts, or a whole way of life. What could culture be for someone like Kittler? To ask this requires us to be specific in the differences between the English word 'culture' and the German *Kultur*.

There are similarities between the histories of the words 'culture' and *Kultur*, but the differences are just as important. In German, the words *Kultur* and *Zivilisation* are related, but do not overlap as culture and civilization often do in English – and *Zivilisation*, unlike civilization, is not a particularly common word (Winthrop-Young 2014: 379). *Kultur* is used in compound words to differentiate, for instance, between plants in the wild and agriculture grown in relation to human care. The word

Kulturwald, literally 'culture-forest', refers to a grove of trees grown through human tending. So, there are major similarities between culture and *Kultur* in associations with agriculture and training. But the emphasis on artistic judgement, while certainly part of the German *Kultur*, is not quite as central. The prominence on a kind of internal cultivation of the soul by training *is* central to the German use of the term. When Theodor Adorno, one of the most important theorists of culture associated with the German Frankfurt School, claims 'Whoever speaks of culture speaks of administration as well' (1991: 107), he should be interpreted in light of the fact that *Kultur* is a form of administration and management of nature. And, importantly for us here, this is not merely training and cultivation through the arts, but also training and cultivation through technical means, or *Technik*.

Like *Kultur*, *Technik* is another problematic German word. *Technik* can be translated both as 'technology' and as **technique**, the latter referring to specific acts or arts performed by a body, the former to a durable manifestation of a technique. The word *Medientechniken* refers to media technologies. But *Körpertechniken* refers to techniques performed by the body, not technologies related to the body. *Kulturtechniken*, while 'linked to mass media, came to include basic skills like reading, writing, or counting' (Winthrop-Young 2014: 382–383). So, cultural techniques can be any number of cultural practices, intrinsically related to technologies and the means of training the body, from cartography and map-making (Siegert 2015), to law with its reliance on documentary evidence (Vismann 2008), to cooking and eating. Bernhard Siegert, the German media theorist who has done most to theorize cultural techniques, locates them in the agricultural history of culture, as 'the development and practical usage of means of cultivating and settling the soil with homesteads and cities' (2015: 9).

Instead of locating culture as a space of ideal perfection, the German tradition focuses on the material practices of cultivation that differentiate nature from culture. The question becomes, what practical means of training, as techniques and technologies of cultivation, make the human a human, rather than an animal? When we focus on cultural techniques, how we make culture is not merely about creativity and meaning but about physical processes through which we understand ourselves, our bodies, and our relations. According to Siegert, 'Every culture begins with the introduction of distinctions: inside/outside, pure/impure, sacred/profane, female/male, human/animal, speech/absence of speech, signal/noise, and so on' (2015: 14). These binary distinctions do not simply happen. They rely on material apparatuses. This means that any understanding of 'culture' is a result of how we use technologies and techniques to manage and control the environment in which we live. It means that the differences that inform how we understand our world are *performative* processes through which we make sense of our bodies, relations, and acts. And we keep performing them in order to make sense of the world in which we live.

This is similar to philosopher Judith Butler's well-known idea of *gender performativity*. Butler argues that bodies come to matter to each other through material practices, be they a specific way of dressing or a specific way of acting. Gender, with its distinction between 'femininity' and 'masculinity', is a result of the clothes one wears and acts one performs, located as they are within larger cultural understandings through which acts are made to make sense (see Butler 1990). Gender is not a 'thing' that exists outside the techniques one performs to make one's body legible to others. The common coding of a girl with the colour pink, and a boy with the colour blue, is not merely symbolic. These acts are material practices – techniques – that work to produce gender as a concept through which we order, understand, and define the capacities of specific bodies, as well as how bodies relate to one another through 'proper' and 'improper' acts and performances. Paul B. Preciado (2013), a theorist of sexuality, gender, and technology, has suggested that gender itself is an effect of twentieth-century biological and pharmaceutical technologies, in which categories like 'female' and 'male' are not inborn biological capacities but are instead dependent on medical means for defining the reproductive capacities of the body, from in vitro fertilization and hormone replacement therapy, to contraceptive pills and Viagra. Practices of hormone therapy, used both as technologies for transgender individuals and cis-female women, demonstrate, for Preciado, not that there is anything like a natural biological gender or sex, but that even biological categories of gender must be shaped and determined by technologies and are, in many ways, dependent on cultural practices and beliefs.

Technique can be said to underpin nearly every action we perform. Changes in how culture is organized – or distinctions between different people and different groups – are often associated with changes in technique. Marcel Mauss gives an example of this in his essay 'Techniques of the Body', in which he discusses different methods of learning to swim, which we briefly discussed in the Introduction:

> Previously, we were taught to dive after having learned to swim. And when we were learning to dive, we were taught to close our eyes and then to open them underwater. Today the technique is

the other way around. The whole training begins by getting the children accustomed to keeping their eyes open underwater. ... Hence, there is a technique of diving and a technique of education in diving that have been discovered in my day. And you can see that it really is a technical education and, as in every technique, there is an apprenticeship in swimming. ... Moreover, the habit of swallowing water and spitting it out again has gone. In my day, swimmers thought of themselves as a kind of steamboat. It was stupid, but in fact I still do this: I cannot get rid of my technique. (Mauss 1992: 456)

In 'Techniques of the Body', Mauss gives examples of a wide range of techniques, and notes how they are often divided by gender and age. Techniques contribute to performing the differentiations that structure social and cultural relations. Different techniques of swimming, for instance, mark a change in age. Different techniques for cooking mark the evolution of different cultures through kinds of cuisine, tastes, and methods, which are themselves bound to the historically contingent availability of kinds of produce, spices, and animals. Different kinds of clothing and different hairstyles, along with different pharmaceuticals and surgical procedures, are techniques for performing gender and identity. One way we can think about technology is that technologies are techniques made durable – techniques are acts that are performed and inhabited in a specific body and are often exceptionally difficult to unlearn once they've become habitual and performed without much thought. A technology persists in its physical form, though it is inevitably bound together with the performance of technique. A technique, strictly speaking, only inheres in being performed, although this performance cannot be thought to be 'ephemeral' or momentary (see Peters 2015: 87).

According to Siegert, cultural techniques are different from techniques in general. First, cultural techniques are material practices that *generate concepts*. Cultural techniques enable us to make sense of the world we live in, in ways that rely on the techniques and technologies we use. Second, cultural techniques *perform symbolic work*. While 'planning, transparency, yoga, gaming, even forgetting' have all been thought of as cultural techniques (Siegert 2015: 11–12), a cultural technique is inherently communicative. The implications of this are that the 'immaterial' world of language and signs depends on material practices and techniques, and the 'cultural' world is not opposed to nature, but rather is bound up with the management and modification of the physical environment in which we live.

Cultural techniques augment Williams' understanding of culture in three ways. First, the documentary definition of culture depends on the technical and technological aspects of media humans use to reinvent and reimagine the physical environment. Writing is not merely a symbolic act, but one that depends on the possibilities of media to write something down and store it over time. Techniques of swimming are not merely skills but are symbolic ways of marking distinctions in age through training and habit. These are all ways that we unintentionally document and record a specific way of living at a specific place and moment in time. The durability of a specific technique (and, perhaps, its ability to become a technology) enables it to become an encoding of culture that serves to perform culture. Second, stressing technique gives us a 'whole way of life' that is reliant on how material practices produce differentiations, which turns us to the production of boundaries and conflicts, rather than the vague 'whole' implied by Williams. The way techniques document and perform differentiations leads us to investigate how culture is a system of differences that is constantly in flux, constantly remade, and constantly rearticulated. Techniques lead us away from a 'whole' towards a fragmented and ever-changing field that emerges through practice. And third, it provides an understanding of cultivation that is not intrinsically linked with 'civilization', associated as it is with British imperialism and other elitist and discriminatory hierarchies. Rather, a focus on cultural techniques demonstrates the multiplicity and plurality of *cultures*, not of culture in the singular. Cultures are produced through the differential application of techniques that enable us to make sense of who we are, what we do, and how we relate to each other.

'LIKING' AS A CULTURAL TECHNIQUE

This definition of cultural techniques is a bit abstract, and it may appear to have little to do with digital media. Thus, an example is in order. On Facebook, a major way we have of relating to others is based on the digital version of the well-known, if culturally specific hand gesture of the thumbs-up, or a 'like' in the language of Facebook. A thumbs-up is a small way of signifying approval in many countries, usually contrasted with a disapproving thumbs-down. While I was writing this, Facebook unveiled a kind of 'dislike' button – a range of possible emotions represented by small images that depict emotions (called 'reactions') – responding to longstanding complaints about using their small, thumbs-up 'like' button when someone shares bad news (which was nonetheless how people often used – and still use – the 'like' button).

Is the 'like' button a cultural technique? On Facebook this gesture was used to express a wide range of emotions, which, until the introduction of reactions, were converted into an act of approval because there was simply no other button than the thumbs-up. (And this is not even accounting for the fact that a thumbs-up means different things in different contexts, and sometimes does not indicate affirmation.) A few years ago, media critic Mercedes Bunz noted that the forced use of the 'like' button was an 'efficient trick: Facebook barely needs to discipline its users, instead it rather designs their actions, and these are positive. It is not that there can't be disagreement on Facebook. It is only that its utterance is made more elaborate as it needs to be declared in the comments. Thus, it cultivates the approach of agreement instead of critique with a design that visually prefers affirmation' (Bunz 2013: 138). I don't know if I completely agree, as there's always been a lot of disagreement on social media. Yet the interface of Facebook and the software on which it once relied gave the appearance of an unbridled positivity, of affirmation, of everyone giving each other a thumbs-up in approval. This is a profoundly reductive way of understanding the purpose of human communication. With their 'reactions' Facebook seems to have changed this, expanding out the symbolic meaning of the like from pure affirmation to include potential expressions of sympathy, sadness, or solidarity.

But the 'like' button does not exist apart from the rest of Facebook. Clicking 'like' is only one of a number of techniques Facebook uses to symbolically map relationships within their 'social graph', the name used by Facebook for their statistical network model that diagrams all relations between people, things, and other pieces of data on Facebook. It is this graph – and the massive amount of data it organizes – that constitutes Facebook's real 'product' of value to investors and advertisers. Likes are used to calculate relationships in order to better target Facebook users with advertising and information. This happens through algorithms that compute the specific value of a like, which pieces of data are most 'relevant' to a specific user's interests, and more (see Bucher 2012).

These algorithms shape what we see on our 'news feed' and contribute to a 'filter bubble' produced by social media's algorithms. The term 'filter bubble' was coined by Eli Pariser, a founder of the websites MoveOn.org and Upworthy. With 'likes' and other pieces of data, Pariser argued, social media create 'a world constructed from the familiar', in which 'there's nothing to learn. If personalization is too acute, it could prevent us from coming into contact with the mind-blowing, preconception-shattering experiences and ideas that change how we think about the world and ourselves' (Pariser 2011: 15; cf. Vaidhyanathan 2011). A like is, in fact, a form of documentation. When you click 'like', you are inscribing information that Facebook then uses to create a profile that records who you are and how you relate to others. This consequentially shapes what you read and see online, which has a relationship with how you imagine yourself and your relations to others – and this is guided by the fact that affirmation becomes the primary way you have of communicating these relationships.

We can argue that the like button is a cultural technique because it is communicative and performs symbolic work, which occurs within the material limits of a specific technology. Clicking 'like' is an act of differentiation – not between 'like' and 'dislike', however, but between a kind of connection and disconnection. Clicking 'like' symbolically links you with whatever it is you've liked. The addition of a wider range of emotions alongside the 'like' doesn't change this; it adds an additional piece of information that differentiates between kinds of links. One link will be coded as affirmative, others will be coded as negative, even though by merely existing all links are, technically, affirmative, inscribing a kind of associative connection. All possible Facebook reactions create kinds of associations between you and something else.

'Liking' on Facebook may seem to be a small, insignificant act, but it is central to how we write down and document culture today. The 'like' button has massive effects in shaping how we relate and understand our 'whole way of life', and it can even be argued that it relates to other forms of 'cultivation' as we learn to use the 'like' to express how we imagine our relations with others. Think about how you use the like button to communicate with other people. What does a 'like' mean to you? What might it mean to another to be 'liked'? And, perhaps even more significantly, what does 'liking' mean to Facebook? What would happen if you stopped 'liking' things? Or, conversely, if you 'liked' everything on Facebook?

I encourage you to try an experiment. Click every 'like' button you can. If you're not willing, this experiment has been performed before. 'I like everything', wrote the journalist Mat Honan in *Wired*, 'Or at least I did, for 48 hours. Literally everything Facebook sent my way, I liked – even if I hated it. I decided to embark on a campaign of conscious liking, to see how it would affect what Facebook showed me' (Honan 2014). Honan found, almost immediately upon beginning his experiment, that his news feed became populated by advertisements and articles from 'content mills' like Upworthy and the Huffington Post. It was packed with political news, often of a highly partisan variety of dubious accuracy. The posts from the 'real people' who were his friends slowly vanished, although this was, interestingly enough, different on Facebook's desktop and mobile platforms. On his phone, he noted, 'I was only presented with the chance to like stories from various websites, and various other ads. Yet on the desktop – while it's still mostly branded content – I continue to see things from my friends. On that little bitty screen, where real-estate is so valuable, Facebook's robots decided that the way to keep my attention is by hiding the people and only showing me the stuff that other machines have pumped out'. Honan discovered that liking *everything* radically changed how Facebook worked.

Honan found that a quote of Andy Warhol's, from a 1963 interview in *Art News*, expressed many of the issues he saw in the widespread use of 'liking' on Facebook:

> *Warhol*:   Someone said that Brecht wanted everybody to think alike. I want everybody to think alike. … Everybody looks alike and acts alike, and we're getting more and more that way. I think everybody should be a machine. I think everybody should like everybody.
>
> *Art News*:   Is that what Pop Art is all about?
>
> *Warhol*:   Yes. It's liking things.
>
> *Art News*:   And liking things is like being a machine?
>
> *Warhol*:   *Yes, because you do the same thing every time. You do it over and over again.* (Quoted in Honan 2014)

This quote reframes how we should think of the Facebook 'like' button a bit. Namely, the technique of 'liking' something is older than Facebook. In fact, it may be difficult to identify an origin for 'liking', although Warhol is here associating liking with a kind of repetitive, mechanical, associative motion that I would suggest is related to the legacy of cybernetics and machines (which we'll discuss in more detail in the next two chapters). Regardless, 'liking' is a technique that generates concepts. Through it, we imagine our relations as being associative, repetitive, and, perhaps, machine-like. This leads to other assumptions about what a human body is and does, that are, nonetheless, embedded in a much larger history of technology and how we conceive of the human body and its capacities.

Let's break down the example of the 'like', summarizing a bit of what we've already noted, making it clear how the 'like' relates to what we've been saying about culture. First, 'liking' can be thought of as a cultural technique because it performs symbolic work. It creates a link, and thus defines and differentiates a specific relationship. It also symbolically shapes the meaning of the gesture of 'liking', and is bound together with larger, often invisible technological and algorithmic structures that are about defining, determining, and predicting actions and relationships. 'Liking' is based on the ability that a specific medium has given us for expressing and recording information, and this information performs an act of differentiation through communication. Second, liking is a form of *documentation*, as it exists as a material, technical method through which information about contemporary life is inscribed. While liking isn't really an example of the creative arts, it nonetheless records something about our 'structure of feeling', which, if you recall, is how Williams referred to how it feels to live at a specific moment in history. Third, liking contributes to how we imagine *social* relations. The 'like' participates in informing our 'whole way of life' as it frames how social media imagine and perform social relations, and it reframes how we see our social relations (as affirmative, as connective). There are other ways of imagining social relations and our whole way of life. But technologies such as the 'like' button shape these relations and how we imagine them to exist. Fourth, liking can even be thought to be a form of 'cultivation', in which the *ideal* of the contemporary moment privileges the expression of positive affirmation, liking and sharing online, and the general generation of data (see Ahmed 2010; Bollmer 2016; Dean 2009). Again, 'liking' is not the only way we can organize culture, but something as simple as the like button plays a massive role in shaping much of how we understand culture today.

There are even examples of people making art about 'liking', and this artwork demonstrates just how much 'liking' shapes cultural practices when it comes to how we use Facebook. For instance, artist Benjamin Grosser's 'Facebook Demetricator' is a simple web browser plug-in that removes all numerical metrics from Facebook. Grosser asks:

> how are the designs of Facebook leading us to act, and to interact in certain ways and not in others? For example, would we add as many friends if we weren't constantly confronted with how many we have? Would we 'like' as many ads if we weren't told how many others liked them before us? Would we comment on others' statuses as often if we weren't told how many friends responded to each comment? (2014)

Grosser's Demetricator is simple. It erases every instance of a number on Facebook. With metrics removed – from timestamps to likes to friend numbers – Grosser found that users often did not know how to use Facebook anymore:

> On the topic of 'likes' and comments, one user wrote me about how, with Demetricator installed, he was no longer able to like anything. 'I found myself not [wanting] to comment on things as often because I wouldn't know if it had a lot of comments or likes already'. This is because he didn't want to be one of the only people to like something that turned out to be unpopular. Another user told me that now she doesn't know what to like because, if something already has say, twenty-five likes, then surely that person doesn't need any more likes from her. They have enough already! (2014)

The 'like' button, as a result, is a powerful tool that dictates what people do on Facebook, where people unconsciously internalize rules for 'liking' in how they negotiate Facebook's use of numbers and metrics.

But the Warhol quote cited above should cause us to question just how new the technique of 'liking' may be. The techniques perpetuated by Facebook's 'like' button did not originate with Facebook. As Warhol indicates, they have a history that goes back to industrialization, at least. There are much larger narratives in the history of technology, of which 'liking' is but one moment. This does not change the fact that the everyday acts and behaviours that produce culture today have been shaped explicitly by the 'like' button and the relationships it produces. Regardless, truly understanding the role of the 'like' button today would require looking back into history to understand how we came to imagine social relations as an instrumental form of connection – a lengthy history, to be sure, and one filled with many things that may or may not seem to relate to Facebook and social media.

CONCLUSION

'Culture' is a very complicated concept. Its many definitions help us to understand the complex interactions between technology, technique, and various forms of symbolic and creative practice. What I hope you take from this overview of culture is that our technologies and techniques shape the way we interact with each other, and they inscribe information, produce differentiations, and participate in the 'whole way of life' – or 'whole way of conflict' – we can think of as culture. Culture is neither another word for art, nor does it merely refer to symbolic acts performed by people. Culture relies on technologies and their materiality. The question of differentiation, central as it is for the theorization of cultural techniques, will continue to haunt us as we now move to questioning the digital in digital culture. If the materialities of media play a key role in shaping cultural relations, then what does it mean to address the specificity of digital media?

NOTE

1. The base is often referred to as 'infrastructure' in the writings of some Marxists. This is not the same use of 'infrastructure' as in this book.

3

DIGITAL AND ANALOGUE

This chapter examines 'digital', problematizing many common understandings of digital media. It first reviews the distinction between digital and analogue, explaining this through a discussion of indexicality in film and photography, and considers a recent attempt to define the digital as a broader process of differentiation. It discusses limitations to these arguments, and then draws on the work of Gilbert Simondon to suggest how his 'mechanology' can contribute a way of theorizing digital media that does not rely on a limiting distinction between analogue and digital.

TERMS: analogue; associated milieu; concretization; digital; epistemology; icon; index/indexicality; individuation (psychic and collective); individualization (technical); mechanology; metaphysics of presence; ontogenesis; ontology; preindividual; symbol; transduction; transindividual

THEORISTS: Walter Benjamin, Gilles Deleuze, Mary Ann Doane, Alexander Galloway, Félix Guattari, Yuk Hui, François Laruelle, Lev Manovich, Charles Sanders Peirce, D. N. Rodowick, Gilbert Simondon, Bernard Steigler

EXAMPLES: Arduino; car engines; Facebook's SharpMask; Instagram photography; modular mobile phones (Google Ara, Motorola Moto X)

Digital would seem to be, unlike culture, a relatively easy word to define. Many accounts of digital culture *do* define what they mean by digital (see, for instance Gere 2008: 15). Commonly, there are at least three different understandings of the digital: the first is related to digital media and its *material specificity*, the second refers to the *cultural associations* provoked by digital technologies, and the third is an abstract process of *differentiation*. The first two definitions are what we usually refer to with the word 'digital'. 'Digital' means computers and their processing of discrete, binary information. The digital is opposed to **analogue**, where digital is discrete and analogue is continuous. This definition extends out to the sheer number of ways that computational media has shaped culture, be it through the arts or a broader whole way of life. The third definition – the digital as differentiation – is far more abstract. It suggests that digital refers to a general process that cannot be limited to computers.

Unlike the last chapter, where I tried to bring together theories of culture that are often thought to be incompatible, my goal here is not a synthetic account of these theories of the digital. Rather, I aim to demonstrate that the digital is far more complex than is often assumed. Beginning with a review of common distinctions between digital and analogue, I'll then discuss larger questions about the digital as a general process of differentiation. These two directions both have significant problems. The assumed material differences between digital and analogue are not as clear as one may imagine, and analogue and digital are often described as an exclusive, binary distinction – digital may mean discrete, but analogue tends to mean little more than 'not digital'. This distinction has some glaring historical problems, and, as I'll suggest, digital and analogue cannot be defined as opposites or even as opposed at all. The distinction between digital and analogue is, quite simply, neither correct nor particularly useful. The framing of the digital as a more general term for differentiation, on the other hand, threatens to make everything digital, as it equates digitality with the existence of difference.

To provide a possible way out of these problems of defining the digital I'll suggest a different distinction, one between the digital and the *mechanical*, a distinction that does not rely on a binary separation between its two terms but rather locates the digital within a larger typology of technical objects, all of which are reliant on the materiality of 'machines'. In doing this, I'll turn to some of the claims of an increasingly significant, long-standing, but generally neglected line of French thought about technology called **mechanology**, focusing primarily on the work of theorist Gilbert Simondon. This discussion of Simondon is difficult, and this chapter is the most complex to understand in this entire book. Part of this is because digital is often assumed to have a simple or self-evident definition, while my goal here is to reveal that it is anything but.

TRADITIONAL WAYS OF OPPOSING DIGITAL AND ANALOGUE

Before we get to the problems with opposing digital and analogue, we first have to define what this opposition is – throughout this discussion, keep in mind that we're reviewing this to ultimately problematize many of these claims. The distinction between digital and analogue has to do with the technical specificity of storage media. Forms of analogue media, be they vinyl LPs, photographs, or film, all have a continuous physical connection between a medium and something else in the natural world, be it light (in photography and film), sound (in audio recordings), or gestures of the hand and body (in writing, painting, or sculpture). This material connection vanishes with digital media, being replaced with a discrete, numerical, computational logic that has no clear relation to nature. Theorists of film and photography refer to this difference with the term **indexicality**. With photography, according to film theorist D. N. Rodowick, the 'photograph is a receptive substance literally etched or sculpted by light forming a mold of the object's reflected image' (2007: 9). In opening the shutter of a camera, one captures on film the actual, physical interplay of light in the world, which is then shaped by physical contact with chemicals. A photograph emerges from the physical contact between light and a medium. Indexicality refers to this material connection between a medium and the natural world, and similar claims can be made about almost all other analogue media.

Indexicality is a concept taken from the American pragmatist philosopher and founder of semiotics Charles Sanders Peirce, and is a key category for how Peirce understood all signs. For Peirce, signs can be divided up into three categories: symbols, icons, and indices. **Symbols** are 'in a conjoint relation to the thing denoted and to the mind' (1885: 180). The link between a symbol and the thing it refers to is produced by convention, and the link is only maintained by the symbolic processing of an individual's mind. The octagonal, red sign for 'stop' is a symbol, for instance, as it has no real connection to the act of stopping. This association is one of convention, and we only make the connection between the stop sign and the act of stopping because we know, in our mind, how to interpret a stop sign. **Icons** are connected because of a resemblance between an iconic sign and what it posits to represent. Most emoji are iconic signs, in that they represent what they look like. We still have to make the connection between an emoji and what it represents, as there is no physical connection between, say, a pizza emoji and an actual pizza (and this does not stop some emoji from becoming symbols, when they mean something other than what they look like). Both symbols and icons are 'degenerate' signs according to Peirce, because the relationship between the sign and what it represents involves a mind to make the connection between the two. There is no direct relationship that links the sign to the thing it refers to.

The **index**, however, is not a degenerate sign, and exists independently of a mind: 'this sign signifies its object solely by virtue of being really connected with it. Of this nature are all natural signs and physical symptoms. I call such a sign an *index*, a pointing finger being the type of this class' (Peirce 1885: 181). Peirce gives a wide range of examples of indices, from which, according to Mary Ann Doane (2007), the index can be divided into two more categories: *trace* and *deixis*. *Deixis* refers to a pointing finger, words like 'this' or 'that' and pronouns (or 'shifters') that refer to specific people but are nonetheless generic, like 'he' or 'she' or 'it' or 'you', the referent of which changes depending on context. Deixis is based on pointing. It is a sign that, in its presence in the here and now, points to something else. A *trace* is quite different, however. It refers to the persistence of evidence, of an imprint or an inscription, like a footprint, or writing in sand, or grease left behind by a piece of pizza. The trace is physically present, but this presence is there to signify an absence, of a presence that exists no more, of a touch that has vanished as time has moved on. Importantly, these two functions of trace and deixis cannot be completely differentiated. A trace still performs a kind of deictic pointing, to that which used to be there, while some deictic indices, like 'he' or 'she' or 'it', are not traces.

In describing analogue media as indexical, the belief is that media record the 'touch' of something – be it sound waves or a visual impression – in ways that combine both trace and deixis, a combination, Doane suggests, that leads to a belief in the truth of an indexical record. Analogue recordings are indexical signs, and the groove on a record or the image of a photograph is equivalent to crumbs in a pizza box – in their material presence, they point to the absence of a physical thing that once was there. The earliest forms of sound recording can be explained in these terms. The phonautograph, the first known sound recording device, patented in 1857, traced lines on paper or glass that were a direct result of how the device registered sound waves. Even though the recordings made by the phonautograph could not be used to reproduce sound (unlike later innovations in sound recording that relied on similar methods), the physical touch of a sound wave was being recorded in the inscriptions made by the device. Vinyl LPs, for the most part, can still be thought of in this way. The grooves on an LP are etchings of sound waves recorded at one point, reproduced whenever you listen to a record. Much of the power of a recording comes from the fact that the person or thing that made the recording once was really there, and when we replay a recording (or look at a photograph) we're hearing or seeing something that once really existed. (This phenomenon has long contributed to the theological and spiritualist understanding of media we discussed earlier – the trace permits an etching of one's body to persist after death, producing a kind of 'immortality'.)

According to Rodowick, digital media do away with this indexicality, replacing the imprint or inscription with a discrete computational logic that lacks reference to physical reality (2007: 10). No longer are there physical traces of bodies, light, sound waves, or chemicals in our media. Rather, there exist computer algorithms and digital processes that render all forms of media equivalent through the numerical processing of computers. Thus, a digital representation is unlinked from any indexical relationship with 'reality', even if, as is the case with a digital photograph or a digitally recorded film, there's no clear simulation going on. What we see is still a simulation because it is little more than a translation of images or sound that, materially, are numerical data processed by a computer. Think of how the film *The Matrix* represents the reality of its titular 'Matrix', and you'll have an understanding of how Rodowick understands digital representations. Rather than 'reality', we have symbols and numbers processed by computers, which create a simulation of reality – one that is flexible and fluid because of its lack of connection to the physical world. Common complaints about digital effects in movies relate to these claims. Digital cinema simply does not 'look real' to many people, even though movies have long relied on effects to simulate environments or places that do not and will never exist. (The world of the original *Star Wars* has certainly never existed in 'reality', and yet it seems more 'real' to many viewers than, say, the digital environments of its prequel *The Phantom Menace*, because its sets, costumes, and effects had some relation to physical reality).

There are problems with these claims, and arguments like Rodowick's should bring to mind what Derrida pointed out when he criticized the **metaphysics of presence**. The loss of indexicality is a loss of presence when analogue media becomes digital. Yet even something entirely digital is 'real' because it has real effects and exists in the real world, even if it may be modified by computational schema. Additionally, even images that are clearly simulated, like digital faces and bodies in videogames and animation, regularly rely on technologies of motion and performance capture that convert the physical movements of human bodies into that which can be manipulated by a computer (Figure 3.1). Even if a photograph is digital, it still relies and encodes something that happened in the 'real world', although the digital tools that can manufacture and modify an image also call into question the ability to differentiate between a 'real' inscription and a simulated one. These are still kinds of indices, encoding the touch and movements of real human bodies, even if they may not be the same kind as found in a photograph.

Regardless, the foundations of media are different with analogue and digital, and the 'touch' registered by digital media is not the same as it has been in the past, along with the ability to suggest an image represents 'reality' or not. As with the distinction between the 'real world' and a virtual one, the problem is in the hierarchy of value attributed to specific kinds of

Figure 3.1 President Barack Obama tries out motion capture cameras after watching a demonstration at the DreamWorks Animation studio, 26 November 2013. Official White House Photo taken by Pete Souza.

Source: Obama White House Flickr. Public Domain.

representations, where one is 'more real' or 'more present' than another, not in the mere existence of a distinction between kinds of media and kinds of representations.

While not everyone is as pessimistic as Rodowick, many still note that the mathematical processing of the computer marks an essential difference between analogue and digital, which seems to do radically different things to a very wide range of media. According to media theorist Lev Manovich, with the computer, 'graphics, moving images, sounds, shapes, spaces, and texts ... have become computable; that is, they comprise simply another set of computer data' (2001: 20). According to Manovich, digital media can be characterized by five principles, even though not every example of digital media will conform to all five principles, and, in some cases, analogue forms of media, especially film, can also be understood in these terms. These principles are as follows:

1. *Numerical representation* – Digital media are inevitably described with a formal, mathematical logic. This happens through *sampling*, which transforms continuous data into discrete data, at a digitally specified *resolution*, which are *quantified* numerically. This enables media to be analyzed and manipulated *algorithmically*.
2. *Modularity* – The discrete elements of digital media can be cut up and recombined, and yet still have their own identity. Or, digital media consist 'of independent parts, each of which consists of smaller independent parts, and so on, down to the level of the smallest "atoms" – pixels, 3-D points, or text characters' (2001: 31).
3. *Automation* – The principles of numerical representation and modularity enable the automation of many elements of 'media creation, manipulation, and access. Thus human intentionality can be removed from the creative process, at least in part' (2001: 32).
4. *Variability* – There is no fixed digital version of anything, but 'potentially infinite versions' and variations (2001: 36). Whenever you open a file on your computer this creates a new file rather than 'opening' an old one, as at least two copies of a file then exist, one on the computer's hard drive, and another in its memory. The standard editing function of 'undo', for instance, can only work because a computer is saving numerous, slightly different versions of the same file in its memory at any one point in time.
5. *Transcoding* – 'Transcoding' usually means changing one file format into another. (If you convert an image from TIFF to JPEG, for instance, you are transcoding the image. This often results in a loss

of data that comes from a change of file format, which is an effect of different compression algorithms and how they sample and organize data. Sometimes you can see the consequences of transcoding with your own eyes, when an image degrades and becomes blocky or pixelated, but much of the time you cannot.) Manovich uses this term to suggest that computers participate in 'cultural reconceptualization', in which categories, concepts, and models derived from the operation of the computer begin to inform other elements of daily life, 'transcoded' beyond the computer (2001: 47).

These five principles are easy to observe in the everyday use of digital media. Let's use the example of taking a photograph with your iPhone, then editing and sharing it on Instagram. While an analogue photograph is the result of light hitting a film negative, which is then printed on photo paper, along with any number of other instances of contact and touch, a digital photograph is fundamentally mathematical. If you look closely at an analogue photograph, you may see the grain of the photo paper, but colors and shades will bleed into each other. The image is continuous, and its specific existence emerges from the hand of the photographer, the photographic apparatus (or camera), light, film stock, chemicals, and so on. But if you enlarge a photo you've taken with your phone, you'll begin to see it broken into discrete pixels, each of which is a specific, discrete colour, which are defined by specific numerical codes that link a quantified colour value to what's expressed on your screen. The resolution of the photograph – and the colours it uses – are based on the technical capabilities built into your phone's camera, its display, and the software that determines sampling rate and how the camera identifies and encodes colour, algorithmically shaping the image through mathematical formulas. So, a picture on your phone is a *numerical representation* rather than an indexical one. It's closer to a symbol or icon than an index.

This image is *modular*. Its pixels can be separated out in any number of ways, and all digital images are composed of the same modular colour pixels. With HTML standards for the World Wide Web, all possible colours are assigned a specific numerical code that corresponds to numerical red, green, and blue values, which are quantified in a range from 0 to 255, represented in hexadecimal code. A specific shade of green, for instance, can be identified with the hex value of #019A01, where 01 refers to the specific quantified amount of red in the colour, 9A to the amount of green, and 01 to the amount of blue. There isn't any singular existence of any one pixel of this colour, and all colours possible on the Web can be computed using these same, modular standards (see Kane 2014a). The image can be *automated*, which we can see if we turn to something like Instagram. An Instagram filter is an algorithmic process that manipulates your original image at a numerical level. The changes you see when you apply a filter on Instagram come from how these filters manipulate these images automatically. While you have some control over image manipulation, your own hand has been removed from much of the work. This image is *variable*. Clicking on different Instagram filters effectively creates different images. Your initial photograph can be remade and remixed into countless different versions with ease. There is no real 'original', in part because the original photo gets copied over and over again; the photo you see on Instagram's interface isn't really the same as the 'original' photo taken with your phone – it's one of many copies.

And, finally, the way we think about these images can be *transcoded* into the rest of daily life. While there are deeper ways that digitization has influenced how we think about the most basic aspects of our lives (see Golumbia 2009), the techniques associated with Instagram and digital photography have changed how we use images to experience and communicate about our world. I've had students tell me about how they intentionally visit restaurants with attractive looking food, all with the purposes of taking a picture to put on Instagram, for instance. These Instagram images are then modified and adjusted in an extreme amount of detail. One may make multiple versions of an image and then have friends comment on which is best, only then choosing which one to post. The techniques associated with Instagram and how it uses digital photography have become transcoded into other ways of acting, relating, and experiencing the world.

Manovich's model is one way of defining what digital media is and does, although it isn't the only way. His principles are an answer to an important question to ask: What are digital media? What is the **ontology** of digital media? An ontological question is simply asking 'what is it?' Or, more accurately, the main ontological question would be 'what is there?' There are, after all, many things that exist even if we do not know of them (Hui 2016: 78). In asking 'what is it?' or 'what is there?' we are attempting to disclose *essences*, trying to define and categorize our world to know what it is. Manovich's categories are an attempt to define the ontological features of digital media. They help us to see how the technical specificity of media enable certain things to be documented, permit certain acts to be performed, and facilitate certain relations. Culture is not just what people do *with* digital media, since the material, ontological qualities of media participate and share in the making of culture. At the same time, ontology cannot be reduced to materiality. While most of Manovich's categories are about the material, technical specifics of digital media, some are about larger ways in which digital media shape beliefs and knowledge that aren't precisely about the material effects of media.

This leads us to a second series of questions, **epistemological** questions, the most general version of which is 'how do we know?' Digital media shape how we come to know things about our world, a point that Manovich makes clear with his principle of transcoding. The models and techniques associated with media are not limited to the computer. Rather, they shape how we view and understand the rest of the whole way of life of culture. Examining digital media epistemologically would be about, in this case at least, how new ways of seeing and manipulating images shape knowledge, awareness, and how we understand and imagine social relations.

The epistemological function of media has long been associated with transformations in the sciences. Photography, for instance, was historically associated with a wide range of scientific practices because of its ability to freeze motion and permit the human eye to observe things that were previously too fleeting to see (see Didi-Huberman 2003). The great theorist and critic Walter Benjamin refers to this as photography's capacity to reveal the *optical unconscious*. Photography allows us to see and examine body movements, postures, emotional reactions, all of which are too momentary to be grasped consciously and too involuntary to be recognized as an intentional act of the human mind (Benjamin 2008: 278–279). Digital media do similar things: they visualize the human body in new ways. Just think about how Big Data visualization permits us to see and know new things about ourselves and our bodies. The capacities of digital media may also lead us to question the truth of the image, as has so long been assumed with photographs being 'true'. The categories that Manovich identified have led to worries about the authenticity of digital images, which seems to disappear as software packages like Photoshop enable the manipulation of images in ways that clearly do not have the same link to 'real life' as before.

THE DIGITAL AS DIFFERENTIATION

As simple as they may seem, these ontological and epistemological questions are difficult to answer. What is true of digital media was often also true of film, and the processes of quantification that have led to today's computers and their numerical forms of representation go back to the late

1800s, if not earlier. A photograph is at least somewhat *automated* because the camera participates in the shaping of an image. Film breaks motion into discrete sequences, and it is thus *modular* and relies on a kind of sampling rate (see, among numerous others, Doane 2002; Manovich 2001: 50–61). So, what's actually digital about digital media? Because of these historical precedents, it's easy to want to detach the digital from digital media, or to stress that digital media are, in the end, inevitably analogue in some form or another because of how digital media are bound up with larger historical and material processes (e.g. Massumi 2002: 133–143). History gets in the way of making clear ontological and epistemological distinctions, as clean breaks that identify distinct historical or technological periods rarely exist. What we may imagine to uniquely characterize our present almost always has an historical precedent.

I now want to turn to a way of theorizing the digital proposed by Alexander Galloway. Galloway has been an important media theorist in the past decade or so and has recently argued that we shouldn't think of the digital as being anchored to technology at all. Rather, the digital is synonymous with general processes of *differentiation*. For Galloway, the difference between the digital and the analogue is the difference between 'the broken and the smooth, the difference between discrete points and continuous curves'. So far, so good. This mirrors the usual way that digital and analogue have been discussed. Yet there's a problem with this seemingly simple distinction:

> But even this forestalls the question: claiming 'discrete points' explains little, because nothing has been said as to how such points became discrete in the first place. So the digital is something more fundamental. *The digital is the basic distinction that makes it possible to make any distinction at all.* The digital is the capacity to divide things and make distinctions between them. (Galloway 2014: xxix, italics added)

Galloway makes this argument through a reading of French philosopher François Laruelle, giving us a provocative and unusual understanding of digital culture. Rather than imply a break with much of the past, as is usually the case with the divide between digital and analogue media, Galloway suggests that 'there simply is no history without digitality … the digital is a basic ingredient within ontology, politics, and most everything in between' (2014: xxxiv). The entire process of distinction is digital, which, as we have suggested in the previous chapter with our discussion of cultural techniques, is central for any act that produces culture. So, all culture is digital culture, not because digital media have transformed anything that can be said to be cultural, but because culture has been digital all along, founded on the production of differences. The computer is only one more machine in a long lineage that separates the world out into discrete elements. Galloway calls this 'the principle of sufficient digitality', which states '*for everything in the world there is a process of distinction appropriate to it*' (2014: xxxiv, original italics).

Rather than suggest that computers and mathematical models are a distortion or reduction of the 'presence' given throughout history, Galloway argues that digitality has prepared the way for digital media and its quantification of everything:

> Computation is not an 'option' available to presence but a precondition of it. It is not simply that computers, artificial intelligence, virtual reality, and the like are predicated on computational decisionism. It is not simply that such and such mundane detail will be rendered computationally, that weather patterns will be modeled on a supercomputer, that stock markets will be migrated over to electronic trading, that we will 'go digital...' The advent of digital being – which is today the only sort of being directly available to us – shows that presence itself is a computational condition. (2014: 111)

Similar arguments can be found throughout media history, in which technological developments from the 1800s and early 1900s can be read as early examples of using technology to make distinctions, inscribe information, and produce mathematical and scientific knowledge about bodies and behaviours (Doane 2002; Schmidgen 2014). The entire history of media, in this view, is a preparation for today's computers. Or, the entire history of media is a history of digitality, in which new forms of media enable new kinds of distinctions, all of which are digital. Galloway stresses that this isn't just about media history, but all history. We are engaged in a process of differentiation that makes it so we are always already digital.

I find Galloway's argument provocative, and perhaps even necessary, although not completely convincing. Histories of digital culture demonstrate both how digital media are part of a broader history of media, but also that there is no singular teleology that can be thought of as technological progress (see Huhtamo & Parikka 2011; Parikka 2012). The history of media is one of many mistakes, errors, and contingencies, and there are alternative histories that were never realized (Zielinski 2006). The idea that there is an underlying digitality that has guided the entire history of media strikes me as a bit too general, or a bit too felicitous. At the same time, it does point to the difficulty involved in challenging the orthodoxies of digital culture. What would it mean to challenge the existence of distinction? If the purpose of theory is to look at the world and question its organization, then Galloway's claims are a provocative effort to do this. Galloway is suggesting that any attempt to critique digital culture can never go too far unless we get to the idea of differentiation as such. As well, any attempt to challenge digital culture and change it without addressing differentiation will seemingly fail, as the condition of digitality has itself not been challenged. While I find the former premise exciting, I find the latter to be fatalistic, and premised on a kind of withdrawal from culture as such. Can we actually have a world without differentiation? I'm not so sure. But merely asking this question may lead us in new and interesting directions.

PROBLEMS WITH THE DIGITAL AND ANALOGUE DISTINCTION

Needless to say, equating the digital with differentiation has problems. Everything becomes digital, because making sense of our world requires us to make differentiations. Specific cultures organize the world in specific ways – not all languages have the same words for colours, for instance, so colours are differently differentiated depending on the language one uses, and many non-Western cultures have more than two genders, differentiating kinds of bodies into more than the categories of 'male' and 'female' that characterize much of the West. The world isn't organized through the same set of distinctions everywhere, and this is one of the major reasons I suggest that there are only digital cultures in plural. Even within specific cultures, individuals organize the world in radically different ways.

Yet getting rid of difference and distinction as such seems, to me at least, to be an impossibility, in which a world of undifferentiated flatness is celebrated as a political move. Because we cannot understand the world without differentiating it into discrete parts, this would mean that we would inevitably be trapped in the digital – at least as defined by Galloway. Rather than doing away with differentiation in general, we should merely embrace different ways of organizing the world and our experience in it. We should focus on the specific ways that culture is organized, questioning which differences matter, which unfairly discriminate, and which can lead to a better, more egalitarian world.

More practically, the mere opposition between digital and analogue also has some significant problems, and not only the metaphysics of presence that characterizes any definition of the digital as a loss of indexicality. First, suggesting that the digital is a loss of indexicality overlooks the history of the word 'digital'. The Latin source of digital literally refers to the index finger. As Benjamin Peters has suggested, this early definition persists today: 'digital media do what fingers do', namely counting, but 'they also point, index, and reference objects at a distance' (Peters 2016: 94). The internet, World Wide Web, and pretty much all social media platforms follow this indexical logic. Links point elsewhere, and the 'social graph' of Facebook is little more than a massive group of indexical links that connect a wide range of data that all seemingly point back to 'you', the user of Facebook. Digital links function like pointing fingers, which means that a loss of indexicality may not be the best way to theorize the distinction between analogue and digital. Now, this understanding of indexicality refers only to deixis, and not to the index as trace. Regardless, it does question just what it means to claim digital media lack indexicality.

A more significant problem with the distinction between analogue and digital is that the digital is assumed to be a form of technology that comes *after* analogue. Yet the idea of analogue as referring to that which is continuous, while the digital is discrete, is a belief that only emerged *after* the popularization of digital media. Instead, analogue has long referred to a specific technological process of simulation, one that uses 'analogue' in a way similar to a deeply related word: analogy. As Jonathan Sterne explains, in its original technological usage, 'A violin is not an analog technology', in part because it is not simulating anything – it is not an analogy of another instrument. But 'a synthesizer is [an analogue technology] because of the defined relationships on which its system is based, such as control voltage and oscillator pitch' (Sterne 2016: 32). The technical components of a synthesizer were intended to shape electricity – at the level of controlling the specific way soundwaves could be generated – in order to be 'analogous' to other instruments. Analogue, throughout most of its history, was a word that indicated one thing substituting for another, which in the 1960s even referred to things like synthetic, soya-based meat and cheeses. In this sense, *skeuomorphism* – the tendency in interface design in which a computer interface is supposed to look like something else (so, a digital notepad or calendar are made to look like a paper notepad or calendar) – is both analogue *and* digital. It is analogue because it is one thing that substitutes for another. It is digital because it exists on a digital computer.

The distinction between analogue as continuous and digital as discrete only seems to have been defined around 1987. One of the most notable instances comes from the futurist Stewart Brand, who, in his book *The Media Lab: Inventing the Future at MIT*, writes:

> Telephones, radio, TV and recorded music began their lives as analog media – every note the listener heard was a smooth direct transform of the music in the studio – but each of these is now, gradually, sometimes wrenchingly, in the process of becoming digitized, which means becoming computerized. You can see the difference in the different surfaces of long-playing records and compact discs: the records' grooves are wavy lines; the far tinier tracks of CDs are nothing but a sequence of distinct pits. Analog is continuous, digital is discrete. (Brand 1987: 18, cited in Sterne 2016: 36–37)

This definition offered by Brand, in spite of it being the commonly accepted one today, is thus *newer* than the digital media it is supposed to define. It suggests that analogue only became 'continuous' when it became a synonym for 'not digital', losing its original meaning as analogy.

A similar objection to the digital as discrete can be seen in some of the claims of Friedrich Kittler. In his essay, 'There is No Software' (2013: 219–229), Kittler argues that the belief in something called 'software' that runs on 'hardware' is an illusion. There is nothing in the physical operation of a computer that sustains this distinction. Everything on a computer can reduce to voltage differences that operate on the physical machinery of the computer itself – the existence of software as somehow different from the physical capacities of computer hardware is misleading. When we get down to the most basic, material qualities of the computer, we only have distinct voltages that are coded as binary. Yet these voltages are not precisely 'off' or 'on', as is usually implied by a discussion of the binary processing of computers, but actually have a level of continuity, in which voltage is continuously on but just increases or decreases in a pattern that is far more continuous than one may imagine, much like the waves processed by a synthesizer. In this sense, then, even a digital computer can be analogue.

THE DIGITAL AND THE MECHANICAL

It seems that defining the digital in opposition to the analogue is a dead end. These categories may still be helpful, at least if we do not take them as being opposites and instead understand that something can be both digital and analogue, and neither category implies a greater 'presence' than the other. After all, we do need to distinguish between, say, kinds of photographs made with computers and those made with film and chemicals. These are not the same thing, and as long as we avoid claims about the analogue being more present or continuous this distinction may still be of use. But I want to briefly introduce one more category that may help how we can understand the specificity of digital media: the *mechanical*. Mechanical may be a better term than analogue, especially given transformations in the meaning of analogue in the past several decades. Mechanical is not something that can be neatly opposed to the digital. It also introduces us to an important line of theoretical thought – **mechanology** – that has long characterized discussions about technology in France but has mostly been ignored in English-speaking countries. Mechanology, or 'the science of machines', is located at the intersection of philosophy and engineering. The work of Gilbert Simondon is, today, most exemplary of this tradition, and it is through Simondon that mechanology has influenced important contemporary writings on technology by those such as Félix Guattari and Bernard Stiegler (see Hayward & Geoghegan 2012; Hayward & Thibault 2013).

We're now going to look at how Simondon defined what he termed the '**individualization** of technical objects', along with how he has been updated by the theorist Yuk Hui to discuss digital media. Doing this requires us to address some larger concerns about ontology as well, as one of the major implications of Simondon's work is a move away from ontology towards **ontogenesis**. Simondon's perspective provides a direction for discussing media that does not defer to the old analogue and digital distinction.

Typically, ontology – in answering the question of 'what is it?' or 'what is there?' – examines the essence of *being*. Essences are eternal – they exist outside history. But, for Simondon, the world does not possess any unchanging ontological stability. Rather, everything undergoes a constant process of **ontogenesis** that stresses *becoming* rather than *being*. Things change based on their relations. Simondon refers to this kind of ontogenesis as **individuation**, in which any individual is in a constant process of becoming itself (1992: 295). Simondon suggests that there are at least two forms of individuation, **psychic individuation**, which corresponds to what we typically think of as an individual, with a specific mind and consciousness. Psychic individuation, for a human being at least, is about the formation of an interiority, an 'I' that speaks as a coherent subject. These psychic individuals do not exist alone. They are inherently part of another process, one of **collective individuation** that enables a 'we' within which the 'I' is a part. Both of these processes of individuation are linked by a relation that Simondon refers to as the **transindividual**. Additionally, there is a space Simondon terms the **preindividual** that isn't precisely before individuation but suggests a field outside the constitution of psychic and collective individuals, as well as the relations between them. The important thing is that no single part of this system to describe ontogenesis can be separated out and isolated, and, at the same time, these different things cannot be collapsed into one another. There are at least three different, distinct domains that interact relationally, all elements of which together participate in ontogenesis.

Simondon is suggesting that 'I' do not exist alone. 'I' do not emerge fully formed when I am born. Rather, I *become* 'me', and that becoming never stops. I am in constant relation with others, a 'we' in which 'I' am formed as a coherent individual. This does not mean that 'I' am not distinct from the 'we' in which I exist. As the philosopher Bernard Stiegler has argued, Simondon shows how '*I* do not exist other than in a group: *my* individuation is the individuation of my *group* ... and, moreover, I may belong to several groups, which may be in disharmony' (Stiegler 2009: 66). Some readings of Simondon stress the transindividual – the relation between the 'I' and the 'we' – far more than either the psychic or collective individual, claiming that Simondon argues that 'I' always overflow myself and am in necessary relation with others, and thus the transindividual is the real subject of becoming (Combes 2013). Others, namely Stiegler and his followers, have stressed the importance of maintaining the distinctions between the many kinds of individuals Simondon has identified. But, Stiegler claims, with contemporary technology the transindividual relation between the 'I' and 'we' has been eroded. Because of the erosion of the transindividual, 'I' am unable to ever achieve any clear coherence as a subject. Stiegler links the many psychic traumas that we face today, such as depression, to an inability to be either an individual or part of a larger collective, a condition that Stiegler relates to how media tend to synchronize time and experience.

Simondon's claims about individuation are linked to but are distinct from his writings about technology. Simondon argues that machines should be thought of as distinct from psychic and collective individuation, as having their own process of **individualization** that produces technical objects. It's significant that Simondon uses individualization, not individuation, to refer to technology. According to Yuk Hui (2016: 14–15), individuation refers to a form of equilibrium – a temporary stability in which an 'I' or 'we' exist as a coherent thing, if only for a moment. Individualization, however, has a hierarchy that relates to defined *functions*. There is no privilege given to the 'I' or 'we' in psychic and collective individuation, while there is a hierarchy that comes from how technologies are individualized into having specific, functional outcomes. Technical objects, unlike psychic or collective individuals, are roughly stable in that they have defined purposes that they perform, and they go through a process of **concretization** in which their technical functions become stable and more permanent. Technical objects are made up of three different levels: *elements*, *individuals*, and *ensembles*. This may seem very abstract, but Simondon was using these terms to describe very real, mechanical technologies, such as an engine, or the development of transistors.

Let's use an engine as an example through which to discuss these categories. In an engine, there are numerous *elements*, such as pistons, cranks, and so on. On its own, a single piston does very little, if anything at all. It is only in linking all of an engine's elements together that it becomes an *individual* with a specific function. In that individual, if any one element breaks it can be replaced and the individual remains the same, performing the same function. The engine, of course, does not exist by itself. It is also part of another, larger *ensemble* that is a car (or boat, or fan, or lawnmower, or anything else that has an engine). These different levels are simultaneously independent yet interlinked. Not all elements work with all kinds of engines, and not all engines work with every ensemble. Simondon is attempting to think through how machines work, and how they change over time. Different engines may, in fact, work in a range of cars, for instance, and a range of elements may work in any one technical individual.

In its development, a technology like an engine moves from the *abstract* to the *concrete*. This means, early on, its elements are less specific and more interchangeable. A specific piston may work in a wide range of engines, for instance. If one were to invent a new kind of engine, the elements one would use would, most likely, be ones that were designed for other technologies, gradually becoming refined as the design was perfected (although this is something that has changed since Simondon's time with computer-aided design (CAD) software, which uses computer simulations to design mechanical parts, so something like an engine would emerge as a relatively concrete prototype rather than the kinds of abstract machines Simondon discusses). As an engine becomes more concrete – more specific, more manufactured – its elements become less interchangeable with other engines. Its parts become more carefully engineered, crafted, and branded, designed to work with only one kind of engine. Its function becomes more designed, perhaps made to work only in a specific ensemble. It is at this point that a specific engine becomes a true technical individual.

An engine is not just a generic engine that can work in any larger ensemble. Rather, each technical individual works with a specific environment, which Simondon terms an **associated milieu**. Something like an engine requires a specific power source (be it petrol or electricity), and it only functions in relation to its larger ensemble (Simondon 2017: 59). Engines that require petrol or electricity are quite different: how a specific technical individual organizes its environment is both built into the object, but also shapes the limits and capacities the object has in the first place given how it relies on specific inputs and materials to perform its given function.

We can easily see a difference between a concretized technical object (like a car) and one that is still fairly abstract. If a part breaks in your car, you'd have to go to the dealer and purchase a part that was designed for a specific make and model of your car to be able to replace it. If a part breaks on your computer, especially if you have an Apple computer, you may not be able to replace it at all. These objects have been designed so their elements are proprietary, part of the intellectual property of a specific company. They are highly concretized. If you've ever had any experience with an Arduino kit, on the other hand, the things you can make are far more abstract. Arduino is an open-source programming language designed to work with simple electronic components. While there are specific parts that are designed to work with Arduino, they are still highly generic and abstract, be they diodes, jumper wires, or capacitors. These different elements are not designed to work in any one, specific technical object. They're made to work in a broad range of projects, toys, and tools that can be crafted with an Arduino kit. At the same time, any technology made in Arduino would require some access to a computer and the Arduino software. You have to code to get Arduino to work. The computer and Arduino software would be part of the associated milieu of the other parts of an Arduino project.

Simondon's understanding of technology, his 'mechanology', has been very influential, mostly through the work of the philosophers Gilles Deleuze and Félix Guattari, who, in their book *Anti-Oedipus*, describe human bodies, societies, and technologies all as machines. 'There is no such thing as either man or nature now, only a process that produces the one within the other and couples the machines together', they claim (1983: 1–2). For Deleuze and Guattari, a machine can literally be anything, and human bodies and societies can all be described as made up of machines. Simondon, however, is clear to differentiate between human and machine, although he also argues that a human can be used as a part in a machine, or a human can be replaced by a machine. These different things are distinct – a psychic individual is different from a collective individual, and both are different from a technical individual.

These different individuals are always related to one another. While transindividual is one important term Simondon proposes to identify the kinds of relations between the many individuals he discusses, another is **transduction**. Transduction refers to a change of energy expressed in one form into another. A transducer, in technological terms, is a mechanism for, say, converting electricity into light, or converting sound into electricity. Our lives are surrounded by a wide range of transducers, be they lightbulbs, which transduce energy into light, microphones, which change sonic vibrations into an electrical signal, speakers, which do the opposite, or an air conditioner, which transduces electricity into a cooler temperature. These technologies are not the only kinds of transducers, however. 'The human being, and the living being more generally, are essentially transducers', claims Simondon. 'The elementary living being, the animal, is itself a transducer when it stores chemical energies and then actualizes them during the course of different vital operations' (2017: 155).

Simondon gives us a wide-ranging vocabulary to discuss the development of many different technologies, along with the varied relationships between humans and technologies. And, while he certainly makes parallels between all of these different individuals, Simondon refuses to reduce the many different domains he identifies into one (unlike cybernetics, which will be discussed in the next chapter). Instead, he stresses the many 'modes of existence' that interact but cannot be collapsed into one another. Simondon's mechanology points us in a direction in which we can look at the similarities between different forms of media, while also acknowledging their differences.

Yet the technologies that Simondon discusses are mechanical – not really what we'd term digital – even though he discusses transistors at length, and transistors are essential for digital technologies. But there is a clear lineage between the machines Simondon theorizes and our computers, and I introduce these concepts because they can help us think about how our computers are often still machines in Simondon's sense. Our computers all rely on different technical elements, be they parts of a hard disk, their various electrical components, and so on. These elements are concretized into specific objects. The ability to replace an element in a computer is, today, something political. As we'll discuss later on, the fact that Apple computers and phones are designed so its individual elements cannot be removed makes them essentially disposable, which has significant implications for the environmental impact of digital technologies. Several companies have recently worked to develop modular mobile phones, including Motorola's Moto X and Google's Ara, in part because the concretization of these technologies is environmentally destructive and economically wasteful. And yet, many of these projects were discontinued around 2017. So, when it comes to the material technologies of digital media, Simondon's categories remain useful, and can help us understand some of the political and economic issues related to our phones and computers, especially when one of the ways corporations such as Apple maintain control over their users is through the inability to change or tinker with its hardware.

Yuk Hui (2016) has suggested that many of Simondon's arguments can be used to describe digital media, though he makes several important claims that differentiate the digital from the mechanical. The digital, for Hui, is explicitly about data and data processing. A digital object, then, is a subset of Simondon's technical objects. Digital objects are concretized through the classification, organization, and definition of kinds of data – through the specification of *metadata*, or data about data. Second, through metadata, a digital object is placed in relation with other kinds of data that generate connections between objects. To put this in less abstract terms, Facebook records a wide range of data about its users. These are not objects, properly speaking, until they are classified and categorized. For instance, Facebook has recently developed computer vision techniques to identify what, precisely, is in the photographs uploaded and shared, which they call SharpMask (Dollar 2016). On the one hand, this helps blind users navigate the massive amount of visual information on Facebook, but, on the other hand, it also classifies the objects contained within a specific image, organizes them, and segments them into specific things. Facebook has generated data through the analysis of digital images – it has created metadata that explicitly define a set of objects within an image. We may think that an image uploaded to Facebook is itself an object, but Facebook makes even more objects out of an image through techniques that identify and separate the many 'objects' within any one photo.

Similar processes exist for any and all forms of data one uploads to Facebook. Status updates are classified according to the appearance of specific words, which are defined as having a specific emotional value. A status update like 'Feeling great today!' only becomes an object once Facebook codes it as, first, a status update and, second, as having an emotional value that is happy or positive. The reactions on Facebook also help to classify the emotional value of a specific status update. Given the wide range of objects that Facebook gathers, it then places its data into relation, which it can use to identify patterns or trends that help it to classify people, tastes, interests, and so on. These techniques involve, for Hui, both processes of individuation and individualization that transduce various energies to create digital objects through which Facebook 'knows' something about its users. With SharpMask, for instance, Facebook suggests that the identification of specific objects in images could lead to a range of practical functions. You could take a picture of a meal, for instance, and SharpMask would identify the different parts of what you're about to eat and tell you nutritional information. A photograph of a retail showroom could be linked to price information about the products on sale. It does this by making 'objects' out of an image, objects that are produced through classification of metadata and the linking to other forms of data.

The point here is not that these digital objects are the same as technical ones. They have their own 'mode of existence', but are also clearly in relation to the mechanical, technical means through which Facebook gathers data about its users. Facebook could not generate data about its users without the mechanical components of a mobile phone, for instance. Data would not exist without the phone's camera, microphone, touch screen, or motion sensing technology. These elements are, following Simondon, mechanical. The phone only exists because of how these different mechanical elements are concretized into a specific technical object that possesses a range of defined, mechanical functions. The digital is, then, not in opposition with the mechanical (or technical), but in relation with it. The capacities of digital media, which, for Hui, are about the gathering and linking of data, are located within the larger analysis of technology given by Simondon. The terms that Simondon provides for us can lead, perhaps, to a way of conceptualizing digital media that accounts both for the physicality of hardware and the specificity of something like a digital image, its functions, and its uses.

CONCLUSION

In this chapter I first reviewed the popular opposition between digital and analogue, introducing Alexander Galloway's recent attempt to theorize the digital as differentiation. These attempts to define the digital have some notable problems. In response, I introduced key terms from the philosophy of Gilbert Simondon to add the *mechanical* as another term that may be of more use than analogue. The digital is too often assumed to have a simple definition, and so this chapter was intended to make the digital far more complex, problematizing many of the ways it has been defined in the past.

We can suggest that digital culture be understood as emerging from specific practices and techniques brought about by digital media. This requires contemplation of the ontology of digital media, which shapes the possibilities for human bodies and relations. The physical materiality of digital media structures culture through the inscription of information and the performance of technique, which, again, contribute both to the 'whole way of life' of culture and its processes that define ideal forms of behaviour. We've discussed several different ways of thinking of how this happens, be it by way of a discussion of cultural techniques or through technical individualization.

At this point we need to bring history into the picture, to think about digital culture less through general theoretical terms and more through a historical lens, which leads us to particular practices and technologies – along with beliefs about them – that continue to influence the present. This will also lead us to a broader set of concepts and issues that are important for our attempts to theorize digital cultures. Thus, we turn to the legacy of cybernetics and how it has guided many of our understandings of technologies, identities, labour, architecture, and more.

PART II

HISTORIES, CONCEPTS, AND DEBATES

4

CYBERNETICS AND POSTHUMANISM

This chapter reviews the claims of Norbert Wiener's cybernetics and the numerous fields influenced by his work. It moves from the invention of cybernetics to recent definitions of posthumanism and transhumanism, along with the claims of second-order cybernetics. This chapter positions the legacy of cybernetics as central to how we imagine many of our digital technologies today, and it suggests that recent theoretical frames derived from cybernetics can be productive for examining the implications of digital media.

TERMS: apophenia; autopoiesis; black-boxing; cybernetics; cyberpunk; emergence; entropy; hylomorphism; imaginary; lag; liberal humanism; posthumanism; second-order cybernetics; system and environment; technological Singularity

THEORISTS: Rosi Braidotti, Peter Galison, Donna Haraway, N. Katherine Hayles, Ray Kurzweil, Niklas Luhmann, Humberto Maturana, Paul B. Preciado, Michel Serres, Alan Turing, Francisco Varela, Norbert Wiener, Cary Wolfe

EXAMPLES: electronic voice phenomena (EVP); Facebook's 'social graph'; lag compensation in online games; *Neuromancer*; *Playboy*; thermostats

We now turn away from the many definitions of 'digital' and 'culture' to a wider range of issues, many of which involve thinking through subjects that are important for digital culture today but are not always directly related to the impact or effects of digital media on culture. First, we will look at the history and continued influence of the science of **cybernetics**.

The term **cybernetics** is derived from the Greek word *kubernetes*, which means 'steersman'. This is the same Greek word from which we derive 'governor'. Cybernetics was the name used by Norbert Wiener, a mathematician who spent much of his life as a professor at MIT, to describe the science he had invented, a science dedicated towards understanding communication in both humans and machines, and how the transmission of messages shapes behaviour, often with the explicit purpose of managing human conduct. Cybernetics is a science of how communication can be used to *control* and *command* – a science of how to govern through messages.[1]

One of the earliest technologies that influenced Wiener's cybernetics was the centrifugal governor of James Watt, invented in 1788 to control the speed of an engine through the regulation of steam into the engine's cylinders. Many of today's technologies operate in a very similar way as the steam engine. For instance, we can use a thermostat to describe some of the general assumptions of cybernetics derived from Watt's governor (see Wiener 1961: 96–97). Let's say you've set a thermostat to 70 degrees Fahrenheit, or around 21 Celsius. The thermostat has a sensor that receives a 'message' from the room in which it is located. That message is the ambient temperature of the room. If the room is too cold or too hot, the thermostat sends a message to turn on either the heat or the air conditioning. It then signals for hot or cool air to stop when it receives feedback that the room has reached 70 degrees.

Of course, this process never really ends, with the heat or air conditioning kicking on and off in response to a change in the temperature of the room and how the sensor receives that 'message'. The different parts of the thermostat send messages to one another, and, consequentially, the temperature of the room remains the same thanks to the 'governance' of the thermostat. The room and the thermostat, along with the heating and the air conditioning, together produce one relatively closed **system** dedicated towards maintaining temperature. This is a simple way to describe how some technologies send and receive messages, and how technology can be used to maintain a kind of static equilibrium. Not only does this describe how thermostats work; countless other technologies use sensors to respond to specific things going on in the larger environment, from refrigerators and water heaters to interactive art installations that respond to light and motion. These technologies receive some message, perform some act, and then wait for feedback to respond to the changes they have caused to happen, all of which is governed according to how they have been set to maintain a kind of equilibrium within the system of which they are a part.

Cybernetics does not only explain these basic technologies. This model of communication has been used to describe countless forms of social, cultural, and biological interactions, be they between humans, brains, parts of bodies, or machines; be they technical, social, or economic. It can explain things as different as drug addiction, or changes in the weather, or cellular evolution. The basic ideas of cybernetics have been used to describe phenomena that may seem to be radically different from a thermostat, but, nonetheless, are framed as obeying similar principles related to the transmission of communication and information for the purposes of controlling and commanding.

Wiener was a child prodigy who received his PhD from Harvard when he was 17. His cybernetics has been one of the most influential bodies of thought of the twentieth century, and understanding both the history and implications of cybernetics are essential for theorizing today's digital culture. Many of the claims we make about digital media still repeat, if in subtle and often simplistic ways, the legacy inspired by Wiener's ideas (see, among others, Dyer-Witheford 2015; Franklin 2015; Halpern 2014; Hayles 1999). Some radical political theories suggest that we're located within a world defined by the assumptions of cybernetics, and that real political change will happen only when we challenge cybernetic theories (i.e. Invisible Committee 2015; Tiqqun 2011). In this chapter, we will discuss some of the foundations of Wiener's cybernetics and a few of the more recent versions of cybernetics indebted to him. We'll examine how these ideas have entered into popular culture and continue to shape how we think of the everyday reality of many of our technologies and our bodies. Finally, we'll review the emergence of **second-order cybernetics**, which has transformed Wiener's theories into a more productive, and often quite strange body of theory that crosses technology, sociology, biology, and beyond, stressing not command and control through communication, but the generative and emergent potential of noise and miscommunication.

What you should take from this chapter is, on the one hand, the historical background of a way of imagining human and technological activity that shapes culture today, one that remains influential. But, on the other hand, you should also understand cybernetics itself as a theoretical model that potentially describes how technology works and affects culture – a model that, as dated as it may seem at times, remains a productive place to look for and discover new ways to imagine and understand the relationship between humans and technology.

THE CYBERNETIC IMAGINARY

I'd like to begin with a fairly long quote from Wiener's 1950 book *The Human Use of Human Beings*. Wiener wrote this book for a popular audience to explain some of his ideas, which may still sound strange or confusing even though they were written to be understood by generalists. According to Wiener,

> ... society can only be understood through a study of the messages and the communication facilities which belong to it; and that in the future development of these messages and communication facilities, messages between man and machines, between machine and man, and between machine and machine, are destined to play an ever-increasing part. ... It is my thesis that the operation of the living individual and the operation of some of the newer communication machines are precisely parallel. Both of them have sensory receptors as one stage in their cycle of operation: that is, in both of them there exists a special apparatus for collecting information from the outer world at low energy levels, and for making it available in the operation of the individual or of the machine. In both cases these external messages are not taken *neat*, but through the internal transforming powers of the apparatus, whether it be alive or dead. The information is then turned into a new form available for the further stages of performance. In both animal and the machine this performance is made to be effective on the outer world. In both of them, their *performed* action on the outer world, and not merely their *intended* action, is reported back to the central regulatory apparatus. (1950: 9, 15, original italics)

Wiener is defining what he understands as fundamental to human life, animals, and communication technology. The social essence of both living being and machine can be found in the transmission of communication and how the physical form of both animals and machines receive, distort, and respond to messages. The human and the thermostat are, in many ways, analogous.

They both have a means for sensing and experiencing the external world. They both have a process for interpreting and understanding the messages they receive from their sensations, be it the mind of a human or the computational processing of a machine. And they use their interpretations to perform actions that have an effect on their external world. Importantly, what matters is what is *actually performed*, not what is intended, and not what ultimately remains inside the individual mind. What matters is what can be seen and sensed by others.

Here, there is an equivalency between the human body and communication technology, an equivalency that, in the years since Wiener's original writings, has been influential and popular in the study of media, communication, engineering, artificial intelligence, psychology, anthropology, government, and beyond. I term this equivalency between humans and machines the cybernetic **imaginary**. One of the reasons I use the word 'imaginary' is because, as a number of recent critics of cybernetics have noted, many assumptions about human bodies and brains made by early cyberneticists are factually incorrect. Neuroscience has shown that bodies and brains do not work the way that Wiener and his followers often assumed, and traditions in the humanities have long claimed that there is more to experience than the transmission of messages. Many beliefs that derive from cybernetics come from misleading metaphors made about technologies, projected onto the human body as if the brain was a computer, information network, telephone, or television. Yet, as wrong as they may be, these beliefs still have power in shaping assumptions about what human bodies are, about what consciousness is, about the 'nature' or 'essence' of the human as a creative, social, and economic being.

How we *think* of computers and technology is not inherently linked to the actual things computers and technology can do (Franklin 2015: xxi). The same goes for our bodies and minds. So, we need to take these ways of imagining human bodies and machines *as being imaginary*, but we also need to understand these fictitious beliefs as having an effect on the real, material practices we perform, practices that repeat an understanding of the human body as equivalent to an information-processing device.

Yet, when I use the word 'imaginary', I'm not simply using it to describe something that is fictional. Much as the theorist of photography Ariella Azoulay (2012) uses it, the imaginary should be thought of as something that exceeds an individual's mind, referring to the ways we understand (and imagine) our relations to each other. The imaginary, then, is a social and political relation. So, with the phrase 'cybernetic imaginary', I am drawing attention to how cybernetics has shaped a way of framing human relations as communicative, and has produced an understanding of collectivity that suggests that our bonds are derived from transmitting and receiving information with other beings who also transmit and receive information. To develop this claim requires a turn to the basic preconditions of, and arguments made by, Wiener's cybernetics.

Anti-Aircraft Guns and Information

According to the historian of science Peter Galison (1994), the foundations of cybernetics should be understood as emerging from the context of Wiener's military service. During the First World War, Wiener apprenticed in ballistic computation. Ballistic computation accounts for the physical limitations of guns and other firearms, improving targeting accuracy through mathematical analysis of gravity, friction, and other physical forces that affect the trajectory of a bullet, missile, or weapon. Because of his nearsightedness and lack of physical fitness, Wiener, while desiring to be of use to the American military in the Second World War, foresaw that he would have 'some sort of job in which I should apply computational techniques to electrical engineering problems' (Wiener 1956: 227), effectively continuing his service in the First World War, if at a different scale.

During the Second World War, Wiener worked on developing anti-aircraft guns that could accurately (and automatically) target and fire in ways that correct for limitations in the gunner's perception and knowledge (1956: 240–241). Wiener attempted to correct these problems with a device he named the 'anti-aircraft (AA) predictor', a practical, mechanical means for identifying and predicting where enemy planes would travel, in order to shoot them down. Wiener's plans to effectively automate anti-aircraft gunning were exceptionally ambitious. They had consequences for the military and much larger, though not particularly obvious, consequences for an understanding of human nature that would dominate a wide range of scientific thought from the 1950s onwards. Wiener was interested in understanding how one could use visible information to predict what was going to happen in the near future, controlling for and managing that which may seem to be unpredictable and beyond our ability to foresee. Wiener would frame both human bodies and technologies as pattern-generating objects that, if controlled for properly, could be predictable and easily managed – and killed, if need be.

As Wiener sees it, the issue is having two things (a plane and a shell, though he doesn't explicitly state this) end up in the same place at the same time. This would make the countless problems of warfare reducible to mathematical calculations of physics – of velocity, position, gravity, and so on. Framing war in the language of physics and mathematics belies what is really at stake: an anti-aircraft gunner shooting a plane piloted by a human, with the gunner shooting down the plane and killing the pilot (who is also, assumedly, trying to kill the anti-aircraft gunner). Wiener frames the human actors and casualties of warfare with the following:

> There are two human elements which must be considered in this control. On the one hand, when the airplane pilot is flying and taking evasive action, his pattern of flight has a great deal to do with not only the limitations of his plane but those of his nervous system. ... On the other hand, the anti-aircraft gunner uses a technique in which he cannot follow his target perfectly but in which he introduces certain random errors because of the limitations of his sense organs and muscles. These two sorts of human elements are combined as part of the semimechanical processes by which the anti-aircraft gunner brings down his target. (1956: 251)

Both gunner and pilot become part of the same cybernetic system, sending each other messages, much like the thermostat described at the beginning of this chapter reacting to the ambient temperature of a room. And, through Wiener's experiments with the AA predictor, this understanding of messages and feedback would become a way to model all human behaviour and cognition. To use the words of Peter Galison, 'Wiener came to see the [anti-aircraft] predictor as a prototype not only of the mind of an inaccessible Axis opponent but of the Allied antiaircraft gunner as well, and then even more widely to include the vast array of human proprioceptive and electrophysiological feedback systems ... the AA predictor ... became, for Wiener, the model for a cybernetic understanding of the universe itself' (1994: 229).

Given how it was formulated during the Second World War, cybernetics should be understood in the context of a specific kind of racism that has often characterized Western beliefs about their enemies from that time. Namely, Axis soldiers were often assumed by Allied forces to be sub-human 'Others' who did not qualify as human beings, and thus killing them could be morally legitimated because the 'Other' was not considered to be fully human, with other races 'thought of as lice, ants, or vermin to be eradicated' (Galison 1994: 230). This kind of Othering is typical in contexts where specific people or groups of people are rendered less than human, unworthy of rights, and functionally excluded from social bonds, be it for social exclusion or for their literal extermination, as is in the case of war and genocide. As a number of philosophers have argued, this racist Othering is foundational for modern forms of community and the State (see Agamben 1998; Foucault 1997). Community and collectivity are based not around sharing something in common, but through the exclusion of others because they do not possess what we consider to be 'essential' for them to be recognized as another human being.

As Galison notes, this Othering is foundational for cybernetics and Wiener's anti-aircraft experiments, although with a subtle and important variation. The enemy Other, for Wiener, was not sub-human and deserving of extermination because of racist assumptions about their humanity – at least not entirely. Rather, the cybernetic Other was physically and morally distant, to be understood through mechanical means that conflated the enemy with technology, 'a vision in which the enemy pilot was so merged with machinery that (his) human-nonhuman status was blurred' (Galison 1994: 233). The enemy deserved exclusion and extermination because the system demanded it. The inability to know anything about the Other meant that much of their humanity would be **black-boxed**, excluded from knowledge, while that which could be observed (the movements of the aeroplane, namely) would account for the Other's location within a cybernetic system that would achieve 'equilibrium' with their destruction, much like a thermostat achieves equilibrium by maintaining a steady temperature. The racism of exclusion, here, had been converted into a mathematical mechanism that suggested that war and the killing of others could be imagined through an 'objective' scientific means that assumed the death of another to be that which naturally, inevitably resulted from the mechanical, physical workings of a cybernetic system.

While initially proposed to explain and account for the behaviour of an unknowable enemy, in which knowledge can only be gleaned through observable information detected and analyzed through technological means, Wiener would eventually begin to explain all human behaviour – and all behaviour, full stop – through this lens that would equate and conflate human and machine. While it may seem callous or inhumane to make the leap between a human being to a thermostat, Wiener makes this leap when he describes human behaviour. The enemy pilot becomes a part of a technical system to be controlled and eliminated, a system that operates analogously to a thermostat controlling the temperature of a room.

A direct descendent of Wiener's experiments with the anti-aircraft predictor may be familiar to you if you happen to play online multiplayer games. While single-player games are usually hosted on an individual's computer or gaming console, online games require access to a central server owned or operated by a game company. These central servers allow for data between many different users across the globe to play a shared game together. Many games are set up differently, but pretty much all online, multiplayer games have different tasks delegated to the user's computer at times, and others delegated to the game's central servers, the latter of which is the authoritative 'world' of the game. It takes time for data to move between computers, which is a massive problem for game designers who want to create worlds in which users from all over the planet can seemingly be in the same virtual 'space'. This is even more of a problem in action-heavy games. The link between the user's computer and the servers can potentially break down at various moments, be it because someone's computer is overloaded or if the network connection is slow.

Whenever this happens in online games, there's an annoying phenomenon called **lag**, when the data transmitted between a user's computer isn't synchronized with that of the game's servers (see Boellstorff 2008: 101–106). Characters may freeze, shots taken may not go where intended, and so on. These errors in gameplay are not due to the actions taken by a player, but because of the time it takes to move game data between the user and the server. Many games, as a result, use 'lag compensation' to deal with the latencies between a user and the server. Some methods of lag compensation work almost exactly like the AA predictor. Using actions that a user *has* performed, the game extrapolates actions that a user *will take* in the future and uses these predictions so the user is still 'playing' even if there is significant lag. Using visible evidence, the software predicts the movements that will happen in the future. And when it comes to the multiplayer modes of games like *Call of Duty*, the militaristic origins of something like lag compensation are even more clear: lag compensation enables a bullet fired in the game to go where intended, accounting for other technical and environmental considerations that may otherwise prevent it from reaching its target.

We can see how some of Wiener's assumptions still remain with us, at least when it comes to games. But the implications of cybernetics are far broader than this. As Wiener's worldview expanded from technology, to the enemy, to all humans, it carried with it a number of assumptions that, together, theorist N. Katherine Hayles refers to as **posthumanism**, which she defines as having four elements:

First, the posthuman view privileges *informational pattern* over material instantiation, so that embodiment in a biological substrate is seen as an accident of history rather than an inevitability of life.

Second, the posthuman view considers *consciousness*, regarded as the seat of human identity in the Western tradition long before Descartes thought he was a mind thinking, as an epiphenomenon, as an evolutionary upstart trying to claim that it is the whole show when in actuality it is only a minor sideshow. Third, the posthuman view thinks of *the body as the original prosthesis* we all learn to manipulate, so that extending or replacing the body with other prostheses becomes a continuation of a process that began before we were born. Fourth, and most important, by these and other means, the posthuman view configures human being so that it can be seamlessly *articulated with intelligent machines*. (1999: 2–3, italics added)

We will now take these four attributes of posthumanism in turn.

Identity as Informational Pattern

According to Wiener, 'One of the most interesting aspects of the world is that it can be considered to be made up of *patterns*. A pattern is essentially an arrangement. It is characterized by the order of the elements of which it is made, rather than by the intrinsic nature of these elements' (1950: 3). 'Content' and 'meaning' are ultimately irrelevant; what matters is how a specific set of basic elements are arranged, which can be mathematically modelled. With Wiener's posthumanism, we are a regular pattern that is divorced from the physical material of the biological body: 'The physical identity of an individual does not consist in the matter of which it is made ...' (1950: 108). The inventor and futurist Ray Kurzweil, who we'll discuss a bit more in a moment, repeats this view when he suggests he is a 'patternist', or 'someone who views patterns of information as the fundamental reality' (2005: 5). This is a common belief among many of those inventing and experimenting with new technologies. But what does it even mean to suggest that we, and the world as a whole, are essentially 'patterns'?

Wiener is presuming a fundamental distinction between form, as a regular pattern that makes up the human mind (or anything else), and matter, as something relatively insignificant beyond its role as the material support in which form manifests itself. This distinction is derived from ancient Greek philosophy, specifically a distinction that Aristotle made between *hyle*, or matter, and *morphe*, or form. This doctrine of **hylomorphism**, as it was later termed by readers of Aristotle, suggested 'the universe of matter is given shape and identity by the forms or essence that imbue it. The intelligibility of material objects owes to the forms that *in-form* them, shaping them from within' (Peters 1988: 10–11). Following from the doctrine of hylomorphism, 'information', then, would be a word that refers to this internal form of organization, the pattern that gives form to matter.

This belief led to one of Wiener's most seemingly outlandish claims: that we can extract a person from their physical body, transmit them through telegraph wires, and reconstruct them elsewhere (1950: 110–111). This has been depicted in *Star Trek* with its transporter, transmitting human bodies from one location to another, in *Willy Wonka and the Chocolate Factory*, when Mike Teavee is beamed into a WonkaVision set, in *The Prestige* (which has a particularly unique and disturbing version of this theme), and has long influenced science fiction.

Wiener's understanding of the relationship between information and energy is also particularly interesting to note. Now, I am simplifying these terms significantly, and Wiener's use of some of these terms is often atypical. The laws of thermodynamics are here important, which explain why hot things get colder, and why perpetual motion machines cannot exist. Specifically, Wiener draws on the second law of thermodynamics, which states that in a thermodynamic system **entropy** always increases. Entropy is a quantitative measure of disorder, and a thermodynamic system is a closed and bounded system, within which energy is transferred between material bodies. Or, to put things differently, in a closed system disorder increases and heat is lost.

Imagine a completely closed room. There are no drafts, windows, or doors in this room, and its insulation is a perfect barrier. Literally nothing comes in or goes out. This room would be a closed thermodynamic system. Even if it starts out as a very warm room, if there's no energy put into it, then it gets colder over time and the things in the room get more disorganized and fall apart. Now, in reality, there are no truly closed thermodynamic systems outside those artificially produced in a laboratory. Even the best insulation cannot keep heat from being lost to an external environment. But in a completely closed system entropy increases until a point of total disorganization and a complete loss of heat. This is often referred to as 'heat death', a point in which there is no more energy and life can no longer be sustained. Some theoretical physicists think that, at some point in the future, the universe will achieve 'heat death' in a kind of inversion of the 'big bang', as energy runs out and the universe achieves a kind of pure disorder.

I'm not as interested in the actual physics behind the laws of thermodynamics here as I am in Wiener's opposition between entropy and information. An example may help explain this. If you're reading a print copy of this book, it is, assumedly, bound together, its pages in a specific order. It has a lot of 'information' because it has a very specific pattern. For it to be this book, *Theorizing Digital Cultures*, the letters and words I am using, the pages that follow one after another, all must conform to this order. Information is not the meaning you get from the specific words you are reading, but the fact that there is a specific arrangement that makes up the content of this book. Following Wiener's understanding of information, *Theorizing Digital Cultures* is not the *specific* book you're currently holding, but that which 'in-forms' the material organization of letters, words, and pages you currently hold. You certainly could think of this book as a pattern that is ordered, and potentially located in countless other material forms (be it a PDF file, or an eBook to be read on a Kindle or iPad). But if you take your book's cover off and throw the pages into the air, when these pages land, they are now disordered. If you go further and take scissors to cut up the pages, disorder increases even more. Entropy has increased, and information has decreased. Of course, there's still some order – but significantly less. And were you to let this book sit for a decade, two decades, a century or two ... the pages would begin to decay away. The actual matter of this book would lose some of its physical organization. The information that in-forms this book gradually loses its battle against disorder as entropy increases.

But, Wiener notes, the beauty of cybernetics comes from how humans and machines can correct for and resist the tendency towards entropy. Through negative feedback, like what we saw with the thermostat, cybernetic systems are able to correct for disorder, maintaining a high degree of information, maintaining order. And, suggests Wiener, the maintenance of this pattern is an act that happens not only through mechanical tools and physical processes, but in the most basic aspects of our biology:

> We are so used to feedback phenomena in our daily life that we often forget the feedback nature of the simplest processes. When we stand erect, it is not in the manner in which a statue stands erect. ... Human beings stand erect ... because they are continually resisting the tendency to fall down, either forward or backward, and manage to offset either tendency by a contraction of muscles pulling them in the opposite direction. ... Our standing and our walking are thus a continual jujitsu against gravity, as life is a perpetual wrestling match with death. (1956: 267–269)

Even standing up can be thought of as a maintenance of a pattern against the forces of disorder. Life, as a cybernetic process, resists disorder (be it entropy, gravity, or death) in the name of the maintenance of patterns. As Hayles notes, this view has been taken up in a massive amount of science influenced by the legacy of cybernetics. In sciences such as Artificial Life, which uses computers to create 'organisms' that simulate life (and are 'alive' in many ways), 'Form can logically be separated from matter; form is privileged over matter; *form defines life*, whereas the material basis merely instantiates life' (Hayles 1999: 231, original italics).

The everyday implications of this may seem vague at this point. But, if we think of ourselves in the language of cybernetics, then our identities effectively become patterns. We can suggest that this is how social media and current forms of marketing understand our identities. Facebook's 'Social Graph' is a mapping of all of the data you've uploaded throughout your time using Facebook. It's a collection of links, of likes and reactions, of friendships, of posts on people's walls, and more. It records what other websites you've been to, and how long you spend looking at specific images and profiles based on technologies Facebook is continually developing to convert your actions into data. 'You', in this case, are little more than the pattern that can be identified by your social media and internet use. So, when Mark Zuckerberg claims that your Facebook profile is the 'real you', he is following a cybernetic understanding of identity.

The Irrelevance of Consciousness

But, you may think, isn't what makes me *me* the thoughts and ideas that I have going on inside my head? The things I keep private? My conscious life? Some interior 'self'? On the contrary, cybernetics suggests that your interior life is ultimately unknowable and has little effect on the external world. As we've already heard from Wiener, in both humans and machines, 'their *performed* action on the outer world, and not merely their *intended* action, is reported back to the central regulatory apparatus' (1950: 15, original italics). The second implication of posthumanism is that consciousness is irrelevant. Instead, what matters is what is performed and made visible to others. A thought is only significant if it is communicated to another.

We can already see how this view works in Wiener's thought, as he reimagines the enemy and the anti-aircraft gunner as part of a system that transmits messages back and forth, as the mind of the enemy pilot is black-boxed and excluded from understanding. This is also similar to some of the arguments made by the British computer scientist and mathematician Alan Turing in his writings on mechanical intelligence, such as the 1950 essay 'Computing Machinery and Intelligence'. In this essay, Turing wanted to reimagine the question 'can machines think?' To do so, he drew on 'the imitation game', a parlour game in which two individuals, a man and a woman, would be hidden in a separate room from a third individual, an interrogator. The interrogator, through a series of questions, would determine the genders of the other individuals, although the two hidden away would be allowed to lie. The imitation game asked a simple question that intrigued Turing. Could one identify the gender of another through nothing but textual evidence, evidence that may be fabricated? Could a man successfully pretend to be a woman once his body is no longer visible?

Turing's game was not intended to be about gender, although it implicitly relies on a specific gender politics (see Halberstam 1991). 'We now ask the question, "What will happen when a machine takes the part of [one of the hidden players] in this game?" Will the interrogator decide wrongly as often when the game is played like this as he does when the game is played between a man and a woman? These questions replace our original, "Can machines think?"' (Turing 1992: 134). The implication of the imitation game, often referred to as 'the Turing test', is that a computer or machine can be considered to think or have a mind as long as it *appears* to have a mind. This is a *performative* understanding of identity and self, as it suggests that what's inside has no real effect on this world, and we should imagine who we are entirely in terms of what we do and how we interact with others. Therefore, a simulation of intelligence is as good as the real thing, as interior consciousness doesn't actually matter.

'The Turing test treats indiscernibles as identicals', claims John Durham Peters, 'A smart machine would be proved intelligent by passing: by the inability of the third part to tell the two veiled interlocutors apart. ... Turing gives us communication as if bodies did not matter ...' (1999: 236). The Turing test suggests that the only thing important in determining intelligence is the ability to textually perform identity. Identity is an informational pattern that exists outside a body; it is explicitly communicated and not kept private inside one's mind. As the British cyberneticist Ross Ashby put it in 1948, 'To some, the critical test of whether a machine is or is not a "brain" would be whether it can or cannot "think". But to the biologist the brain is not a thinking machine, it is an *acting* machine; it gets information and then it does something about it' (quoted in Pickering 2010: 6). While these different theorists I've referred to here had different views about the specificity of the human body and the function of the brain, the end results of their claims are similar. In taking up questions about the ability of a machine to think, consciousness was no longer a sign of intelligence, but instead intelligence becomes about visible acts and their performance.

The Body as Prosthesis

The third implication of posthumanism is an effect of the first two implications, although it brings them together in a way that may also seem contradictory. If identity is a pattern that can be removed from physical matter, placed into other bodies, and what matters is what is performed, not what is inside, then the body itself becomes a flexible and fluid 'thing' that is merely in-formed by the 'pattern' that is 'me'. The 'real me' is the pattern, though that pattern only exists through the visible means through which it can be observed. What does this mean for 'me'? Where is my 'identity'? Am 'I' merely the visible patterns that I perform? Does my body really matter at all, beyond being a specific way that these patterns are made visible? By framing the body as inessential, as a prosthesis that provides the material instantiation of the pattern that is 'me', the roboticist Hans Moravec can then claim, as he does in his influential book *Mind Children*:

> It should be possible to reconstruct many missing pieces [of identity] from other information – the person's genetic code, for instance, or filmstrips of the person in life, samples of handwriting, medical records, memories of associates, and so on. ... The pattern-identity position implies that a person reconstructed by inference would be just as real as one reconstructed from an intact tape. The only difference is that in the former case some of the person's pattern was temporarily diffused in the environment before being reassembled. (1988: 122)

You are what can be observed – your pattern is both inside you but is, in reality, completely there in the visible, recorded data you slough off in daily life. But what of the physical human body, then? The body is one way of performing a pattern, one that is ultimately inessential for defining who you are and what you do. As a prosthesis it can be replaced by, say, a robot body, which is what Moravec ultimately argues (1999: 77).

This dimension of posthumanism often receives objections. Beginning with the philosophers Edmund Husserl and Maurice Merlau-Ponty, among others, the physical human body has been positioned as central to how we understand our world and our location in it. Who 'I' am is directly founded in the physical, embodied capacities I have for movement. Recent work in neuroscience and cognitive philosophy has supported these claims, demonstrating that a separation between mind and body, as implied by posthumanism, is untenable. Mind is not separate from body; it cannot be downloaded from the body and uploaded into a robot. Mind is what the body does, not a program that 'runs' on the brain like a piece of software runs on a computer. But some of those following posthuman traditions have then suggested that, while we may never be able to completely discard the body, we are nonetheless 'in the grip of a seductive but quite untenable illusion: the illusion that the mechanisms of mind and self can ultimately unfold only on some privileged stage marked out by the good old-fashioned skin-bag' (Clark 2003: 27). We'll return to these questions in Chapter 6, because they're more complex than I'm suggesting here (for instance, Andy Clark, whom I have cited above, does not argue that we can completely get rid of the body, unlike Kurzweil and Moravec). For now, just know that posthumanism makes the necessity of the physical, biological body questionable. While a complete loss of the body may be a mistake, the body nonetheless becomes a prosthesis interchangeable or augmentable with any other technical prosthesis.

The Technological Singularity

The fourth implication of the posthuman identified by Hayles is that humans and machines can be seamlessly articulated. If the essence of both human and machine are informational patterns, patterns that can be observed and performed by any prosthetic body, then there is a fundamental equivalence between human and machine implied by posthumanism. 'I have spoken of machines, but not only of machines having brains of brass and thews of iron', notes Wiener near the end of *The Human Use of Human Beings*. 'When human atoms are knit into an organization in which they are used, not in their full right as responsible human beings, but as cogs and levers and rods, it matters little that their raw material is flesh and blood. *What is used as an element in a machine, is an element in the machine*' (1950: 212–213, original italics). Wiener was uncomfortable with the implications of his theory. He saw cybernetics as revealing an equivalence between human and machine that made the human body into little more than a cog that could then be used by others.

While Wiener was sceptical of the implications of his own theories, in recent years the articulation of human and machine in cybernetics has emerged as a kind of theological desire for a **technological Singularity**, where technology serves as a metaphysical saviour that enables us to escape the physical limit of death. Associated most notably with Ray Kurzweil, the inventor and futurist I briefly mentioned above, the technological Singularity is a moment predicted to happen around 2048, at which time the technical capability of technology is believed to exceed that of the human body and brain. Kurzweil, who has played a foundational role in the development of many digital technologies, such as optical character recognition (or the ability of computers to 'read' through the recognition of text characters), speech recognition, and synthesizers, has argued that humans will become combined with technology as our storage and processing hardware become more effective than our brains. The technological Singularity

> will allow us to transcend [the] limitations of our biological bodies and brains. … Our mortality will be in our own hands. We will be able to live as long as we want (a subtly different statement from saying we will live forever). We will fully understand human thinking and will vastly extend and expand its reach. By the end of this century, the nonbiological portion of our intelligence will be trillions of trillions of times more powerful than unaided human intelligence. … There will be no distinction, post-Singularity, between human and machine or between physical and virtual reality. (Kurzweil 2005: 9)

The idea of the Singularity has been influential for a great deal of science fiction, venture capital, and art (see Krysa & Parikka, 2015), and – in my opinion, at least – is perhaps best represented in the *Black Mirror* episode 'San Junipero' (2016).

The possibility of the Singularity ever happening has been heavily criticized, not merely for its technical feasibility but for problems of class and a seeming lack of concern with the physical reality of the planet Earth. Assumedly, these technologies will not be available to all. Even if they were, would we then live in a virtual world and let Earth waste away from the pollution produced by servers and technical infrastructure? Who would maintain these computers? Kurzweil seems to think that these processes would be automated, but the actual construction of the Singularity seems to be rife with countless political issues and problems. But I do agree with Kurzweil when he suggests that a 'primary political and philosophical issue of the next century will be the definition of who we are' (1999: 2). The posthuman reveals how the science and technology developed after the Second World War seriously call into question just what a human is or can be, along with the relationship the human has with technology.

Transhumanism versus Posthumanism

It's difficult to make complete sense of posthumanism. Wiener seems to assume that human beings are little more than information processing devices, interchangeable with computers, an argument that also disturbs his own beliefs about the value of human life. There is a significant reason to doubt this view of human nature and biology, as it doesn't mesh with a great deal of what current neuroscience claims about the human body and cognition, for instance. Nonetheless, cybernetics has been massively influential in science, popular culture, and serves to generally define many of the ways we think of ourselves on social media (see Bollmer 2016). If it doesn't happen on Facebook, after all, who's to say if it actually happened at all? Much of our online identity is entirely based out of what we upload and transmit. Our identities online are often thought to be completely informational. Additionally, Hayles is somewhat positive, or at least ambivalent, about posthumanism:

> But the posthuman does not really mean the end of humanity. It signals instead the end of a certain conception of the human, a conception that may have applied, at best, to that fraction of humanity who had the wealth, power, and leisure to conceptualize themselves as autonomous beings exercising their will through individual agency and choice. What is lethal is not the posthuman as such but the grafting of the posthuman onto a liberal humanist view of the self. (1999: 286–287)

What we should be wary of is not a view that questions the boundaries of the human and the overlap between human and machine, but of a perspective that positions this overlap in the service of **liberal humanism**, of a view that suggests we're isolated, rational, and free individuals in competition. Donna Haraway, the renowned feminist theorist of science, makes a similar claim. Haraway notes that the transformation of biology between the First World War and the present has increasingly thought of the biological in terms of cybernetic systems, which are themselves framed in terms of the demands of capitalist markets (1991: 62, 68). But Haraway nonetheless notes that the intersection of cybernetics and biology produces a new figure, a *cyborg*, that, as she argues in her famous 'Cyborg Manifesto', could undermine historical systems of domination and oppression through a commitment to hybridity that questions the boundaries between humans, animals, and machines (1991: 149–181).

In recent years, the more hopeful interpretation of cybernetics and its legacy offered by Haraway and Hayles has proven to be quite influential, often through different attempts to define the posthuman from the one offered by Hayles. Theorists such as Cary Wolfe and Rosi Braidotti have been explicit in differentiating posthumanism from what they term *transhumanism*. For Wolfe and Braidotti, transhumanism is the belief we have sketched above – the dream that technology and information permit us to transcend the human body (Braidotti 2013: 91). In fact, as Wolfe argues, humanism has historically been defined through reference to 'animal' others and is 'achieved by escaping or repressing not just its animal origins in nature, the biological, and the evolutionary, but more generally by transcending the bonds of materiality and embodiment altogether'. Thus, the view espoused by Wiener and his followers is actually 'an *intensification* of humanism', an attempt to purify the human through a deliberate and continual attempt at excluding anything and everything that could be thought to acknowledge how the human is a biological, animal being (Wolfe 2010: xv). In its attempts to define the human as a kind of informational pattern, extractable from matter, cybernetics is an extension of modern humanism that suggests that the essence of the human being is in thought, mind, and rationality, rather than a physical relationship to the body and the environment.

The posthuman, for Wolfe and Braidotti, is a way of undoing the most limiting aspects of the legacy of liberal humanism. Rather than a human defined through the exclusion of the animal and the technological, the posthuman becomes a way of imagining the world in which nature and culture are not clearly separated, in which life includes life beyond the human, acknowledging the role of other beings in the creation of the world. The posthuman is, thus, not really about the end of *humans*, but the end of a perspective that suggests humans exist outside the rest of the world, making the world little more than for the use of humankind. As we attempted to demonstrate in our discussion of culture, the posthuman likewise shows how culture is made up of material practices that involve technologies and techniques, and how the human is itself a product of these cultural techniques through which we come to know our own bodies, our relations, and identities.

POPULAR CYBERNETICS

The influence of cybernetics has not just been on science, technology, and philosophy; its implications for popular culture should not be understated. Probably the most significant influence cybernetics has had on popular culture, or at least the most visible, has been in science fiction, and particularly a version of science fiction from the 1980s and 1990s referred to as **cyberpunk**. William Gibson's canonical *Neuromancer* (1984) took the model of the human proposed by cybernetics and linked it with a kind of digital space divorced from physical reality. Gibson explains this by way of a television show in his novel:

> 'The matrix has its roots in primitive arcade games', said the voice-over, 'in early graphics programs and military experimentation with cranial jacks'. On the Sony, a two-dimensional space war faded behind a forest of mathematically generated ferns, demonstrating the special possibilities of logarithmic spirals; cold blue military footage burned through, lab animals wired into test systems, helmets feeding into fire control circuits of tanks and war planes. 'Cyberspace. A consensual hallucination experienced daily by billions of legitimate operators, in every nation, by children being taught mathematical concepts. ... A graphic representation of data abstracted from the banks of every computer in the human system. Unthinkable complexity. Lines of light ranged in the nonspace of the mind, clusters and constellations of data. Like city lights, receding...' (1984: 67)

Beginning with the assumptions of cybernetics, Gibson proposes an online world that emerges from the conjunction of military technology and videogames, in which we become data that can be uploaded into a world separate from the physical one we inhabit. Like *Neuromancer*, other cyberpunk novels depict a seemingly dystopian future in which human bodies and information machines are interchangeable, such as Neal Stephenson's *Snow Crash* (1992), much of which takes place in an online world called 'the Metaverse'. Not only were these novels influential for shaping an entire generation of science fiction films (including, but not limited to, the various *Matrix* films, *Strange Days*, *Lawnmower Man*, and the more recent movies *Gamer* and *Transcendence*), they also influenced the design of actual online spaces. We once called the internet 'cyberspace' because of *Neuromancer*, and *Snow Crash*'s Metaverse has served as a model for countless online virtual worlds. Even though many of these representations seem dated, they increasingly appear to be returning with the renewed dream of an online virtual reality, now managed through social media and Facebook's Oculus Rift, which promise a return to cyberspace rather than social networking platforms. Many episodes of *Black Mirror*, as well, return us to many of these concerns, if more clearly grounded in everyday anxieties about mobile phones and social media.

The worlds depicted in cyberpunk do not exist and, most likely, cannot exist. Cyberspace is, as the literary critic Fredric Jameson puts it, 'a literary construction we tend to believe in … there are certainly historical reasons for its appearance … which greatly transcend the technological fact of computer development of the invention of the Internet' (2015: 222). Gibson draws on the legacy of cybernetics and transforms it into an imagined world, one that emerges at a specific moment – and is taken up in popular culture more broadly – because of how it happens to map things that are happening elsewhere in culture. If we think back to our definitions of culture, *Neuromancer* and cyberpunk happen to *document* a specific way of understanding daily life at a specific moment in time. They may appear to be about technology but are, in fact, using technology to discuss much larger contextual transformations. In this way, cybernetics and the fiction it has inspired should be thought of less as a scientific imagining of how human bodies and technologies will operate in the future, and more as a way of understanding a present filled with the increasing presence of apparently lively machines while, at the same time, the agency of an individual human appears to wane away. For Jameson, Gibson gives us 'a picture and a sense of our individual relationships to realities that transcend our phenomenological mapping systems and our cognitive abilities to think them' (2015: 234–235). The future depicted by cyberpunk (and cybernetics) is a charting of specific desires and anxieties of a world remade through technologies determined to transform the body into data, a world remade into a space permeated by information.

Even beyond cyberpunk and science fiction, the way of imagining the relationship between the human body, technology, and communication proposed with cybernetics has been widespread in Western culture since the 1950s. For instance, theorist of sexuality, technology, and architecture Paul B. Preciado has suggested that we should understand the cultural significance of *Playboy* magazine in relationship to the intertwining of the body, information, and technology proposed by cybernetics – the lifestyle depicted in *Playboy* was not just about the invention of mid-century (male) sexuality, but one that imagined the body as a cybernetic system. While we may think of *Playboy* as completely divorced from our discussion of cybernetics and cyberspace, it too depicts specific elements about bodies, behaviours, and technologies that are effectively 'posthuman'.

Focusing on the architecture and furniture design of the bedrooms and kitchens depicted in *Playboy*, Preciado notes that the bed became a space for work, leisure, and entertainment – a space that does this because of its intertwining with information flows and communications media (2014: 146, 161). *Playboy* transforms the bedroom into a space for the transmission of data flows, in which video enables various streams of information to enter (via television, the VCR, and so on) and exit (through video cameras, surveillance technologies, and, today, social media). The body becomes modified by pharmaceuticals that alter the chemicals in one's brain to transform the physical capacities of what a body does and why, be it to stay up all night, to have more focus while working, or to have sex (or all three). Quite literally, the body is synthesized with technologies that transform its physical capacities.

Playboy is just one example, one that was particularly early in framing the human body as a thing in dialogue with media technologies, transmitting flows of information throughout the world. Today, the varied technological infrastructures that are central to everyday technology and large-scale city planning and logistics alike demonstrate how we conceive our world as one in which information flows are ultimately what matter (see Bollmer 2016; Easterling 2014). Our world has been remade through the beliefs supplied by cybernetics about human nature, the material world, and the essential organizing properties of information. The world we inhabit came into being through the articulation of material reality with a set of ideas that remake everything into circulating flows that blur the distinction between human, animal, and machine.

FROM FIRST- TO SECOND-ORDER CYBERNETICS

It is easy to be dismissive of cybernetics, given how many of its claims appear to be associated with the legacy of the military, and how it seems to fear or disdain the human body in favour of dematerialized information. But the legacy of cybernetics is far broader and more interesting than a focus on Wiener alone would indicate. As with the more 'positive' understanding of the posthuman discussed above, there are many permutations of cybernetics that draw on Wiener in order to challenge some of his assumptions about the human brain and body, and, especially, the relationship we have to our environment and 'control'.

A major difference between Wiener's cybernetics and more recent work in cybernetics is the move from 'first-order' systems to 'second-order' systems. A first-order system is something like the thermostat we've been discussing throughout this chapter. Through communication and feedback, the thermostat and room create a 'closed' system that maintains a balanced, controlled temperature. But, there's a problem here. These kinds of systems almost never exist in reality. It's not really possible to completely seal off a room to create a closed system. Think about the old cliché where a parent gets angry because one of their children has left the door open, which then lets out heat (if it's too cold out) or lets in heat (it it's too hot). Keeping a house climate controlled, after all, costs money. This is because a house may be temporarily sealed off from outside, but doors and windows do open, after all. The room is never completely sealed off and self-contained. There's always a larger **environment** or 'medium' in which these systems take place.

Second-order cybernetics stresses the importance of this larger environment, bringing back issues of materiality, questioning the ability of messages to fully control a system. A system is always embedded in a larger medium, which is itself material and shapes the possibilities for a system to constitute itself. At best, the closure of a system through a technology like a thermostat only makes sense because it is in constant interaction with a larger environment that causes the room's temperature to change. The door may open, people may move in and out. The first-order system is only functionally or operationally closed in relation to the larger environment with which it interacts. So, to conclude this chapter, I want to review some of the key concepts of second-order cybernetics, concepts which serve to open up our understanding of cybernetic models in describing contemporary digital culture beyond the dematerialized, deterministic models offered by Wiener.

System and Environment

The most significant concepts developed by second-order cybernetics are those of **system and environment**. Let's once again return to our example of the thermostat. It's not just that the sensor in the thermostat is understanding the temperature of a room and adjusting the heat or air conditioning in relation to it. In the movement of information from the room, to the thermostat, to the heating or air conditioning devices, the elements in this system are constituting themselves *as a system*, as distinct from a larger environment that is outside the boundaries of that system. The system is not intrinsically closed, *but closes itself*, and, through feedback, constantly attempts to maintain its boundaries and coherency as a system. So, as doors and windows open, and people move into and out of the room, the thermostat works to make sure that the system remains closed, even though it effectively cannot be. The relationship between system and environment, then, is one of *differentiation*, defined by the social theorist Niklas Luhmann, one of the most significant writers to use the tools of second-order cybernetics to describe social relations, as 'nothing more than the repetition within systems of the difference between system and environment' (1995: 7). This act of differentiation is self-referential, meaning that the performance of differentiation is about identifying a 'self' as clearly distinct and defined. While we may not think of a thermostat as a kind of 'self', its actions are about maintaining a system's boundaries and consistency, a 'self' that is distinct from the environment in which it exists.

Autopoiesis

Another term for this self-referential act of distinction is **autopoiesis**, a concept that comes from the work of biologists Humberto Maturana and Francisco Varela. Autopoiesis means self-producing or self-making. According to Maturana and Varela, all living beings are characterized by an autopoietic form of self-organization, which is a kind of 'bootstrapping' mechanism through which an entity differentiates itself from a larger environment. 'The most striking feature of an autopoietic system', they state, 'is that it pulls itself up by its own bootstraps and becomes distinct from its environment through its own dynamics, in such a way that both things are inseparable' (1987: 46–47). Autopoiesis means that the actions I take differentiate me from the world I inhabit, but also means that I am foundationally embedded in my environment. I become the 'system' differentiated from the 'environment' assumed by second-order cybernetics. As a result, every system is, to use the words of Maturana and Varela, *structurally coupled* with the environment. A system is never fully or permanently differentiated; in fact, it can only maintain its differentiation in relation to the larger environment (so, for instance, I have to eat food and breathe air to survive – the boundaries that differentiate me from my environment are constantly regulating the relationship I have with the environment, and the acts of eating and breathing transform part of my environment into my body).

Maturana and Varela begin with the assumption that the clear existence of 'any being, object, thing, or unity' comes from 'making an *act of distinction* which distinguishes what has been indicated as separate from its background. Each time we refer to anything explicitly or implicitly, we are specifying a *criterion of distinction*, which indicates what we are talking about and specifies its properties as being, unity, or object' (1987:

40, original italics). Much as we saw with Galloway and his discussion of the digital in the previous chapter, we begin by making distinctions in this world, sorting out one thing from another negatively. But Maturana and Varela extend this act of distinction further – my own self-identity involves a self-reflexive act that differentiates me from my environment. And, because this is not about consciousness, this act is potentially performed by any living entity (or, if we take the posthuman implications of cybernetics seriously, any 'active' entity capable of sending and receiving messages, full stop). As is the case with Wiener, life is a performative act, not about internal thoughts and an inner life, but about exterior behaviours. These acts make distinctions between system and environment that sustain the autonomy of an entity, but also reveal how that entity is in relation to others.

It's easy to see how these acts of differentiation occur in biology. Cell division, for instance, involves acts of distinction that not only produce multiple cells, but eventually group cells into organs to create the various systems of the biological body. The body maintains itself through small acts of differentiation that separate one cell from another. Maturana and Varela were fairly adamant that their theory of autopoiesis should not be used to describe things beyond biology, although that has not prevented their followers from extending this concept to broader social and economic systems. Nonetheless, we should always question whether or not a concept like autopoiesis, developed to describe biological development, can or should be extended out to other, non-biological phenomena. The differences we make are about specifying what things are and how they relate: when something ceases to make a difference, be it between the biological and the social or the biological and the technological, then there are significant implications for how we imagine and act in our world.

In spite of Maturana and Varela's objections, we *can* use autopoiesis to describe much of our world. If systems are constituted by making and performing acts of differentiation and distinction, then the thermostat certainly can be thought of as a self-organizing, autopoietic system. If we think back to our discussion of cultural techniques, we can also suggest that these technical practices, given how they are about the act of making a distinction, are ones through which our world becomes 'self-organized'. Facebook's likes and reactions serve to perform a specific relation that is involved in the self-organization of Facebook as an autopoietic system. Likes perform not only a conjunction (when we like something we are linked to it), but a differentiation (creating that link means that we are not linked to other things). If we stopped contributing to Facebook, it would effectively disappear, given how it relies on user-generated content (see Gehl 2014). The acts through which we contribute to our social networking websites help perpetuate them as systems. And whenever we attempt to distinguish between our online and offline identities, we are effectively performing an autopoietic distinction through which our identities are differentiated and made stable. The moment something happens and we cease to perform these distinctions, then the system we're maintaining may wane and disappear.

Noise and Emergence

At this point we can see how second-order cybernetics is a bit different from some of the ideas proposed by Wiener. No longer is it about the transmission of information and messages, collapsing human and machine into one another, but about acts that perform distinctions, acts that separate different systems out from one another and temporarily maintain their existence. And, likewise, second-order cybernetics ceases to have such a determinist relationship to information and control. One of the most interesting deviations from the original theories of cybernetics has happened with the celebration of *noise*. For Wiener, along with many early discussions of information, there's an assumption that noise is a bad thing. Noise, after all, stops a message from being transmitted correctly, it prevents a cybernetic system from constituting itself through feedback, and so on. Information is often explicitly opposed to noise (e.g. Terranova 2004: 10), as if the distinction between information and noise were the same thing as the opposition between order and disorder, or sense and nonsense.

The French philosopher Michel Serres (1982) has provided a fascinating reinterpretation of how to think about noise and information. Playing on the fact that the French word *parasite* means three things – a biological parasite, a social parasite, and, literally, static – Serres uses the 'parasites' of cybernetics to cross different technological, social, and biological relations. But rather than discuss how social order is maintained through communication, and that we should strive for a clear and accurate transmission of information, Serres celebrates the moments that parasites cause these systems to break and fracture. The moments that rupture the system are transformative, and potentially reframe and invent new relations that could potentially change society.

Noise, for Serres, is something *generative*, it produces new phenomena by interrupting the systems that are currently in place. This system involves others as well, parasites that feed off its imperfections and ineffi-ciencies. But these parasitical systems are temporary. Interruptions effect a transformation in the ways we make distinctions, effectively changing them and inventing new things. Managing the parasites, the noise in the system that feeds off of its inefficiencies, or the interruptions that prohibit smooth communication, effectively requires the system to be transformed, to become something else.

In second-order cybernetics and the various sciences influenced by cybernetics and information theory, this is referred to as **emergence**. New patterns and new forms of organization emerge from disorder, from stat-ic, from noise. Relations may become increasingly complex, which then produce new systems and new forms of order. This is fairly literal when it comes to sound and images. When we see static on television, or hear noise in sound, we often nonetheless attempt to make sense of the patterns that may or may not be there. Our minds project order onto something that may otherwise be disordered – a phenomenon called **apophenia**. We create systems out of disorder in the search for order and patterns, differentiating out a system from the noise.

We can take as a brief example what's generally referred to as elec-tronic voice phenomena, or EVP. In the history of media, EVP were usu-ally found by placing recording technologies in an empty room, and then playing back what was recorded at a high volume, reversing it, slowing it down, or manipulating it otherwise. What's revealed on the tape is, sup-posedly, the voices of the deceased, returning to haunt us and talk to us through our technologies. According to media historian Jeffery Sconce, some of the earliest examples of EVP seemed to be surreal statements in a variety of languages, with spirits making such declarations that could be translated as 'Now, now she-wolf! I want air', or 'Bring a halibut!' Early critics of EVP suggested that 'psychic researchers ... were merely project-ing their own fears and desires onto the hissing static, fashioning "spirit voices" from the debris of their own psyche and, in the end, hearing what they wanted to hear' (Sconce 2000: 88–89). Sconce does not suggest that this interpretation of EVP is the incontrovertible truth, but it follows from how second-order cybernetics understands the imposition of pattern onto disorganized noise. We 'hear' something because we attempt to find pat-terns in what we're listening to. This means that a 'system' has emerged, and the perpetuation of that system (convincing others that the voices recorded say something specific, documenting what has been 'heard' in various ways) perpetuates its existence as something 'ordered'. Has some-one ever directed your attention to a specific sound? Have they played music backwards and directed you to hear 'voices' speaking to you? If not, then I suggest you view one of the many reality TV shows available today about ghost hunters, who regularly employ EVP as a technique to listen to the deceased. Usually, the recordings on these shows, or the voices identified by manipulating songs, just happen to be nonsense as sounds are played backwards or otherwise manipulated (unless there's actually 'backwards masking' going on). Yet we assume there to be 'meaning' in what we hear as we impose patterns onto the noise. The inefficiencies in our recordings have allowed a new order to emerge, one that we experience as 'voices' that come from the beyond.

CONCLUSION: BETWEEN SCIENCE AND SCIENCE FICTION

In this chapter, we have introduced Norbert Wiener's cybernetics and followed its history through the creation of posthumanism and its uptake in popular culture. We then discussed some of the key concepts of second-order cybernetics, and how it often differs from Wiener's original vision for cybernetics. Weiner's cybernetics blurred the boundaries between human and machine by making the body inessential, instead celebrating the maintenance of patterns over time. This has been a view taken up in a wide range of popular culture, and implicitly informs many understandings of identity we have today, both in the legacy of cyberpunk literature and film, and in assumptions about identity made by social media's data analytics. Second-order cybernetics expands the work of Weiner by stressing how patterns happen in an environment – in a medium that involves the performance and perpetuation of distinctions. Second-order cybernetics highlights the physical and embodied relationship produced through the materiality of mediation, emphasizing that we cannot just focus on the transmission and movement of the pattern that is information.

The popular interpretation of cybernetics is foundational for how we imagine digital culture, even though it presents a fictitious view of bodies, identities, and the boundaries between machines and humans. It nonetheless charts how we imagine our relations with technology. And, likewise, some of the assumptions about bodies and identities derived from cybernetics still influence how our digital technologies frame who we are and how we relate. Second-order cybernetics additionally provides theoretical elements on which we can draw to theorize digital culture, as the concepts of autopoiesis, emergence, system, and environment are all excellent tools for describing how we make sense of much of our world, in a way that refuses to let the physical reality of medium vanish in favour of disembodied information. The next chapter turns to a discussion of identity and embodiment, fleshing out some of the relations between digital media and the body provoked by the posthuman implications of cybernetics.

NOTE

1. As these terms suggest, cybernetics also has a relationship to the military and warfare. 'Command' and 'control' are terms associated with various military protocols, often abbreviated as 'C2', an acronym which refers to how those in the military must obey the authority of their commanding officer. With cybernetics and other applications of technology in the military, C2 has been expanded to 'C3', which stands for 'command, control and communications', although this is only one variation of the numerous abbreviations that have followed in recent years.

5

IDENTITIES AND PERFORMANCES

This chapter explores the performance of personal identity online. I argue that identity online is not a fluid, flexible thing – as many have claimed about online identity throughout the past several decades – but relies on how the materiality of a medium permits identity to be performed. After reviewing more general theories of identity and performance, this chapter examines the history of online identities through text-based and graphical environments, along with more recent kinds of identity performances found in online games and social media platforms.

TERMS: avatars; essentialism and anti–essentialism; interpellation; subject position

THEORISTS: Louis Althusser, Karen Barad, Gilles Deleuze, Erving Goffman, Alice Marwick, Theresa Senft, Allucquère Rosanne Stone, Sherry Turkle

EXAMPLES: anonymity in blogging; LambdaMOO; Lucasfilm's *Habitat*; *Rust*; service work; *Snow Crash's* Metaverse

Digital media – particularly online, networked media – are regularly linked with transformations in how we understand personal identity. Some of the earliest work that paid serious attention to digital media argued that online interaction was the realization of a more flexible, fluid identity. Identity was not inherently linked to the biology of the human body, but to the play of textual identities, multiple personalities, and active self-creation via the construction of avatars. Recent discussions of identity online, however, have called into question these arguments from the 1980s and 1990s. Identity online is not inherently fluid anymore – if it ever was – because of the role of digital surveillance and the political economy of social media. Social media platforms regularly demand that you have one identity rather than multiple ones. Many believe larger threats to online civility and order, such as cyberbullying and trolling, will be rectified by forcing people to use real names, guaranteeing consequences offline for actions taken online. In light of this, one of the questions digital culture implores us to ask is 'what is identity'?

Bringing together a number of the concepts and concerns we've introduced thus far, this chapter reviews the different ways we conceptualize identity online, arguing that the materiality of technology constrains how we interact, and, in the process, produces the possibilities for bodies, their differences, their relations, and, crucially, *how they come to matter to and for each other* (Barad 2007: 143, 180). Our identities and bodies are quite literally shaped by the material and technical means we have for recording information and communicating. This does not mean that we are nothing other than our data, or that we do not exist outside the technologies we use. But it does mean that our sense of self and our physical sense of embodiment are both shaped by the media we use. Our identities are reimagined according to how media permit our bodies to interact.

This chapter covers a general history of online identity, from text-based virtual worlds to social media, reviewing concepts we have for understanding identity online. It demonstrates how our identities are shaped by the physical capacities of technology, even in the most mundane, everyday interactions online. Throughout this chapter, identity will be linked to, or contrasted with, the fact that humans, as biological, animal beings, *have bodies*. Some of these issues about the body will be bracketed for now. The next chapter continues with the claims proposed in this chapter to investigate more general questions of embodiment, asking how digital media transform the possibilities and limits of the human body.

THE PERFORMANCE OF IDENTITY

Before we discuss online identities, I'd like to think a bit more generally about identity as such. Who are you? How do you come to understand yourself? Is identity about something inside you? About some interior *essence*? Or is identity about what you do? About what is visible to others? About what you *perform*? We've already used this term 'perform' a number of times in this book. In the last chapter we noted how, with cybernetics, interior consciousness doesn't really matter. There is no 'essence' inside you that makes you 'essentially' human, or 'essentially' a man or a woman (or, to use another term, there is no 'ontological stability' to the categories of 'human', or 'man', or 'woman'). Instead, what matters is what is performed. A similar view of identity is taken up by many of those who discuss the social and cultural aspects of digital media. Identity is not what you *are*, but rather is something you *do*. This is a *performative* understanding of identity, contrasted with an **essentialist** understanding of identity. Most theorists of digital media do not place much emphasis on some essential nature that exists inside you. As was the case with cybernetics, what is made visible to others – what is performed and observed – is your identity. The identities you perform may be different depending on context. You appear to others, and that appearance matters.

The relationship between interior states of the mind and exterior relations with others has long been a problem for understanding human psychology and social relationships. We have no real access to the interior states of other people aside from what's made visible and public. Identity, in this case, is not about what you keep to yourself, but about how you present yourself to others. This understanding of identity goes back, at least, to Erving Goffman's classic work of sociology, *The Presentation of Self in Everyday Life* (1959). For Goffman, our social world is a drama in which we perform roles and manage the various impressions others have of us. Our identities derive from how we interact and relate, and our ability to perform specific identities depends on the relations in which we find ourselves.

One of the most common examples we can use to explain how we perform our identities comes from work – in particular, service work. You may have worked in a restaurant or café at some point in your life. Think about all of the different ways you present yourself when working at a restaurant. Whenever a server goes out to attend to their customers, entering the 'front of house', they will usually put on a performance of professionalism, elegance, or friendliness. This is especially true in the United States where these performances are linked to pay through tipping. As well, these performances are themselves shaped by the kind of restaurant in which a person works. A server's performance will be very different if they work at a fine dining restaurant, a family restaurant, or a restaurant that has some sort of theme. Once the server moves from the front of house to the kitchen, or 'back of house', the performance may change. A previously well-mannered server may become angry. They may swear when dealing with line cooks, who may make rude comments. The context has changed, as has how a person presents themselves to others. When a person is alone, the performance may change as well – maybe the server talks to themself in a mirror, for instance.

So what's the real identity here? The well-mannered server, or the angry, swearing one? Or the one alone, at home? Do these parts bleed into one another? Or do we perform a lot of work to make sure they remain separate? How might these performances shift depending on the physical architecture of the restaurant? How might things be different if there's a closed door between the dining room and the kitchen, or if the kitchen is open for the restaurant's guests to look into and observe food being prepared? Let's extend these questions out beyond restaurants. How do you present yourself in the class you're in? What about at home with your parents? What about at a bar or pub with your friends?

The point here is not to say that one of these performances is more 'you' than another. Rather, they're all part of you. We break up and parcel out who we are depending on context, which is about how we encounter others and present ourselves to them. These contexts are shaped by our physical environment and, today, how that environment is permeated with digital media. Differentiating our social roles may be helped by our technologies. But our technologies may also make it more difficult to parcel out these roles. The everyday use of social media, for instance, has often resulted in what Alice Marwick and danah boyd (2011) refer to as *context collapse*, in which social media erode our ability to maintain the boundaries between contexts, so our parents or bosses see photos of drunken nights out because our Facebook friends may include people we know from any and every context of our lives. While these stories about context collapse regularly characterized discussion of social media, now different platforms are often used to mitigate against context collapse, maintaining the boundaries that were previously marked by different physical spaces. If you use Facebook to talk with your family, make a LinkedIn or Twitter page for class, and use Snapchat to send videos to friends, you're working to make sure context collapse does not happen, perpetuating a way of performing identity that was first identified by Goffman in the 1950s.

Now, you may think that you perform the same identity in every single situation, not hiding anything from anyone. This is possible, but most of the time we do subtly change how we act because of who we imagine may be watching. Even the most visible celebrity works to keep things out of view. In a world defined by reality TV, social media, and other forms of surveillance, we are often told to be authentic all of the time, to be 'real' in all of our relationships (cf. Andrejevic 2004). But this is, quite simply, not the usual way that people have acted in social relationships.

Many of these roles we play are far more ingrained into who we are than others. The term **subject position** refers to how we inhabit some roles quite deeply as they move from a daily performance to the very foundations of how we understand who we are. According to the Marxist theorist Louis Althusser, many of the institutions we move through in life, from school, home, work, and the church, along with the various forms of media we use, are dedicated towards teaching us how to behave in specific roles. The goal is not merely to teach proper ways to behave, but to get us to identify with these roles. We are, to use Althusser's term, 'interpellated' into a specific subject position. For Althusser, **interpellation** works quite simply. It's like someone yelling at us, *hailing* us with the statement, 'Hey, you there!' (Althusser 2001: 118).

This is, for Althusser, how various institutions work as well, and it is central for how power and social control operate. We obey because we *recognize ourselves* as fulfilling a specific social role. As a student in class, you are hailed into the role of student, a role you presumably embrace as really you, even if you may not think that the subject position of 'student' defines who you are. But you nonetheless act as if it does. You walk into the classroom and find your proper location, which is most likely behind one of many small desks or tables, set up to face a blackboard or screen, and not behind the desk or table at the front of the room. Your participation in the class perpetuates the performance of your role as student, rather than that of another role, such as that of teacher. At the same time, there are various institutions and techniques in place to make sure you know your role. You are given assignments, which you have to complete and submit to your teacher. Your teacher, likewise, performs their role in assigning work, marking it, giving feedback, and so on. You could argue that the entire system of university education is focused around teaching and enforcing specific performances of identity. Imagine if any one of these roles ceased to be performed properly. What would happen? What would it be like if you stopped having assignments that were marked for credit? What would your education be like? How would your roles be performed? (I should note, some – not many – universities do not have marked assignments. Getting grades is not a necessary part of a university education.)

Your entire life is filled with roles you are hailed into, be it a child or a parent, a student or a teacher, a man or a woman. All of the various identity categories you can think of are subject positions that you are hailed to embrace, and you may or may not identify with the categories into which you've been hailed. You've learned how a 'man' is supposed to behave, or how a 'woman' is supposed to relate to a 'man'. You know how 'men' are supposed to act towards each other, and what it means to 'properly' appear as a 'man'. You know how 'women' are supposed to act towards other 'women'. I assume you've heard the phrase 'Be a man!' or 'Man up!' before. These statements interpellate a specific, gendered body into being something that is called 'a man', although this is often only defined through an implied negative: certain behaviours are assumed to be inappropriate for a specific subject position. These categories and performances are not inborn, which means the often discriminatory and restrictive relations they perpetuate can be changed. In the case of gender identities, knowing and behaving like a proper 'man' or proper 'woman' perpetuates the system of inequalities referred to as patriarchy. You've learned these things because of school, church, media, and beyond. These institutions teach you how you are supposed to act and relate to others. Yet there is no one proper way of being any identity – or, there is no *essence* to a specific identity. You've been interpellated into these categories, which, if the interpellation has been successful, you identify with and embrace as part of who you are.

'You' are continually identified and called into being 'something' based on how you appear to others and how you relate to other people. Those who do not conform to a specific subject position (or cannot be successfully identified as being 'something') are often considered a threat to the dominant social order, and can be subject to exclusion, prejudice, or violence as a result. This is, according to many queer theorists, one of the reasons that sexualities and relations that deviate from heterosexual norms are considered to be a threat. There's nothing inherently visual that performs sexuality, even though there are many stereotypes that are identified to police the boundaries of, again, 'proper' forms of how sexuality and gender appear (cf. Edelman 1994). Additionally, what these categories mean, along with the proper performance of any specific identity, is historically and cultural specific. What it means to be a 'man' or a 'woman' may be dramatically different in the United States, New Zealand, Germany,

Brazil, Egypt, or Japan, or, for that matter, these identities may differ between different communities that, with the internet, may not be clearly bound by geography. This means that identity categories are political, and changing the acts and behaviours associated with a specific identity, or claiming identities that refuse traditional categories (such as 'nonbinary' or 'asexual'), may be a place for social change. And when identities become ever more rigid (when being 'something' carries with it increasingly specific assumptions), merely having an identity can be a reason for restrictive limitations to be placed on the actions one performs. Having an identity is not intrinsically empowering. Rather, being 'something' means that you're expected to know your role and how that role is supposed to act. Naming an identity is one way of controlling and managing bodies through the definition of how bodies are supposed to act and appear to others.

ONLINE IDENTITIES

One of the strange things about online identities is that, historically, they have allowed people to refuse, question, or otherwise play with the identities that come with their bodies. They seem to challenge many of the ways that institutions hail us into being 'something', and they do so because our physical bodies often disappear from visibility. We get to construct identities based on **avatars**. This leads to a fundamentally different way of understanding how identity is performed, one based less on physical context and the relations we have with others and more on intentional self-creation. As the psychologist Sherry Turkle noted in her foundational *Life on the Screen*, when online, 'The self is no longer simply playing different roles in different settings at different times, something that a person experiences when, for example, she wakes up as a lover, makes breakfast as a mother, and drives to work as a lawyer'. Instead, computers and online spaces permit us 'parallel identities, parallel lives' (1995: 14). On the internet, Turkle claims, our performances are not about relatively discrete identities that we shift between as the context varies. We are not hailed into distinct subject positions that change based on the institutions around us. With digital media, something about identity fundamentally changes, something that appears to leave the body behind, in which we perform multiple identities simultaneously.

Of course, technology has *always* had an effect in transforming how we interact and become present to another. Our performances (and thus, our identities) have always been about the materiality of technology and how it mediates our interactions. In a different context, the philosopher of science Karen Barad has suggested that our relations are always shaped by material apparatuses that 'leave marks' on our bodies (2007: 176). Our modes of interacting and presenting ourselves to each other are, quite literally, framed by the technical and material support we have for relating and communicating. This means that we have to take the technical specificity of human interaction very seriously, as what identity is becomes an effect of how we encounter each other through the varied materialities of mediation we use to communicate and perform identity. Our identities are intrinsically shaped by how technologies permit our bodies to become present to another, through which we can – or cannot – perform identity in specific ways, either permitted or prohibited by the materiality of the device or platform we're using. The internet isn't something that conceals the body. Rather, it permits the body to become visible in specific ways.

Performing Textual Identity

If we take this claim seriously, then many of the arguments Turkle and other early theorists of identity online made about the fluidity and flexibility of online identity should be related to the specific technologies people used to perform their identities. So, we should review how online identity has been theorized in the past, but also emphasize how these historical claims about identity are, in fact, about how a specific technology or platform enabled bodies to appear to others at a specific moment. Many of Turkle's arguments were based on early text-based online worlds, called MUDs or MOOs, acronyms for 'Multi-User Dungeon' and 'MUD Object-Oriented', respectively. Her claims emerged from interviews or observation, often of disparate groups of children, scientists, or students at her home university of MIT. These interviews were first about the use of these early text-based computer programs, and more recently have been about interactions with robots. Turkle has charted how we imagine our own identities based on how we interact with computers, with others over computers, and with artificial intelligences. Who 'we' are depends deeply on *how* we interact and *with what* we are interacting.

For Turkle, computers are 'objects-to-think-with', technologies that provide metaphors for how we imagine who we are and how we relate. In her book *The Second Self* (2005), those Turkle interviewed used the model of a computer to suggest that a single, coherent thing called an identity was an illusion, and that human cognition was equivalent to a distributed set of computational, algorithmic processes. This belief makes impossible any clear way of saying that there is such a thing as an 'I'. Rather, 'I' am a set of disparate, if overlapping mental processes that interact to produce 'me'. Any coherent sense of an 'I' is an illusion, a side effect of what's happening in the body's (ultimately computational) cognition. As was the case for Norbert Wiener's posthumanism from decades before, consciousness is a side effect that covers over the fact that the human brain operates in a way analogous to a computer. 'A model of mind as multiprocessor leaves you with a "decentralized" self: there is no "me", no "I", no unitary actor', suggests Turkle, 'But theories that deny and "decenter" the "I" challenge most people's day-to-day experience of having one' (2005: 265).

Yet, as she ventured beyond people's personal relationships with computers to relationships they carried out on the internet, Turkle found that these 'decentered' identities characterized how many individuals described most interactions online. People would log on to MUDs and MOOs and perform as different genders and different sexualities, or as different beings completely unlike the human body in front of the computer. In their interviews, these individuals would often suggest to Turkle that their online performances felt more real than their offline bodies. Being able to distribute their identities away from a single, centred 'I' was liberating, and it permitted early users of the internet a more 'real' engagement with the identity they imagined themselves to 'really' be, even if that identity did not appear to conform to their physical, biological body.

However, while Turkle saw in this a decentred, distributed understanding of identity, in which no 'real me' could be stated to exist, her interviewees often assumed an essentialist understanding of identity, in which one's interior essence did not inherently conform to one's performances – or, their body and their performances in daily life would *not* be 'the real me', but a 'real me' would nonetheless exist, hidden underneath one's skin, invisible to others were it not for communication via computers. Online spaces were often suggested to be more real than daily life beyond their computers because of the freedom to let the 'real me' become visible. One of the things Turkle found was that men would regularly perform as women, and women as men, with her interviewees telling her that 'virtual gender-swapping enabled them to understand what it's like to be a person of the other gender' (Turkle 1995: 238). Thus, these online spaces seemingly enabled people to challenge the institutions that they usually faced, their usual interpellations, and to experiment with identity in a way that seemed to leave the biological body behind.

The theorist of digital media Allucquère Rosanne Stone has been even more explicit in her claims about the potentialities of identity in online spaces than Turkle. For Stone, when people performed identity online, or acted as a different gender, or even had virtual sex while performing a different identity, what was sent over communications infrastructures 'wasn't just information, it was *bodies*' (Stone 1995: 7). According to Stone, bodies are intrinsically bound up in textuality and language, and while the 'real' physical body never disappears, what gets uploaded online and communicated is still a fully present, 'real' part of the physical body sitting behind the screen, even if it may have little to no relation to that body's physical biology. According to Stone, we are textual, and the ways that we textually perform identity online demonstrates how our bodies can extend themselves out through textual prostheses, 'connecting' with others that are long distances away. While we may perform online as someone with an identity that has little to do with our physical biology, our online identities are nonetheless an extension of our physical bodies and are part of the 'real' identity of the person behind the screen.

These claims have been massively influential in any discussion of identity online. For decades, identity online has been thought to be more fluid, more flexible, and a kind of 'distributed' identity that happens as we speak through an avatar or persona we've created, in which the 'real me' has little to do with the physicality of the biological body. Yet these arguments about identity need to be placed into the technical context of early computer gaming and the initial development of MUDs and MOOs, the technologies both Turkle and Stone used to formulate their claims.

Some of the earliest computer games were developed by programmers working at MIT and other ARPANET-connected institutions. Text-based games like *Adventure* (Will Crowther, 1976) and *Zork* (Infocom, 1980) were not merely created for the amusement of these programmers and students. They were experiments derived from early artificial intelligence combined with an attempt to invent digital versions of the popular role-playing game *Dungeons and Dragons*. These programmers invented the idea of a playable, digital world that was influential for future understandings of both games and so-called 'cyberspace'. The common name attributed to these games today – 'text adventure' (see Montfort 2003: 65–93) – points directly to the way the game itself inscribes information, bodies, and relation through a textual interface.

These early games were designed for single players. MUDs and MOOs transformed these games into multi-user spaces, the most notable of which was LambdaMOO, founded in late 1990 or early 1991 by Xerox PARC researcher Pavel Curtis. But, even though they were seemingly populated by 'real' people, the spaces, identities, and interactions of MUDs and MOOs were still limited to what could be described textually. As a result of relations mediated through simple textual descriptions and a verb-object input mechanism (called a parser), a body in the game would be almost completely undefined aside from the text users input to describe themselves. LambdaMOO, for instance, allowed for custom gender descriptions, and included in its gender presets the following categories: 'neuter, male, female, either, Spivak, splat, plural, egotistical, royal, and 2nd person'. Considering how some of these genders do not correspond to the human body in any clear way reveals how textuality is central to the identity experiments described by Turkle and Stone. If the physical body only becomes present through text, then the possibilities for embodiment seem to have little to do with the physical human body. Thus, 'embodiment' in these games is consequentially open-ended (if mostly invisible) aside from the registration of bodies through language (and, specifically, typed language) recognized by a computer program.

The flexible and fluid identities described by Turkle and Stone are not an essence of human identity disclosed through technology, but a material effect of how these text-based worlds happen to work. Stone, in particular, has to claim that identity is essentially textual for her arguments about these online spaces to make sense (1995: 41). On the one hand, this is true – much of our identities are entirely derived from what can be written down, stored, and communicated. We often make ourselves visible and legible to others through textual means. But, at the same time, it is a mistake to then completely reduce the body to textuality. Not all forms of media are textual, and the textual inscription of a body is not the precise equivalent to the body. Perhaps more importantly, *textuality is not only about words, but about the materiality of a medium of communication.* When we assume identities online to be fluid, flexible, and in some tentative relationship to the physicality of the biological body, we're making assumptions about identity and embodiment that emerge from how various technologies enable matter to come to matter. Technologies are required for our bodies to perform identity, and these performances only occur through the materially specific channels through which the body becomes present to others.

One of the things that Turkle identified from her research on identities – one that continues to resonate with us today – is that we *'have learned to take things at interface value'* (1995: 23). As was the case with cybernetics, if something appears and performs as living, we treat it as alive. If something appears and performs as if it has emotions and feelings, then we treat it as if it has emotions and feelings. Turkle saw how people could feel emotions for others based merely on textual description, or confide in (rather poorly made) computer simulations of psychiatrists, or even fall in love with simplistic artificial intelligences called 'bots', which, today, are increasingly prevalent throughout the internet (Bollmer & Rodley 2017; Gehl and Bakardjieva 2017). These AIs today – perhaps most popularly represented in Spike Jonze's 2013 film *Her*, where a man falls in love with a Siri-like AI on his mobile phone – are far more developed than the little pieces of text that characterized online interaction in LambdaMOO. And yet, then, as now, we approach others and value them based on their performances. What matters is not some interior essence, but performances and projections, our willingness to believe that performances are real or authentic, and that visible evidence for intelligence, emotion, and creativity is good enough.

In her early work, Turkle was somewhat positive about the potentials revealed by computers and the internet. In recent years, however, the problem of taking things at interface value has greatly disturbed her. This cybernetic understanding of identity has led to people preferring the company of robots and artificial intelligences to other people. As a fifteen-year-old interviewee informed her, 'People' are 'risky', while robots are 'safe' (Turkle 2011: 51). Turkle now fears that we're replacing humans with simulations because dealing with the emotional complexity and unknowability of the inner lives of others is difficult and often painful. Robots and AIs, programmable as they are, are easier to deal with than other humans. At the same time, having an emotional, intimate relationship with another can be intensely fulfilling – but the ups cannot be separated from the downs. The pain and joy of being close to another human being requires an openness, an openness that involves losing some control over one's own body (as emotions and feelings are about the body, after all) in favour of making a world with another, in which togetherness involves uncertainty, unpredictability, and the difficulties of dealing with people who have their own desires and wills that may not coincide with our own. As we've grown used to accepting performances as evidence, performances that often abstract or reduce the body in any number of ways, are we somehow forgetting something about our relations with other people, replacing them with software that can be easily programmed and manipulated? Are we preferring predictability and control, desiring devices that can easily bend to our own will?

While I think Turkle's fears are completely justified, the materiality of communication has *always* influenced how we interact, and, I think we can argue, we've always taken things at interface value. We assume the words we read in a hand-written letter are sincere, even though we may have little evidence to support our beliefs. We assume them to be written by the real person who signs the letter, rather than a forgery. We assume that the voices we hear on the telephone are capable of communicating 'real' emotions to us, even though the body only becomes present through sound that is, in all honesty, of rather poor quality. We assume that the tears from another's eye are truthful, although we have little way of actually knowing if they are heartfelt or false. It's true that, in reducing the body through technology, we can mistake software for a human being, as is the case when people have lengthy conversations with bots. Perhaps the grounds upon which we evaluate these changes should not defer to questions about presence or the 'fullness' of specific relations and experiences compared to other relations and experiences that seem to be 'degraded' or 'incomplete'. Perhaps what's at stake is the need for a different set of terms for evaluating the ethics and politics of human relations when we relate to each other primarily through technology.

Avatars and Visual Identity

Of course, our online worlds are no longer merely textual. We have complex **avatars** designed to mimic the human body, and yet expand its possibilities in ways that may appear to mirror the potentials given by textual description in LambdaMOO. An avatar is an online representation of a human user. The term is derived from the Sanskrit word for the physical incarnation of a Hindu god, *avatāra*, which translates as 'descent'. It was first used to describe the digital version of a human user by the designers of Lucasfilm's *Habitat*, an early virtual world from the 1980s (Morningstar & Farmer 1991). Along with *Habitat*, one of the most influential ways of imagining online interactions via avatars comes from Neil Stephenson's cyberpunk novel *Snow Crash*, which depicted a virtual reality called the Metaverse, where an individual's social position was determined by the appearance of their avatar. Here, Stephenson is describing the Metaverse and avatars, specifically the avatar of the book's main character, the irreverently named Hiro Protagonist:

> As Hiro approaches the Street, he sees two young couples. ...
> He is not seeing real people, of course. This is all a part of the
> moving illustration drawn by his computer according to specifi-
> cations coming down the fiber-optic cable. The people are pieces
> of software called avatars. They are the audiovisual bodies that
> people use to communicate with each other in the Metaverse. ...
> Your avatar can look any way you want it to, up to the limita-
> tions of your equipment. If you're ugly, you can make your avatar
> beautiful. If you've just gotten out of bed, your avatar can be
> wearing beautiful clothes and professionally applied makeup ...
> (Stephenson 1992: 35–36)

In these early examples, an avatar was always a visual, graphical representation of a user, one that may or may not correspond to the 'real' body
of the user. And, especially in *Snow Crash*, there is an ideal of *crafting*
identity with avatars. Identity relates to the mediated body and its presence for others, along with the *techniques* required for anything called
'identity'. With the avatar, identity is a cultural technique, something that
involves cultivation directly associated with the use and knowledge of
technology.

Recently, the term avatar has been used to describe nearly any representation of a user – textual, visual, or otherwise – not only in virtual
worlds, but in forms of social media as diverse as internet forums, blogs,
or social networking websites. So, while the text-based descriptions of
LambdaMOO were not initially described as avatars, we may now think of
them as such. As we've moved past these text-based worlds our identities
online are no longer just forms of textual description. They now include
images and animations, and, with voice chat, perhaps sounds as well. Our
avatar is a representation of our identity, but its specific form depends on
the platform or technology we may be using, along with the techniques
demanded by that platform or technology.

We still have a tendency to think of the self-fashioning of avatars as
a kind of identity play, attributing these visual representations the same
fluidity and flexibility as textual descriptions, even though the ways that
bodies become present to others has challenged many of the arguments
outlined by authors like Turkle and Stone. Because of the fluidity offered
by the avatar, some, drawing on the findings of Turkle, forecasted a future
in which racism, homophobia, and other forms of discrimination based on
identity would wane because of the ability to remake one's identity online
through 'disembodied' avatars.

Turkle, however, was sceptical of the claims people made about the seeming egalitarianism of performing another identity online:

> But as I listened to this boast [of 'understanding' the experience of another through online identity play and gender swapping], my mind often travelled to my own experiences of living in a woman's body. These include worry about physical vulnerability, fears of unwanted pregnancy and of infertility, fine-tuned decisions about how much make-up to wear to a job interview, and the difficulty of giving a professional seminar while doubled over with monthly cramps. To a certain extent, knowledge is inherently experiential, based on a physicality that we each experience differently. (1995: 238)

Our lives are grounded in our physical bodies, along with the techniques required for the performance of identity and the management of a body's biological rhythms and behaviours. Having an avatar cannot replace or transform the simple fact that I inhabit this world through my body and the physical practices I perform because of my body.

Sexism, racism, and homophobia persist online, in spite of the seeming flexibility and fluidity of the avatar. Many recent authors have determined that possibilities enabled by avatars are not as fluid as initially thought. Prejudice against non-normative avatars, such as those that are non-white or overweight, still remains even with the variable, virtual body of the avatar. Because identity can be changed online, marginal identities are often completely erased in virtual worlds – when given the option, people rarely choose to have avatars that do not conform to 'desirable' identities (Nakamura 2002). Rather than enabling a more equitable way of understanding identity through digital representations, avatars reproduce – if not exacerbate – the prejudices about identity already present in the offline world. Because prejudices still exist online, users may choose to represent their identity in a way that simply repeats privileged identity categories.

If and when marginal identities are represented online, often they are so via drop-down menus that do not permit fluid manifestations of identity. Because of the visual aspects of avatar creation, instead of open-ended textual description we are now presented with (often elaborate) character-creation applications for online worlds and games, which, while highly customizable, are limited, and certainly do not include a range of imaginative categories for gender like that of LambdaMOO. There is a fetishizing of the 'skin' of the avatar (Hillis 2009: 157), and non-white and non-male avatars tend to be represented through reductive, stereotypical, and often sexualized caricatures, especially when users 'pass' as a race or gender that is different from that of their own body.

Rust, a multiplayer survival game known for being chaotic and anarchic, reveals some of these issues regarding identity in games. Initially, the game only had white, bald men as avatars, many of whom were naked. When the game's designers added race and gender for the game's avatars, instead of allowing players to customize their characters, as is the case with almost any other online, multiplayer game, *Rust* randomly assigned race and gender (along with the size of genitalia), permanently associating these categories with a player's account. 'We wanted a way to recognize people beyond their names, kind of a fingerprint', according to *Rust*'s lead designer Garry Newman. 'We already kind of have this; players recognize each other via their voice, and that's pretty interesting. So we wanted to push it further'. And even though the options initially built into the game were limited, Newman noted that 'There's a lot of skin colours in the world, and it's really easy to appear racially insensitive when doing this', but, 'Our ideal scenario is one in which no two players look the same, so you'll recognize someone in game by their face to the extent that nametags will be redundant' (Quoted in Grayson 2015).

Rust is, perhaps unintentionally, making a significant statement about identity online. On the one hand, *Rust*'s designers affirm that an avatar is not particularly anchored to the 'real' body of the player. It is, nonetheless, something that can be used for purposes of identification. Ideally, these identities will not be defined in terms of biological identities or generic classes, but in terms of a wide range of diverse bodies that are completely unique and differentiated. This means that *Rust* is operating with a kind of anti-essentialist understanding of identity. Even though it includes race and gender as categories, its designers want to extend these categories to be so diverse that identities are not listed as a set of fixed options on a drop-down menu. There is no essential or fixed understanding of identity, but rather pure diversity – at least in an ideal future when the software actually achieves the complexity needed to realize this goal.

The example of *Rust* also emphasizes that the open fluidity promised by online identity has become another way to perpetuate racism, sexism, and other forms of discrimination. Being able to choose identities has actually reduced the different ways that identities are performed online. The avatar becomes something that players must 'see' as similar to themselves, or at least 'see' as something over which they have control – or else they may get exceptionally angry, as many *Rust* players did in reaction to the forced identity categories they were required to use. Newman noted that the inclusion of a broader range of races led to the increase of racial slurs and hate speech in the game itself – it didn't seem to do anything to challenge or question the racism or sexism of many of the game's players. And, we again see how the materiality of the technology itself permits (or prohibits) specific ways that bodies become visible to others. The medium itself is that which shapes and transforms the limits and possibilities for identity performed online.

'You Only Have One Identity'

Rust is only one of many recent attempts to undermine the fluidity of online identity. By linking a randomly generated avatar to a specific account, the game, while still pseudonymous, is attempting to control some of the possibilities once enabled by digital interaction online. *Rust* is, in part, attempting to negotiate having a clear, set identity with the anonymity that characterized early online interactions – and still characterizes identity on places like the message board 4chan. With anonymity, because there's no inherent consistency in how one becomes present to another (usually via text), then one can effectively change identities over and over again, embracing a multiplicity of identities instead of one that is anchored to the body (although, of course, we've already seen that bodily identity itself is neither unified nor consistent). *Rust*'s designers want to make this fluidity difficult, if not impossible. Your avatar in the game is your *only* identity in the game. At the same time, *Rust*'s players are not truly the same as their avatar; there is a clear distinction between the two, even though the avatar may be linked to the user's 'real' identity (if only an identity that is 'real' because it comes from the online account required to play the game).

The fear of complete anonymity online is understandable. Because the body only makes itself present to others in a limited way, the possibilities for identity expand. But, at the same time, the obligation to others may also vanish as we only encounter another as a textual abstraction or graphical representation that, some may imagine, is less than real. Anonymity, once celebrated as something that permits political agency online, is now more often thought to be a tool used by trolls to harass and harm others. This has, increasingly, led to attempts to permanently fix identity online, linking it to a specific body, limiting the fluidity once celebrated by Stone and Turkle.

Much of the early celebration of blogging, for instance, was often centred on how blogs permitted individuals to speak online, to have a voice, and yet remain hidden and outside the boundaries of state surveillance.

This was clearly the case for bloggers in the Middle East during the late 1990s and early 2000s. Bloggers from Iraq and Iran, who went by names like Salem Pax, Riverbend, and NHK, used the anonymity and veiling of digital media to have a clear voice. NHK, an Iraqi teenager, wrote on her blog, 'I don't put my real name on this blog because I'm not allowed to have a free opinion in this life. I can't tell the truth until I am sure that no one knows who I am' (quoted in Bollmer 2016: 163). Political agency, here, was equated to the ability of digital media to veil the speaker. The ability to speak 'truth' was a by-product of being hidden.

With social media, these celebrations of anonymity have long vanished. A social networking website like MySpace (to use an example that may seem long dated) allowed users to customize their profile in countless ways, and even to use names that had little to do with one's real name, perhaps even changing this name at will. This level of potential anonymity is certainly not the case for many social media platforms today, and the moral panics surrounding various (often short-lived) messaging apps, such as Kik and YikYak, come from the seeming anonymity afforded by the platform, which can lead to brutal harassment and bullying. Solutions to this problem have been to permanently link one's account to a specific expression of identity, just as in *Rust*. Facebook has been exceptionally vocal about maintaining these links between one's 'real' identity and what's uploaded online. 'You only have one identity', Facebook's CEO Mark Zuckerberg stated in a 2009 interview, 'The days of you having a different image for your work friends or co-workers and for the other people you know are probably coming to an end pretty quickly ... the level of transparency the world has now won't support having two identities for a person' (quoted in Bollmer 2016: 169).

These changes can be described though Alice Marwick and danah boyd's (2011) concept of *context collapse*, as mentioned earlier. With any form of communication, we generally have an 'imagined audience' in mind, or a general *public* that we address (Warner 2002). As is the case with any performance of identity, the strategies we use for communication change depending on how we imagine our audience. But social media websites, be it Facebook, Twitter, or any number of other platforms through which you are supposed to publicly perform 'you' for other people, multiple audiences and contexts are collapsed into one. Today, we are interpellated into performing a single identity, all the time, and anything other than that single identity is somehow 'false'. Hopefully, at this point, you can see how strange this way of thinking of identity is. Our identities have long been partial and fragmentary. But, today, we're increasingly told that we only have one identity, and we should make that single identity visible to others.

We are even told that having a single, fixed identity is something that has actual economic value. Many of the practices of identity online seem to follow what Theresa Senft has described as *microcelebrity*, or 'the commitment to deploying and maintaining one's online identity as if it were a branded good, with the expectation that others do the same' (2013: 346). Alice Marwick, drawing on Senft, has suggested that this is a general strategy for using social media, especially if one wants to be popular, attract followers and friends, and get likes and attention. Individuals tend to apply 'market principles to how they think about themselves, interact with others, and display their identity' (Marwick 2013: 7), imagining 'authenticity' and 'being yourself' not merely as self-presentation strategies, but as a means to make oneself a commodity and potential celebrity. Considering how many new jobs, such as social media manager and social media 'influencer', appear to have economic viability, there is certainly truth to this. But, even for those who do not seem to want to be 'microcelebrities' via social media, the belief that one should 'be yourself', perpetuating one 'true' identity via Facebook, Twitter, and Instagram, is certainly far more common than the multiple contexts and identities that were once celebrated by Turkle.

Near the end of his life, in 1990, the philosopher Gilles Deleuze published a short essay titled 'Postscript on Control Societies'. In it, he argued that we were no longer in a world defined by clearly differentiated institutions like those discussed by Althusser. Instead, we were entering a new society, a 'control society', defined by 'ultrarapid forms of apparently free-floating control' (Deleuze 1995: 178). For Deleuze, school, once with a clear end point called 'graduation', is becoming 'continuous education' or 'lifelong learning' with no clear end. Health care is becoming preventative and about calculation and prediction, as is finance. And, in terms of identities, instead of a clear 'individual' we become *dividuals* – who we are is divided up into discrete units, where 'masses become samples, data, markets, or "*banks*"' (1995: 180). What once was a unitary, undividable 'self' (an in-dividual), has been divided up endlessly into smaller and smaller bits of discrete data, the totality of which is thought to be 'you'. Seemingly constant surveillance, designed to analyze statistics and prevent sickness, disorder, and crime before it happens, is implemented nearly everywhere, in which we are constantly compelled to generate personal data, which is analyzed by software and computer systems beyond human awareness. I mention Deleuze and his control society because it appears, to me, that the transformations in identity that we see with social media also demonstrate this shift from institutions (in which we have many, contextual identities) to a general-ized system of 'free-floating control' (in which we have one identity that can be broken down into countless permutations of digitally-analyzed data). So, you may only have one identity, but it is one that can be divided up in countless ways.

This understanding of identity can be seen in the rise of self-tracking via smartphones and wearables. The past few years have seen the growth of health tracking via iPhones and the Apple Watch, FitBits and more, along with apps designed to monitor movement, exercise, sex, and diet in any number of ways. These devices suggest that there's something about our own bodies and behaviours that we're blind to in our everyday lives, only made visible through the quantification of the body and the analysis of data (see Lupton 2016). We are assumed to be little more than our data, which can be uploaded, analyzed, and understood in ways that we remain blind to without the help of our digital devices (see Bollmer 2016). While we may not think of the things we track via our phones and wearables as part of our identities, they nonetheless frame 'who we are' in terms of data that can be gathered, understood, and statistically analyzed. This, again, follows a cybernetic understanding of identity and imagines the human body as a constellation of data points that can be interpreted and used for purposes of control and management.

CONCLUSION

What I've described here can be thought of as two different, but inter-twining arguments. First, 'identity' should be understood in relationship to the technologies we use to *become present* to another. The possibilities of identity are related to how we interact, and the elements of our bodies that become present are either relatively fixed or relatively flexible based on how we can communicate. Second, as digital media move from pri-marily textual interactions, to graphical avatars, to social media profiles and Big Data, we've seen fluid identities shift to a single, fixed identity made up of an assemblage of data that can be uploaded and shared online. This perhaps leads us back to cybernetics and the assumptions it makes about identity and the body. This isn't an ontological argument about identity, but an historical claim that suggests we may be imagining iden-tity in a way that equates a true self with data that can be recorded and analyzed. This hopefully demonstrates how a cybernetic understanding of identity is not the only way we can imagine identity, but also shows us that the way we imagine identity today seems to repeat the logic of cybernetics in everyday life.

Throughout this chapter, the idea of having an *identity* has been linked with, or contrasted with, the fact that we intrinsically have a *body*. But what is a body? Like the possibilities we have for identity, digital media transform the capacities and possibilities of the human body. It is to this problem that we now turn.

6

BODIES AND EXTENSIONS

This chapter continues our discussion of identity from Chapter 5, drawing on a phenomenological definition of embodiment. I claim that a key function of technology is to transform and extend (or amputate) the sensory capacities of the body. From this claim, a number of authors suggest that networked media produce the possibilities for collective bodies and collective intelligences. This chapter presents a sceptical view of these possibilities, however, and concludes by drawing attention to issues of power and inequality that may be obscured in the name of 'collective intelligence'.

TERMS: body schema; collective intelligence; embodiment; metaphysics of presence

THEORISTS: Andy Clark, Marshall McLuhan, Maurice Merleau-Ponty, Brian Rotman, Sherry Turkle

EXAMPLES: Auto-Tune; Hatsune Miku; holographic performers; Twitch Plays *Pokémon*

Today's social media platforms may seem to be vastly different from Wiener and his cybernetics. Yet many perpetuate a cybernetic understanding of identity, in which 'you' are little more than informational patterns in the form of personal data and associative links, and your body matters little – at least beyond that which can be converted into data. You may still think to yourself that this is a misguided or simply incorrect way of understanding who we are and how we relate. 'You' are not the same thing as your Facebook profile, your Instagram pictures, or the filters and videos sent over Snapchat – 'you' are not your data. There is something important about a physical body that cannot be reduced to information. But why might you think this? Why are 'you' something other than the data observed and collected about your identity? Why aren't 'you' ultimately a mathematical, computational pattern?

Cybernetics suggests that human bodies can be linked seamlessly with technologies; there's nothing that prevents us from becoming technologically augmented cyborgs. Both human and machine are informational, pattern-based things, and thus can be combined easily. Yet many of us may still think of our bodies as the fleshy, biological stuff that *must* be linked to the physical limits of our skin. Why do we assume this? Why might cybernetics be wrong about the human body and its relationship to technology? Is it because you might imagine the physical, biological body to be 'natural', while technology is 'unnatural'? Why would you accept there to be something about your body that comes from 'nature', and messing with or transforming your body is somehow a perversion of this nature? Could you – or should you – transform your sensory capacities through technology, augmenting your body through tools that, for instance, would allow you to see ultraviolet and infrared colours, invisible due to the physical limits of your eyes? Could you – or should you – use tools that allow you to hear sounds that are beyond the ability of your ears to sense? What would this do to your understanding of who 'you' are? Would this transform the human body into something that may no longer count as 'human'?

But haven't technologies *always* changed the human body and its capacities? A telephone allows you to hear someone who is not physically near, and a television allows you to see things that are far away. An exercise machine allows you to radically reshape and train the physical capacity of your body's muscles. Glasses or contact lenses may allow you to see when you otherwise could not. And we use technologies on the inside of our bodies, as well. An immunization may prevent you from becoming sick. A pacemaker or artificial joint may allow you to move – or simply stay alive – when your biological body may have failed. Why don't we consider these technologies to be perversions of 'human nature'? These technologies have already transformed what bodies are by reinventing how we see and how we hear, how we move, and how we live. If we think back to our discussion of cultural techniques, any form of cultivation can be thought of as an artificially invented technique, which are often solidified into the objects and things we think of as technology. This not only includes computers and appliances, but the most basic ways of manipulating the land in the history of agriculture, or the most basic ways of shaping our built environment in the history of architecture. Human beings are in constant dialogue with the technological. What counts as human is constantly reinvented through inhuman means – the techniques and technologies we use to rationally order our world and our bodies (Bollmer 2016; Lyotard 1991). Human nature, as defined by the sensory, cognitive, and biological capacities derived from the human body, is only realized in relation with the materiality of the technological.

Yet, what would it mean to completely leave the body behind, as seems to be the suggestion that follows from cybernetics? Is this desirable, or even possible? If, as I'm suggesting, there is no natural human body that exists without technology, then where is the boundary between human and technology drawn? Can one even be set? In order to attempt to answer these questions we have to elaborate the relationship between the body, identity, and digital media, a relationship we've already hinted at through-out this book so far and began thinking through in the previous chapter. We should follow cybernetics in asking, *what, exactly, is a body*? But, at the same time, we cannot conclude that a body is inessential, and that our essence is nothing other than information. In this chapter I claim that the body is the primary way we experience and encounter our world, and we can never assume the essence of identity and embodiment to be disem-bodied, informational patterns, as cybernetics often imagines. At the same time, what counts as a body cannot be limited to what's contained within the skin of the biological body. Understanding the relationship between biology, technology, and experience questions just what it means to have a body and, additionally, what it means to have an identity.

The biological capacities of our bodies – specifically, how they move and how they perceive the world – are reliant on and reshaped through the technologies we use. While it is a mistake to follow cybernetics and assume a loss of the human body, our bodies are certainly transformed and remade in relationship to the media we use to experience the world we inhabit. We cannot naïvely assume that our bodies end at the limits of our skin; but, at the same time, we cannot assume that this fact means our biological bodies are inessential and will vanish over time.

THE BODY OF HATSUNE MIKU

Before we launch into our discussion of embodiment, we should still acknowledge that both cybernetics and its fantasies of disembodiment have had a strong influence on how we think about identity and the body. If we accept the cybernetic imaginary, the 'people' of digital media may no longer rely on human bodies but are rather about informational patterns that may seem less than physically real. Let's begin with an example of the problems that emerge from a cybernetic understanding of the body and identity. The Japanese pop star Hatsune Miku is one of the most noteworthy examples of how cybernetics has affected our everyday reality, at least how we imagine the relationship between digital media, embodiment, and, interestingly, celebrity. Unlike most celebrities or musicians, Hatsune Miku is not a person, but a vocal synthesizer designed for music production professionals. Developed by the software company Crypton Future Media, Miku's name can be translated as a combination of the words for first (*hatsu*), sound (*ne*), and future (*miku*). She is the most popular of Crypton's *vocaloids*, a term used to describe software synthesizer packages that rely on samples of a voice actor, which are accompanied by a cartoon representation of the persona to which that voice supposedly belongs. Crypton describes Miku as a 'beloved collaboratively constructed cyber celebrity with a growing user community across the world. She is also often called a global icon or "hub", because the culture around her encourages a worldwide creative community to produce and share Miku-related content' (Crypton Future Media 2016).

Through a keyboard interface, combined with her library of vocal samples, Hatsune Miku 'sings' based on the various ways her software has been configured, which change pitch, tone, and any number of other musical vocal elements, creating a reasonable simulation of human singing, although the synthesized sound of her voice is also part of her popular appeal. Hatsune Miku has been a successful software package for musicians. She has been used to compose the original Nyan Cat song, a vocaloid opera entitled *The End*, created by fashion designer Louis Vuitton and director Toshiki Okada, and over 100,000 original songs written using her voice. But Hatsune Miku is not just a voice. 170,000 YouTube videos and one million artworks have used her image. A three-dimensional hologram version of her has become a popular live performer, selling out concerts in Los Angeles, Taipei, Hong Kong, Singapore, and Tokyo, opening for Lady Gaga, and even appearing on *Late Night with David Letterman* in 2014. Miku's synthesized voice and holographic body, in many ways, seem like a logical outgrowth of contemporary pop music, as reliant on digital record-ing methods and visual spectacle as it is. But one cannot say that Miku is 'fake' or 'imaginary'. Here, we see an image from a live performance given by Hatsune Miku (Figure 6.1). We can see that she is little more than a holo-graphic digital image, but she nonetheless possesses a kind of presence, and is able to affect her audience through sound, visuals, and motion. Taking to the stage in a wide range of outfits, she even seems to interact directly with her live band, all the while igniting the passion of countless fans who, with glow sticks in their hands, dance and sing along to her music.

Figure 6.1 A live performance of the vocaloid hologram Hatsune Miku.
Source: YouTube.

We should refuse a quick dismissal of Miku as a weird aberration, whose fans are unable to distinguish between 'reality' and 'simulation'. She's not that different from the 'resurrection' of Tupac Shakur as a hologram at the 2012 Coachella music festival, in which a three-dimensional version of the deceased rapper performed alongside Snoop Dogg and Dr. Dre (see Fusco 2015) (Figure 6.2). She's just one of many 3D hologram performers that have appeared in recent years, from Michael Jackson to the 'virtual band' Gorillaz. Gorillaz typically perform live in the form of two-dimensional, projected cartoon animations. Yet they appeared at the MTV European Music Awards in 2005 in what is considered to be the first 3D hologram performance. So, the concept of having virtual performers is, at this point, not a particularly strange idea.

Figure 6.2 A hologram of Tupac Shakur performs at Coachella in 2012

Source: YouTube.

Many of these hologram performers are anchored, in some way, to 'real' human bodies. Digital animation recreates the bodies of the deceased in accordance with what has been recorded and stored at some point in time. Tupac and Michael Jackson were recreated through various past recordings and manipulated using computers. These techniques have also been used in film, television, and advertising. In Bryan Singer's 2006 *Superman Returns*, for instance, Marlon Brando portrayed Superman's father, Jor-El, even though Brando died in 2004. For *Superman Returns*, footage from the 1978 *Superman* was digitally edited to make Brando 'act' and perform new dialogue. The members of Gorillaz are articulated to the voices and performances of 'real' musicians, namely Blur's Damon Albarn, who provides much of the singing, songwriting, and instrumentation for the 'virtual band'. But while Miku's voice is based on vocal samples, her existence as a vocaloid means that these samples are heavily edited. Does this suggest that the 'body' that provides this voice vanishes, the body of the singer who supplied the samples? What about Miku's 3D holographic body she uses in her performances? Is this anchored to anything 'real'?

Hatsune Miku and these other holographic performers all call us to ask questions about how digital media transform the human body. Why is Hatsune Miku any more or less real than a live human performer?

142

What's the difference? Clearly, we may think she is a digital simulation that never really existed in any physical form, although she is based on someone's real, sampled voice. And isn't she still real for her fans? Isn't she still, at some level, making real sound and music? We do literally hear her music, after all. Even though she is simulated, her voice and performance have very real effects on our senses. What's the difference between her digitally manipulated voice and the voice of a singer or rapper that has been processed through Auto-Tune or other form of pitch correction software, be it Cher, Kanye West, or Daft Punk? Auto-Tune is a common form of software-based pitch correction, which is easily heard on a song like Cher's 'Believe' or Kanye West's *808s & Heartbreak*. The use of Auto-Tune is widespread in the contemporary music industry and treats the voices of pop stars and rappers in ways that are functionally analogous to how vocaloid software treats its samples. When we listen to most recorded pop music today, we are not hearing an indexical recording of the voice of a singer, but a heavily edited and manipulated product of digital software and sampling. What differentiates Hatsune Miku's voice from these other pop stars and rappers? What differentiates her body from a hologram of Tupac Shakur? This *does not* mean that there are *no* distinctions between a human body and a hologram. Hatsune Miku *is* different from a human singer. But how should we understand these differences, especially if we want to avoid relying on any **metaphysics of presence**, suggesting that digital media are less real or less present than something else?

These ways of reinventing and reimagining the body have political and practical consequences. If we do not think of how our identities, bodies, and technologies relate, we can begin to think of virtual pop stars, holograms, and human beings as potentially interchangeable because of assumptions we make about who we are and how we interact, which are often legitimated with reference to human nature. At the same time, we can never simply defer to a natural human body that is more present than something else – things are far more complex than that, and our bodies and identities are too closely bound up with technology to make a binary distinction between the human body and technology. Thus, we now turn to discuss how technology has long related to our bodies, hopefully to answer some of these questions.

FROM IDENTITY TO EMBODIMENT

While we may imagine our identities as informational patterns and our bodies as inessential, these beliefs about disembodiment are a mistake. In the last chapter, we already saw an example of why we should never forget the body. Sherry Turkle was uncomfortable with people saying that online performances enabled them to experience how things 'really are' for another gender. Think back to her statement, 'To a certain extent, knowledge is inherently experiential, based on a physicality that we each experience differently' (Turkle 1995: 238). Your understanding of the world is implicitly guided by the orientation of your body and everything that your body carries with it. Performing as another identity online may open up one's experience. Yet these performances do not supersede the experiences that one may have because of biology, or the experiences one has had merely appearing as a specific identity in daily life. And one's past cannot be forgotten merely because they have a different identity online from the identity they have offline. Our past experiences accumulate in our bodies and shape how we understand and relate to our world (cf. Ahmed 2006).

'The body is our general medium for having a world', says the philosopher Maurice Merleau-Ponty (1962: 169). The way we understand the world is guided by our experiences and our perceptions, which are fundamentally about the physical capacities of the human body. The body is a medium because it frames how we experience the world. Much like text or graphical avatars frame how we become present for another, our bodies frame how the world becomes present to our own experience. And, just as each medium permits or prohibits the specific ways in which our relations can be made present, the different ways we experience the world – the fact that people literally perceive the world in different ways because different bodies have different capacities, or because people have different histories which shape how they relate and experience the world in which they live – means that our bodies should be placed at the absolute forefront of any understanding of who 'we' are as specific beings.

We never experience the world in its totality. We can only experience it from a particular position, and that position is guided by our body, what it experiences, and how it experiences it. But the inherent partiality of our experience does not mean that the world only exists in our head, or that any sort of synthetic knowledge of the world is impossible. 'The world is not what I think, but what I live through', claims Merleau-Ponty, 'I am open to the world, I have no doubt that I am in communication with it, but I do not possess it; it is inexhaustible' (1962: xviii–xix; cf. Zahavi 2003: 98–99). Beginning with the body reveals to us how our knowledge is inevitably guided by our own histories and memories. Our experience is different from the experience of another. Our experiences are shaped by how we appear and become present to others. We interact and react based on the relations we have. But we live in and share the same world together. We must acknowledge the partiality of our experience and attempt to collaborate and communicate with others in order to better understand the different ways of living in and experiencing the reality we share. At the same time, we must always acknowledge that we will never truly be able to understand what it's like to be another person because we always inhabit a specific body.

One of the dreams of cybernetics is that we can finally transcend the body and achieve a kind of universal knowledge, in which the limits and boundaries of experience erode away as the body vanishes. This is what we see when people performing as another gender online think that they may 'really understand' what it's like to be another person. The internet and digital media seem to promise this possibility, teaching through a form of empathy that requires one to literally experience how it feels to be another person. But why do we think we need to experience what another person experiences? Why can't we try to understand their claims about how they experience the world, without attempting to replicate it, virtually, for our own experience?

In placing the body first, however, we do little to define what a body or **embodiment** even is. Technologies literally transform how we experience the world, how we see, hear, touch, and perhaps even smell and taste. If we claim that the body should come first, and that our bodies shape how we experience the world, then we also need to acknowledge how technologies fundamentally transform what it means to even *have* a body.

Media as Extensions (and Amputations) of the Human Body

For the foundational media theorist Marshall McLuhan, 'Any invention or technology is an extension or self-amputation of our physical bodies' (1964: 45). Quite literally, McLuhan suggests, media reshape the body and its capacities. They may permit us to see at a distance (as with television), move in new, faster ways (cars and bicycles, for instance), or see and hear the events of the past (as with photography and sound recording). At the same time, each medium imposes limits to our bodies, selecting and shaping experiences in ways that 'amputate' the body. Wearing a virtual reality headset transforms what you see, hear, and (potentially) touch by placing you in a different, simulated environment. The possibilities afforded by VR reshape and reimagine your body and its capacities in a number of different ways, permitting you to experience worlds that may be far away or places and stories that may be completely unlike your daily life. These experiences and sensations are most assuredly real. Any experience is equally real because it has real effects that transform what a body is and does. But, at the same time, your capacities of sensation are limited because you no longer sense what's immediately around you. The sounds, images, scents, and other sensations of the world have been replaced by that which we experience through media. These senses have been *amputated*, to use McLuhan's language.

It's impossible to step outside the technological and have an unmediated experience, however. For McLuhan, a medium is any technology that can be thought of as an extension of the body, 'from clothing to the computer' (1995: 239), which reshape the relationship the human body has with the world. This includes things like spoken language and light bulbs. A medium is, quite simply, that which affects human perception and human interaction, both with other humans and with the world itself. 'Any technology tends to create a new human environment', claims McLuhan (1962: vi). This means that our bodies, and the relations we have with others, are fundamentally informed by the technologies we use, and technologies do not so much 'mediate' as they provide the grounds for any experience of our own selves and relations with others. Electric lights, for instance, completely change how we experience space and time. The fight against night-time darkness transforms how space is used, and how safe or dangerous specific places may be (and for whom). It even makes night-time 'productive' as people work at night with electric lights. With the invention of the electric light, the environment was completely reorganized. And it's not like we have a choice in accepting or rejecting these ways that technology reshapes our environment, as if there's some 'natural' state we can achieve by refusing technology. 'To behold, use or perceive any extension of ourselves in technological form is necessarily to embrace it', says McLuhan, 'To listen to radio or to read the printed page is to accept these extensions of ourselves into our personal system and to undergo the "closure" or displacement of perception that follows automatically. ... Physiologically, man in the normal use of technology (or his variously extended body) is perpetually modified by it and in turn finds ever new ways of modifying his technology' (1962: 46). The use of any medium requires a specific sensory experience, using specific capacities of the body at the expense of others.

Body Schema and Body Image

The way we imagine our own bodies is fundamentally bound together with technology as well. Close your eyes and picture your body. How do you see yourself? We commonly think of this as something we can call a *body image*.

You have a way of seeing and imagining how your body appears. This image is probably visual, and if we compare it to the actual experience we have of our body then it clearly doesn't match up. For instance, you cannot see your face without the help of a mirror or, perhaps, a smartphone. There are large parts of your body, such as your back, that you cannot visualize without the help of some medium that reflects your appearance back towards you. You simply do not see yourself as an external observer would see you. So how do you get a sense of your own body?

The term 'body image' isn't particularly good at capturing the lived reality of having a body. According to Merleau-Ponty, body image 'was at first understood to mean a *compendium* of our bodily experience … it was supposed to register for me the positional changes of the parts of my body for each movement of one of them, the position of each local stimulus in the body as a whole, an account of the movements performed at every instant during a complex gesture, in short a continual translation into visual language of the kinaesthetic and articular impressions of the moment' (1962: 113). But in stressing the visual, the range of bodily experiences that are not visual – the movements and sensations that involve touch, for instance – are rendered secondary to a way of visualizing and imagining the body.

The term **body schema** accounts for these different, non-visual ways that a body moves, revealing and making a world present to experience. You have a felt sense of your body in space that isn't entirely reliant on sight. If you close your eyes and touch your nose (or other part of your body, for that matter), you'll probably succeed. You have a felt sense of where the different parts of your body are, and you know how to inhabit your body even if you do not imagine your body visually. As Merleau-Ponty noted, amputees often feel as if parts of their body still exist as 'phantom limbs', even though they know and can see that their limbs are no longer part of their bodies.

The body schema includes the different technical extensions that reframe how a body moves through space. The body schema is 'a flexible, plastic, systemic form of distributed agency encompassing what takes place within the boundaries of the body proper (the skin) as well as the entirety of the spatiality of embodied motility' (Hansen 2006: 38). This means that, as is the case with McLuhan, we should think of technology as that which transforms how we move through space and interact with a larger environment. Our 'bodies' do not end at our skin but are extended through the technologies we use to move, touch, and sense.

The way we visualize our bodies – our body image – is therefore a product of our body schema. The body schema includes the mirrors and cameras we look at and employ to understand and imagine our body. The way we come to understand our bodies inherently overflows the limits of our skin, using our technological extensions to reflect our bodies back towards us. A mirror becomes part of the way we visually sense our face and body, and we literally use the mirror to come to understand how our body relates and becomes present to others. We can say that smartphones perform a similar function. We may take a selfie in order to visualize how we look, and we come to understand our bodies in relation to the technologies we use to visualize who we are and how we become present to others (cf. Bollmer & Guinness 2017). Certain facial expressions and other gestures may become common because of how we visualize and understand our bodies – a performance that is both directed to others as well as ourselves.

Collective Bodies, Collective Minds?

According to the cognitive philosopher Andy Clark, 'The human mind, if it is to be the physical organ of human reason, simply cannot be seen as bound and restricted by the biological skinbag. In fact, it has *never been* thus restricted and bound' (2003: 4). Clark, while he dismisses the physical human body as a 'skinbag', nonetheless claims that the human use of technology is something inherently physical, and distributes the mind into the larger environment. Whenever we purchase a new technology, we are 'not just investing in new toys', Clark claims. Rather, we are 'buying *mindware upgrades*, electronic prostheses capable of extending and transforming [our] personal reach, thought, and vision' (2003: 10). In many ways, this is what we've been arguing so far. Technologies permit the body to be extended in specific ways, enabling it to perform specific identities that expand or transform the body in specific ways. So, when we communicate online, we are 'really there', our bodies are distributed outward. Our minds, if we understand them in physical terms as fundamentally embodied, are therefore also distributed outward, beyond the limits of our skin. Thought, for Clark, is something that takes place both within and beyond the limits of the physical body because the body is extended through technology.

Many of our online platforms today, Wikipedia being the most notable, are believed to produce a form of shared, collaborative intelligence based on the synthesis of a wide range of partial, individual knowledge. The suggestions of Amazon or Netflix, which tell you what you may like based on what you've previously read or watched, are not the product of individuals making suggestions. They're based on a body of collective data that is analyzed to predict what you may like to read or watch in the future, based on the acts and evaluations of many, many others. Wikipedia is thought to generate 'truth' out of the swirling maelstrom of countless individuals participating together on its website, not because of the authority or research of any one individual, but because of the apparent 'objectivity' that comes from uniting a multitude of different perspectives. So, while my specific body limits and frames the world I experience, network technologies are often believed to enable a form of **collective intelligence** that unites individual bodies through collaborative networks (cf. Lévy 1997). Because of the interrelation between the human body and technology, should we then assume that Wikipedia, Amazon, and the rest of the internet are, effectively, parts of the human body? Andy Clark suggests that, because these technologies rely on collective information generation, then the internet is creating a larger, collective body, the intelligence of which becomes a part of our own mind whenever we read, contribute, and upload information online.

Brian Rotman, a theorist of media, science, and mathematics, makes a similar point. With network technology, we can no longer suggest that there is a stable, coherent thing called an 'I' or 'me'. In the past, our identities were based on the fact that there were relatively clear limits to our technologies. A mirror only projects 'me' back to myself. If I wrote into a diary it was an expression of 'me' that emerged from my own hand, speaking back to me. While my diary could be read by others, my writing still contained the trace of me, the individual who wrote it in the first place. But with the internet, 'Now the "I" bleeds outwards into the collective, which in turn introjects, insinuates, and internalizes itself within the "me": what was private and interior is seen as a fold in the public, the historical, the social as outside events enter (and reveal themselves as having always entered) the individual soul' (Rotman 2008: 99). The ability to define what is specifically individual about myself becomes difficult, if not completely impossible. Both my knowledge and my experience become an expression of collective writing and collaboration, which transform both how I relate to myself (there is no clear 'I' doing the writing) and my relation to others (other people become part of 'me' as agency is distributed outwards).

Yet again, we seem to be back at Turkle's observation that the internet distributes the 'I' into 'parallel selves', a suggestion of which she was nonetheless sceptical. This time, however, the 'I' is so thoroughly dissolved that any attempt at defining 'I' is, at best, a mistake, or, at worst, a denial of the distributed and collective nature of identity. Henry Jenkins, a scholar of fandom and popular culture, has suggested that fan communities online should be thought of in terms similar to these. When people gather online to discuss a television show, be it *Survivor* or *Game of Thrones*, Jenkins claims that they are producing a collective body of knowledge in which the agency of any one individual is subsumed into the collective (2006: 26–29). Our knowledge is intrinsically linked to a collective body, which shapes and transforms any attempt to define 'me' and my own interior thought and knowledge. While Jenkins does not go as far as Clark or Rotman, literally claiming that these online forums are a part of the mind of a user, given the relationship between technology and the body we've been discussing we should wonder: what, then, constitutes the boundary between my mind (and body) and the mind (and body) of another on the internet?

As Turkle suggested in the 1980s, this distributed understanding of identity and embodiment does not really mesh with the everyday experiences of most people. So, let's have one final example in this chapter to explain the kind of collective bodies and agencies enabled by digital media that these authors discuss. In 2014, an anonymous Australian programmer used the online video streaming platform Twitch to create a way to play the videogame *Pokémon* collectively. The experiment, named 'Twitch Plays *Pokémon*', began with the game *Pokémon Red*, which was originally released for the Nintendo GameBoy. Twitch Plays *Pokémon* attracted over 80,000 viewers and had at least 10 per cent of those 80,000 viewers participating, collectively playing *Pokémon Red*, beginning on 12 February and completing the game 16 days later, on 1 March. Twitch collectively 'played' *Pokémon* using a relatively simple app developed with JavaScript. The members of a chatroom watching the Twitch Plays *Pokémon* video stream would input different commands that coincided with the GameBoy's buttons. We can see an example of one of the many incarnations of Twitch Plays *Pokémon* in Figure 6.3.

On the right-hand side of the image, we observe how people type in 'A', 'B', 'select', 'start', or directional commands to interact with the game. The JavaScript app identifies these commands, and then inputs them into the game. Initially, this meant that the gameplay via Twitch was quite chaotic. After a few days, the designer of Twitch Plays *Pokémon* added two different modes for gameplay, 'Democracy' or 'Anarchy' (which we can also see input by some users in this specific example). Anarchy proceeded as the gameplay interface was initially designed. Democracy, on the other hand, added a voting mechanism that would tally all inputs received over a set amount of time, and then play the one with the highest number of votes.

Twitch Plays *Pokémon* proceeds in short bursts, in chaotic ways that make it seem like forward progression is impossible. Menus open

Figure 6.3 Twitch Plays *Pokémon*.

Source: YouTube.

and close almost at random, the player's avatar moves around aimlessly, perhaps backing into corners and getting stuck. And yet, Twitch Plays *Pokémon* has successfully completed not just *Pokémon Red*, but most of the different *Pokémon* games available, and similar collective gaming experiments have attempted to complete games such as the notoriously difficult *Dark Souls* and the open-world role-playing game *Fallout 3*. While most of these games involve some sort of interface or modification to be developed so they can be played over Twitch with a large number of different individuals, they demonstrate how network technologies work to produce a 'collective' player that unites a wide range of different people, creating a 'collective body' that plays the game. No one individual could be said to be 'playing' Twitch Plays *Pokémon*. Rather, it was an act of collective will, filtered through a technological apparatus designed to harness different gestures and acts of a wide range of human bodies, networked together through the internet. Whether or not Twitch Plays *Pokémon* was a particularly successful example of collective intelligence (as, even though the game was completed, it took longer than it would have for an individual player), it nonetheless reveals how technology can produce a kind of collective agent that brings together different bodies to act as one.

I find Twitch Plays *Pokémon* interesting because it is one of the few examples in which a kind of collective intelligence really does emerge from the potentials of networked, digital media, at least beyond Wikipedia and a few notable works of contemporary art. At the same time, I am wary of the suggestion that our bodies actually become 'collective' with digital, networked technologies. Accepting this 'collective body' as fact has a tendency to cover over political investments involved in these collective projects, for instance. Wikipedia is often named as one of the great successes of collective intelligence – a collaborative environment that produces 'truth' out of the input of a vast range of diverse individuals. Yet, in spite of its rhetoric otherwise, Wikipedia is not truly an 'open' or 'collaborative' environment, and it has long had a tendency of veiling many of its discriminatory practices. Wikipedia's editors are almost entirely male, many of whom work hard to silence the few women who do contribute to Wikipedia. Rather than work to rectify these problems, the ideals of an open, collaborative intelligence serve to blame 'nonexistent female contributors for "not participating"' (Tkacz 2015: 11). Here, we see how the ideal of a collective body erases from view the very real issues that emerge from having a body and appearing towards others. Again, we see how one way of making a body visible towards others – which, perhaps unsurprisingly, is primarily text-based in all of these collective examples – tends to ignore the physicality of a human body for the specific way it becomes visible towards another.

CONCLUSION

Any discussion of the body and digital media is difficult, in part because we must acknowledge that our technologies extend our bodies, transform how we experience and relate to our environment, and reshape how we become present to others. Our identities and bodies are clearly bound together with our technologies. At the same time, the ability of our technologies to transmit information across vast distances, to make us present in places that we may not otherwise be, too often drifts into fantasies of disembodiment, in which our technological extensions substitute for the biological fact of having a body. At best, this can produce kinds of collective, participatory agencies via the internet. At worst, this can lead to some horrendously problematic takes on the politics of identity, in which we supposedly can understand someone else by pretending to be another identity online – which can literally erase the body of another and any acknowledgement that embodied experience matters.

In the previous chapter, we discussed different ways of understanding identity, suggesting that identity can be conceptualized as emerging from the specific ways technologies allow us to perform 'who we are' by enabling us to become present to others in specific ways. The different ways technologies do this, be they textual, visual, or about the data extracted from the human body in any number of ways, transform how we become present and the possibilities we have for performing identity. In this chapter, we moved from these claims about identity to a larger discussion of embodiment, arguing that technologies fundamentally transform what a body is and does, extending out – but also limiting – the body in its sensory capacities. In recent years, this fact has led a number of theorists and writers to suggest that we are experiencing a 'collective' form of embodiment, perhaps best illustrated with projects like Wikipedia and Twitch Plays *Pokémon*, in which individual agency is subsumed into a collective will, and the actions of any one body are distributed into a larger 'body' of which that individual is part.

So, what can we say about Hatsune Miku now? She is, in many ways, an extension of a body, based on technologically recorded samples that are then manipulated. The holographic technology used for her performances transforms what we see and hear and make present for our experience something that would otherwise be impossible without that technology. Perhaps we can even say that there is an aspect of collective embodiment with Hatsune Miku, as these samples are taken up and used to produce all sorts of creative products by many different people, in collaboration, across the planet. Hatsune Miku is not the creation of one individual but of many, networked together via the internet. At the same time, can we say that Miku really has a body? She may be present to our experience, but what is being transmitted to us? Is she merely an image? What is being performed? How is the body being augmented, extended, or transformed? How is the body being amputated in her performances? Again, I do not think we can come up with clear, definitive answers for these questions. But we have a better way of thinking about them than a simple distinction between 'real' and 'false', one that acknowledges that Hatsune Miku is present and real, but is present in a different way from a human singer.

7

AESTHETICS AND AFFECTS

Since digital media transform the perceptual capacities of the human body, we should think in detail about the aesthetics of digital media. Aesthetics refers to the understanding and judgement of what can be perceived and sensed. This chapter reviews key concepts from the general field of aesthetic theory, including the relationship between aesthetics, form, and politics. It concludes with a discussion of affect as it relates to aesthetics and sensation. The next chapter continues this discussion with an overview of specific forms that characterize digital culture.

TERMS: aesthetics; affect; distribution of the sensible; hypermediacy; ideals; immediacy; medium specificity; remediation; three regimes of images (ethical, poetic/representative, aesthetic)

THEORISTS: Leon Battista Alberti, Walter Benjamin, Jay David Bolter, Eugenie Brinkema, Richard Grusin, William James, Rosalind Krauss, Caroline Levine, Jacques Rancière, Baruch Spinoza

EXAMPLES: Aziz 'Zyzz' Shavershian; Kanye West's 'Welcome to Heartbreak' music video; Kazimir Malevich's Black Square; James Bridle's 'New Aesthetic'

Marshall McLuhan argued that media can enlarge, reframe, or hinder our perceptual capacities. Media literally transform what we experience – capacities that have long been associated with the philosophical field of **aesthetics**. Aesthetics comes from the Greek *aisthetikos*, which refers to perception, feeling, and sensation. When we examine how digital media shape perception and sensation we ask aesthetic questions. This requires us to situate digital media within a larger history of aesthetic theory, a task we'll begin to take up in this chapter and continue in the next.

When we talk of aesthetics we are often describing the way something appears to our experience, seemingly a synonym for 'style'. But a better word than style would be *form*, and McLuhan is often thought of as a 'media formalist', concerned more with the material form of media than any specific 'meaning' or 'content' transmitted. But form is not precisely a synonym for medium. Form, following literary critic Caroline Levine, refers to '*an arrangement of elements – an ordering, patterning, or shaping*' (2015: 3, original italics). Form can refer to a very broad range of things, whether it is the materiality of a medium or specific artistic techniques or whether it is the specific, material dimensions of an object or the kinds of colours used in an image (and it can also refer to a kind of pattern, as we saw with cybernetics, but refers to more than informational patterns). The formal elements of something define the aesthetics of a specific artist or set of artists, or a set of design principles that characterize a brand. There is a relatively consistent set of forms that distinguish 'modernist aesthetics', or 'Facebook aesthetics', or even 'post-internet aesthetics'.

But aesthetics does not only refer to these formal similarities. There are specific categories we use to judge forms, which are often about the feelings and emotions evoked by a work of art or an object. Traditionally, the judgement that philosophical aesthetics has concerned itself with is beauty – what formal characteristics make something beautiful? Those discussing contemporary aesthetics, however, are not as focused on beauty as they are on other judgements. Digital technologies have been associated with a set of formal properties that produce the feeling of 'coolness', for instance, although what produces coolness is often difficult to identify (Liu 2004). Apple's products are objects made of sleek lines and brushed metal. They may appear 'cool' today, but coolness changes over time. What was cool in the 1990s may not be cool anymore – unless it is recontextualized and reinvented to become cool again. The candy-coloured iMac G3, which was produced from 1998 to 2003, was exceptionally cool in its own time, although it may not be cool anymore, aside from a kind of retro kitsch.

So, aesthetics are defined by, first, a set of *formal consistencies* that characterize artworks or objects made during a specific period of time or place, made by a specific person or group of people, or, in some cases, associated with a particular brand. Second, they are defined by the *value judgements* made about these formal consistencies, which are implicit in the categories we use to describe formal elements, categories like 'cool', or 'beautiful'. These judgements reveal something about how we order and make sense of the world, and how we come to understand our position within it. Third, these forms and judgements are often less about what something clearly means than about a feeling or intensity that cannot be clearly articulated in language – aesthetics have something to do with **affect**, which refers to the way a body moves, or the way it affects and is affected by other bodies. When we say something 'moves us', we are *affected* by it.

In this chapter, I'm going to begin to define a way of thinking about aesthetic categories as political categories. This happens to be a general way of thinking about culture at large, rather than just a discussion of the aesthetics of digital media. This discussion of aesthetic theory is intended to supplement how we've been thinking about culture, and moves towards the subject of the next chapter, which reviews a number of formal elements of digital media that often characterize art about the internet and social media, along with art made with digital media. In these two chapters, I am primarily interested in recent ways of thinking about aesthetics, as many discussions of aesthetics in cultural theory have been dedicated towards examining how we make sense of a world permeated by digital, networked information, especially when 'information' and 'networks' are seemingly too large to experience in any coherent way (Galloway 2011; Jagoda 2016). Additionally, we will be reviewing some of what is referred to as 'affect theory' in this chapter. Aesthetics are about how we make sense of our world, but they do so less through rational thought than through intensities that we feel, intensities that shape how the body moves and acts. Affect theory can help us to describe these intensities.

Let's now discuss a few examples to pull apart how these different definitions of aesthetics may work in practice, beginning with one that may appear to have absolutely nothing to do with art.

THE 'FATHER OF AESTHETICS' AND THE 'NEW AESTHETIC'

The first example I will discuss is Australian internet microcelebrity Aziz Shavershian, better known as 'Zyzz' to his online followers, who died in 2011 at the age of 22. Online, Zyzz was often referred to as the 'father of aesthetics'. 'Aesthetics' here refers to an internet subculture that emerged between 2006 and 2007 and peaked in popularity around 2010 (Fuller & Jeffery 2017). Zyzz was one of the most visible individuals associated with this subculture, using 'aesthetic' to refer to a kind of bodily perfection, achieved not only with exercise but with an elaborate regimen of drugs, such as anabolic steroids (Underwood 2017: 84). He served as an ideal for a kind of bodily practice (often associated with a broad range of online memes and images) that was aspirational for a number of others in the 'aesthetics' subculture.

Zyzz may seem like a silly example with which to begin a discussion of aesthetics, especially since many of us would not take a combination of weightlifting and steroids to be 'art' in any coherent sense – although the theorist Hans Ulrich Gumbrecht (2006) has described the more traditionally legitimate kinds of athleticism associated with sport as one of the clearest ways we have of experiencing and judging aesthetic beauty today (also see Taussig 2012). Yet, we can argue that Zyzz and the 'aesthetics' subculture are following a relatively traditional understanding of aesthetics. This example begs us to ask, how do we evaluate something, especially in terms of its *formal* qualities? Implicitly, in the usage of Zyzz and his followers, 'aesthetics' refers to an idealized bodily form, one to be obtained through specific – often pharmaceutically augmented – practices that would transform one's own body into that which mirrored an ideal body, which was, in this case at least, the body of Zyzz himself.

But this understanding of aesthetics – the judgement of forms and how they relate to **ideals** – is something of a problem. Who gets to define the criteria upon which we evaluate these forms? Who says something is an ideal? These ideals of beauty are defined by a group of people brought together through internet message boards. What gives this group the right to judge these forms? What makes one form better than another? Or, what makes something more closely adhere to an ideal than something else? Are these even appropriate ways of evaluating art, bodies, and experience? Following Caroline Levine, our lives are filled with multiple forms that overlap and intersect. How do we make sense of the sheer number of forms implicit in shaping how we make sense of our world? While this would appear to be about taste, suggesting that one may prefer how one body looks to another, a judgement that is ultimately subjective, there is an explicit politics here, one that suggests the various categories we use to describe and evaluate carry with them assumptions about proper bodies and ideal actions. Taste is not just about personal preferences, but about the ways we think of others and relate to them.

Zyzz and his followers adopted a shared commitment to the development of a specific kind of body, along with a sense of ideals about beauty and perfection shared by the members of the online 'aesthetic' bodybuilding community. But aesthetics can refer to more than these kinds of shared ideals and judgements of taste. The British writer and artist James Bridle coined the phrase 'the New Aesthetic', which is also the name of his well-known Tumblr blog, to refer to a way of visualizing the role of the internet and digital media in everyday life (Berry & Dieter 2015: 5). The 'New Aesthetic', like art associated with other, similar terms, such as 'post-internet' or 'post-digital', is about making the often-invisible ways digital media shape our everyday experience into that which is visible and sensible to human perception. When we look at some of the forms associated with the 'New Aesthetic', we can understand them in terms of a coherent style (which often appear as things like digital glitches, animated GIFs, or dated images that come from the history of digital media). These formal elements are supposedly revealing to us, in a way that humans can understand and sense, the inner workings of technologies and the role they have in shaping daily life.

These ways of visualizing digital culture have already had a significant impact on popular culture. As just one particularly notable example, we can refer to Kanye West's 'Welcome to Heartbreak' music video from 2009 (Figure 7.1). In this specific shot from the video, we see different images laid over each other, bleeding into each other, although not in any smooth, clearly intentional way. While West can be made out in the middle of the screen, he is obscured by blocky distortions that come from other shots in the video. In the video itself, these different shots are seen as explosions of colour and partial figures, which are not reminiscent of human intervention into direction and editing, but of corrupted images that come from problems in a digital file. Instead of clear or coherent editing, we have visual glitches suggestive of those that come from poorly encoded digital video. What we're seeing in this image is a result of the misuse of video compression – not fully intended by any human, and still potentially 'beautiful' to many, but derived from a way of visualizing and making sensible the operations of digital video. These images were made for a song that heavily relies on Auto-Tune, manipulating West's voice in ways that are obviously an effect of digital technology. The assumption with Bridle's 'New Aesthetic' is that these visual, stylistic changes challenge and critique that which is invisible in daily life. Artists use the mistakes and limits of digital technology, supposedly, to critically reveal the technological elements underpinning the infrastructures we regularly ignore.

Figure 7.1　Glitch in Kanye West's 'Welcome to Heartbreak' music video.

Source: YouTube

　　Glitch art, which relies on the errors and mistakes of technology in its form (cf. Cubitt 2017b; Krapp 2011), is intended, like the works of those associated with the 'New Aesthetic', to reveal what we overlook, denaturalizing the media environment of digital media. Many glitch artists assume that their art disrupts the 'smooth' surfaces of digital media, revealing what's really going on underneath, showing us the function and limitations of hardware and software. This is positioned as a challenge to the logic of contemporary capitalism, reliant as it is on digital media, and some of these artists were upset with West's seeming appropriation of glitch for his video (see Kane 2014b). Does 'Welcome to Heartbreak' demonstrate a way of disrupting or challenging the everyday ways we have of engaging with digital media? Or does it demonstrate how the various forms associated with digital media merely become new ways of engaging and sensing our world?

We should take glitch as provoking a few questions about how we define aesthetics and how we understand their politics. The assumption here is that a specific way of visualizing or representing digital media is political. But what can we say about this politics? What makes a specific aesthetic form political? Is it about how art can make us see something in everyday life that we usually neglect, challenging our preconceived understanding of our world, as is the case with the New Aesthetic and glitch? Or, is the politics here about how specific artistic and stylistic forms, along with their judgements, draw lines and make associations between specific groups of people, as is the case with Zyzz and the 'aesthetics' subculture (and the artists upset about Kanye West's appropriation of glitch)? These are both ways of thinking about the politics of aesthetics – either by visualizing and exposing reality, or by assembling groups of people (and differentiating them, placing them in conflict) through shared commitments to the judgement of taste.

These two examples demonstrate a number of key elements of aesthetics we will continue to elaborate below. Aesthetics are about *formal* elements that differentiate kinds of art, kinds of bodies, kinds of actions. They are associated with *taste*, in that they are linked to specific judgements that evaluate based on adherence or achievement of an ideal (such as 'beauty'), but they are often related to weaker kinds of judgements (such as 'cool' or 'interesting'). Finally, they are dependent on specific technological contexts, but are also about how communities come to judge and understand form. While glitch may have been cool at one time, and supposedly 'political' in its disclosure of the operation of digital technology, its use by Kanye West may transform how a specific formal element is judged. The judgement here is used to perform membership in a community, in which taste represents a kind of belonging (or, for that matter, a kind of exclusion). But we cannot limit the politics of aesthetics to inclusion and exclusion based on shared taste. Rather, we should discuss how the very ability to express and experience specific forms is, in and of itself, political.

THE POLITICS OF AESTHETICS

Politics and aesthetics are often opposed, a distinction that goes back to the famous essay by Marxist theorist Walter Benjamin, 'The Work of Art in the Age of Mechanical Reproduction', which was initially written and revised during the rise of the Third Reich in Germany, between 1935 and 1939. In the essay's epilogue, Benjamin claims: 'The logical result of Fascism is the introduction of aesthetics into politics. … All efforts to render politics aesthetic culminate in one thing: war' (1968: 241). Benjamin is referring to beliefs like those of the Italian Fascist Filippo Tommaso Marinetti and the Futurists, who claimed that war and violence were intrinsically beautiful. But Benjamin's claim has resulted in a longstanding distinction between aesthetics and politics, one that opposes the sensory envelopment and absorption of beauty with a kind of disaffected and distracted political alienation. In the 'Work of Art' essay, Benjamin argues that mass production destroys the 'aura' of an object, with aura defined as a kind of energy that emerges from a specific object being unique and located at a specific place and time. The viewer is often entranced in the presence of an art object because of its aura, and the value of an object – its 'cult value' – often comes from how access is prohibited, and the object may be difficult to access and view. Mass production, in democratizing the art object by reproducing countless copies that are more or less the same, transforms 'cult value' into 'exhibition value' – the value of an object comes from its wide distribution of being seen. Mass production also opens a space for the political, since we are no longer enrapt with the aura of the original. It is in becoming alienated from an original and its 'cult value' that political agency happens, opposed to how Fascism tends to 'aestheticize politics'. Aestheticizing violence – stressing its beauty and form – leads to an uncritical embrace of war, Benjamin suggests. It is in alienation that we become critical, seeing through any fetishizing of the original.

There have been numerous challenges to Benjamin's distinction in recent years. The theorist of photography Ariella Azoulay, for instance, suggests that 'political' is itself an aesthetic judgement, and that the politics of art – specifically photography – comes from how an image makes visible specific relations between the people documented in an artwork (Azoulay 2012: 54). Others, such as Samuel Weber (1996), have noted how our desire for aura – for an intense experience of uniqueness, for a 'reality' unmediated by technology – has only increased in recent years. Rather than aura being destroyed by mass production, we now demand aura all the time. Regardless, a simple distinction between aesthetics and politics may not be very helpful. Instead, we should attempt to think through how politics and aesthetics are related.

The Distribution of the Sensible

One of the most significant theorists to discuss the relationship between aesthetics and politics is the French philosopher Jacques Rancière.

Rancière's primary concern is with the **distribution of the sensible**, which he defines as 'the system of self-evident facts of sense perception that simultaneously discloses the existence of something in common and the delimitations that define the respective parts and positions within it. A distribution of the sensible therefore establishes at one and the same time something common that is shared and exclusive parts' (2004: 7). What Rancière means here is that our world is *partitioned*, and partitions are literally about what can be experienced and who can experience it – what can be seen and who can see it, what can be said and who can say it, what can be heard and who can hear it, what can be felt and who can feel it. This distribution is foundational for who becomes part of a specific community, and how that community exists in space and time. 'The distribution of the sensible reveals who can have a share in what is common to the community based on what they do and on the time and space in which this activity is performed ... it defines what is visible or not in a common space, endowed with a common language, etc.' (2004: 8). Politics for Rancière, then, are literally about how these partitions and relations change. He uses the term *police*, which does not intrinsically mean the people and institutions of law enforcement, to refer to that which enacts and maintains these partitions ('police' here is more clearly related to a phrase such as 'policing the boundaries'). The police and politics are conjoined – the police enact and maintain partitions, politics are about questioning and transforming partitions.

This does not mean that the arts and the political are the same thing. We cannot say that all art is political. Nor can we say that politics and the arts are inherently linked. Instead, there is a politics to aesthetics and an aesthetics to politics. If we think about 'actual' political acts, which would include things like protest, democratic deliberation over governmental policy, and the institutional task of creating and enforcing law, we can ask questions about what can be seen, who can talk, and what spaces are permitted for specific people. (Or, to phrase this another way, what parts of your government can you see? What is hidden from you? In which conversations can you participate? From which are you excluded?) The ability to protest in the street rather than a demarcated 'free speech zone', to occupy a specific building or space to be heard, or to hear and have access to the debates that elected representatives have in official meeting, these all involve an aesthetic dimension because they rely on partitions that define where people can go and what can be experienced. We can say that there is an aesthetic dimension to politics, because politics relies on partitions that form communities and collectives out of what can be experienced.

But this is not precisely the same thing as the politics of aesthetics. What we call 'art' has radically changed throughout the history of Western culture. And 'art' in non-Western contexts would refer to other practices, which may or may not be understood as art in the West (or understood through the norms of Western art). As the category of 'art' changes over time and differs from place to place, there have been shifts between what gets identified as 'art', which are linked to other changes in what can be seen and said. The partitions that define 'art', and the way that this boundary is policed, have changed over time. These changes tell us that there is a politics to aesthetics, a politics that involves struggles over what we can say is 'art' and how we evaluate it as 'art'.

The Three Regimes of Art in Western Culture

Rancière differentiates between three 'regimes' of art in Western culture. While these are historical, he doesn't imply a clear progression, or that older ways of evaluating artistic representations have completely vanished when a new regime arrives. These different regimes 'emerged' at a specific point in history, and they persist as that which is 'residual' later on (Rancière 2004: 46–47). The first, which is associated with Plato and the Ancient Greeks, is the **ethical regime of images**. In this regime, 'art' is not identified as such. There are only 'arts', specific practices of producing images, which include painting, poetry, and theatre. These images are understood as lesser imitations of reality, and they are evaluated in terms of how well these images *educate* both children and citizens, or how well a specific image fits in and effects a more general *ethos* – the 'mode of being' of a community and the individuals in that community. For Plato, there is a distinction between *true arts*, which imitate with specific ends in mind, ends that resonate with the ethos (and are, thus, 'ethical'), and *simulacra*, which imitate reality without this ethical dimension, merely appearing as true. Plato illustrates this with the example of a classical Greek sculpture which is made larger on top than on the bottom. Viewers at the bottom of the sculpture would see it as accurate when it is, in fact, malformed, duping and confusing the viewer in the name of an assumed 'truth' that is not actually true. Simulacra appear true, but are, in fact, distortions.

The second regime Rancière discusses, which emerged with Aristotle and persisted for much of history until the emergence of modernity, is the **poetic** or **representative regime of the arts**. This, he claims, is defined by the coupled terms *poiēsis* and *mimēsis*, which refer to creation and imitation, respectively. In this regime, the arts can be evaluated based on how well an artist is able to mimic or make a copy of a model from reality. Evaluating art in this way

> develops into forms of normativity that define the conditions according to which imitations can be recognized as exclusively belonging to an art and assessed, within this framework, as good or bad, adequate or inadequate: partitions between the representable and the unrepresentable; the distinction between genres according to what is represented; principles for adapting forms of expression to genres and thus to the subject matter represented; the distribution of resemblances according to principles of verisimilitude, appropriateness, or correspondence; criteria for distinguishing between and comparing the arts; etc. (Rancière 2004: 17)

Whereas the ethical regime of images evaluated the arts based on the lessons taught and the alignment with the general values of a community, the poetic or representative regime of the arts instead celebrates how a specific art form – its technical and material existence, its limitations according to genre – enables specific ways of representing reality, of replicating reality, of imitating reality.

We can understand how this regime operates fairly easily. Under it, a 'good' work of art can be understood in terms of how well it is able to replicate or mirror reality. We can evaluate a painting based on how well it copies human perception and experience, or a building or sculpture can be evaluated in terms of how well it mirrors nature and, especially, a set of ideal, formal elements derived from a way of understanding the human body. We can see some of these ways of evaluating art in Leon Battista Alberti's *On Painting*, originally written in the 1430s. *On Painting* is one of the most foundational documents discussing this way of evaluating the arts. Alberti wants to 'explain the art of painting [as] beginning from Nature's principles themselves' (2011: 22). These principles are derived from the human body and the human figure, filtered through the mathematics of Alberti's own time. 'But since the human figure, or all things known to man, perhaps Protagoras, in saying that man is the model and the measure of all things, meant precisely this: that the incidentals of all [objects] are correctly measured and are known by man's incidentals' (2011: 38). So, the arts, following Alberti, could be evaluated not just in terms of how they visually mirrored reality, but in terms of how their formal elements could be thought to mirror the human body, in terms of both proportion and how the human body perceives space. This system of evaluation refers not only to painting, sculpture, and architecture, but to music as well. Human bodily perfection, as described by Vitruvius and encoded in the ideals of the Vitruvian man and the golden ratio, were transferred into all arts, in which beauty and pleasure were assumed to emerge from a work that accurately repeated the ratios of nature and the human body.

Rancière's third regime is **the aesthetic regime of the arts**, which, he claims, is a more accurate label for what we often call modernism. This third regime is characterized by a move away from *mimēsis* and the representation of reality, instead privileging *abstraction*. Evaluating art, in this case, is often about a search for its 'essence', or, following the art historian Rosalind Krauss, is a way of looking at how an artwork engages with its **medium specificity**. Media, for Krauss, are 'specified by the material support they supply for artistic practice: the way canvas and stretcher support the images of traditional painting and plaster wall those of fresco, or the way metal armatures support the material of sculptural volume' (2010: xiii–xiv).

Figure 7.2 Kazimir Malevich's *Black Square* (1915). Oil on linen, 79.5 cm x 79.5 cm.

Source: Wikimedia Commons

So, in this way, the evaluation of a work of abstract, modern art would not be evaluated by how well it *copies* reality, but in terms of how well it discloses some 'essence' of the material thing in which the work exists.

An iconic example of how these regimes of art have moved away from representation towards abstraction can be seen in Kazimir Malevich's famous painting *Black Square*, from 1915 (Figure 7.2). *Black Square* is not about any sense of representation, any mirroring of reality. Rather, it is about the specific medium of paint on canvas. Any attempt to evaluate it on the basis of the representative regime – in which art and painting are judged on the model of the human body and its experience – would seemingly fail, given how the painting doesn't *represent* or *mirror* 'experience' in any way. The painting itself is what is experienced, as a painting. We understand this work as 'great' (and as 'art') because of what it tells us about itself as a painting, and what it reveals about its medium that may have been previously buried. *Black Square* has been found to have been painted over at least two other, more representational images. In painting over these images, Malevich has seemingly denied the ability of a 'representational' image to represent at all. The 'reality' of the painting can only be expressed in its most basic, medium-specific expression of paint on a canvas. The aesthetic regime of art, then, is about questioning the formal elements of the medium itself, looking at a painting for what it tells us about painting, or looking at a sculpture for what it tells us about sculpture.

Immediacy and Hypermediacy

The aesthetic regime of the arts did not do away with the representative regime. The relation between these two regimes can be seen in how theorists Jay David Bolter and Richard Grusin describe the interplay between different media forms as a dialectic of **immediacy** and **hypermediacy**, which also helps us understand how these different aesthetic regimes relate to digital media.

Immediacy relies on judgements similar to those that characterize the representative regime of the arts. Representations and images should 'promise us transparent, perceptual immediacy, experience without mediation' (Bolter & Grusin 1999: 22–23). The medium itself should be invisible, and our experience of a work of art (or any other form of representation) should reach ever closer to a duplication of reality. We can see the drive towards immediacy in virtual reality and videogames. These representations are intended to be true-to-life simulations, copying reality in ways that make us forget that the 'representation' is a representation at all.

A game like *Grand Theft Auto V* takes painstaking effort to recreate a fully authentic 'world' in which the player is (mostly) free to do whatever they feel. (Though, admittedly, this freedom is an illusion given how it is necessarily programmed into the game, and games like *GTA* disrupt their own realism through the use of things like mini-maps or directional indices, without which it would be difficult, if not impossible, to play these games. *GTA* attempts to hide these aspects of its interface by imitating, for instance, GPS systems on phones, but they're still not presented as a true-to-life replication of reality). The terms we use to evaluate games, such as 'immersion' and 'world', suggest that the way we judge them is often reliant on how well designers craft a simulation that 'feels real', transcending mediation (see Ryan 2015).

Hypermediacy, on the other hand, like the aesthetic regime, instead 'makes us aware of the medium or media and (in sometimes subtle and sometimes obvious ways) reminds us of our desire for immediacy' (Bolter & Grusin 1999: 34). Hypermediacy, when it comes to digital media and television, is seen when something may exist in multiple windows on the same computer screen, when we have to use countless menu-based interfaces online, when user comments stream past a video, when alerts or notifications pop up on our iPhone screen, or when various tweets from Twitter show up in a feed at the bottom of a television show. Rather than getting lost in a 'realistic' simulation, these examples of hypermediacy draw our attention to the screens we use, showing us the 'reality' of our devices and interfaces. For Bolter and Grusin, the drives towards immediacy and hypermediacy are intertwined, and they both represent an attempt to get beyond mediation and approach the real. Immediacy is about a 'real' or 'immersive' copy of 'reality'; hypermediacy is about identifying the 'reality' of the medium one is actually using.

In the case of modernist paintings like *Black Square*, 'by eliminating "the real" or "the world" as a referent, modernism emphasized the reality of both the act of painting and its product. Painters offered us their works as objects in the world, not as a representation of an external world. ... Modern art was often regarded as real or authentic, precisely because it refused to be realistic ...' (Bolter & Grusin 1999: 58). In fact, we can suggest that whenever a new medium is invented that has a closer attachment to a kind of 'immediacy', then older media are freed to explore their own affordances and limitations, their own **medium specificity**, in which the aesthetic dimensions of the work are not about verisimilitude towards 'the world' but about exploring the potentials of the medium in and of itself.

The invention of modernist painting, resulting in works like *Black Square*, happened after the popularization of photography, which certainly mimics 'reality' more fully than painting every could.

As is clear from Bolter and Grusin, neither immediacy nor hypermediacy are 'more real' than the other. They express an intertwined attempt to represent 'reality', if in ways that are vastly opposed, a process they refer to as **remediation**, in which formal elements of newer media are imported into older media and vice versa. A photograph may aspire to look like a painting, for instance, or a videogame may include elements derived from film (such as cutscenes or actors), while a film may include elements derived from games.

Form and Order

The transformations between Rancière's three regimes – the ethical, the poetic/representative, and the aesthetic – are political, in that they rely on transformations in what can be seen, what can be experienced, and what can be said about what is seen and experienced. These transformations in the definition of 'art' demonstrate how radically representation can change over time. What art permits us to see and experience is not uniform throughout history, and the politics of aesthetics are precisely in challenging and transforming these ways of experiencing the world, alongside the claims we can make about these changes.

These changes are not inherently about 'politics', but they are political. Caroline Levine makes this explicit when she links aesthetic and literary form with social and political structures (2015: 14). She suggests that we should look towards aesthetic form – the way a plot is structured, the way a film shot is composed, the way we interact with a videogame, and so on – to examine the many ways we have of making sense of daily life. Aesthetic form imposes order, an order that both constrains and permits specific possibilities, be they for experience or for action. These artistic forms and social forms, while not precisely the same thing, intersect and come into contact, precisely because they demonstrate ways we have of making sense of the world and acting within it. How do we organize what we experience? How do we communicate it to others? How do we agree upon how we imagine this world to be? These are aesthetic questions. But the point is not just to agree, to note that something is, in fact, beautiful or interesting. We should examine our forms and judgements and the implicit politics in our categories, especially as our categories change over time. How can we challenge form in order to allow new things to be seen, said, and experienced?

THE QUESTION OF 'AFFECT'

The way we judge forms isn't always rational, however. Judgement is often about how something feels, or how it moves us. In other words, aesthetic judgements are linked to **affect**. Before we conclude this chapter, I want to briefly provide a definition of affect and discuss a body of literature that's been increasingly significant for any discussion of digital media and digital culture – 'affect theory'. This is a difficult task for a number of reasons, most significantly because affect is often opposed to conscious experience and linguistic meaning. Because affect is contrasted with meaning and sense, it is hard to talk about in any direct way. But at its most basic level, affect is a kind of intensity and movement, an intensity that is about affecting something else and being affected by others and objects. This definition is a bit tautological. Affect also has something to do with emotion, but the two aren't synonyms.

Affect, in its contemporary usage, is derived from a number of historical sources, the most notable being the philosopher Baruch Spinoza and the philosopher and psychologist William James. For Spinoza, as defined in his classic work *Ethics* (1994), originally published in 1677, affect refers to the body and its capacity for acting. So, from Spinoza, affect is about a body, what it does, and how it moves. James argues something similar but he was more interested in defining the emotions for the emerging science of psychology, arguing that human experience should be explained through the brain rather than subjective, conscious experience or something like a soul. While we typically imagine that we think something or feel something first and then react, James argued the opposite:

> Common-sense says, we lose our fortune, are sorry and weep; we meet a bear, are frightened and run; we are insulted by a rival, are angry and strike. The hypothesis here to be defended says that this order of sequence is incorrect, that the one mental state is not immediately induced by the other, that the bodily manifestations must first be interposed between, and that the more rational statement is that we feel sorry because we cry, angry because we strike, afraid because we tremble, and not that we cry, strike, or tremble, because we are sorry, angry, or fearful, as the case may be. (1890: 450)

While this may seem like it flies in the face of common sense, a great deal of neuroscientific research on the function of the brain has subsequently repeated the claims of James. The theory of emotion presented by James, now termed the 'James–Lange theory', named for James and Carl Lange, a contemporary of his who made a similar argument at around the same time, has seemingly stood the test of time in scientific research about cognition.[1] So, with both Spinoza and James, our brain and body *act*, and it is only *after* we act that consciousness steps in to help explain and understand what is happening.

While James used the word 'emotion', those following James and Spinoza have used the term 'affect' to describe what is implicit here, namely, that our conscious knowledge of our world – our judgements, named emotions, 'meanings', and so on – is secondary to intensities that move and are moved by our bodies. For Brian Massumi, one of the most influential affect theorists in recent years, an 'emotion' is explicitly named, it is 'qualified intensity' that is placed into 'semantically and semiotically formed progressions … into function and meaning. It is intensity owned and recognized' (2002: 28). Affect, unlike emotion, is preindividual, moving between bodies divorced from language and meaning, with its own 'autonomy' that cannot be limited to the subjective. It is something that moves between bodies and overflows the experiences of an individual.

There are numerous implications of a turn to affect rather than emotion (or 'meaning'). First is a stress on the physicality of the body rather than meaning, sense, or language. Affect requires us to look at how a body moves instead of conscious interpretation. This emphasis on the body likewise becomes about the biological capacities of the body and, more specifically, on the brain and specific process of cognition that happen prior to consciousness. Second, as affect is not limited to a single body, the body itself becomes a set of 'brain-body-world entanglements' with unclear boundaries 'between the human and non-human, self and other' (Blackman 2012: 1).

In its early days, affect theorists seemed to suggest that this turn to the affective was, in and of itself, a political move. Affect seemed to resist a kind of formalism and, instead, pointed towards an openness that existed prior to meaning and sense-making. Yet, when it comes to digital media, it's been increasingly clear that new platforms and technologies have been designed to modulate, control, and direct the affectivity of the human body (Andrejevic 2013; Clough 2008; Hillis, Paasonen & Petit 2015). As media theorist Mark Hansen has suggested, 'contemporary advertising aims to capture our attention without our awareness, to manipulate us subliminally and outside of our control; and today's digital networks possess the capacity to gather and exploit all kinds of data without us having any knowledge, and, to a great extent, any possibility for knowledge, of such activity' (2015: 71). The body's movements are directly analyzed by Facebook and other forms of social media, for instance, which can identify how long one is looking at an image (by pausing in a web browser, or by identifying how a cursor is moving), data which are gathered without the awareness of a user, which are then analyzed and used to direct attention, desire, and so on, all prior to any conscious awareness or meaning-making.

While affect was often celebrated because of its seeming escape from formal logics, developments in digital media have revealed that, even when turning to these kinds of non-signifying, non-representational intensities, there is a formalism to the affective. As film theorist Eugenie Brinkema (2014) has suggested, affect and form are conjoined. Forms are designed to produce specific intensities and feelings prior to any clear 'sense' or 'meaning', and, even more important for us, forms direct and shape affects as well. This means that affect, rather than escaping the logic of aesthetic form and judgement, is essential for any possible understanding of aesthetics. Aesthetic judgement is about how specific forms move the body in specific ways. Form, then, becomes a specific way that affect is mobilized, analyzed, understood, and directed. So, when we talk about affect, we aren't just talking about an unformed intensity that exists prior to systems of meaning. Rather, we are thinking about the particular, formal means through which our body encounters a specific object. Our response to a work – our aesthetic response – is not just about what's in our individualized mind but is also about our experience with a work of art (or another body). Our experience of form, expressed in how something appears to experience, moves intensities between bodies. While we then come to judge these formal intensities (using terms like 'cool' or 'beautiful'), these judgements are there to help us make sense of how form shapes and directs the affective capacities of the body.

CONCLUSION

In this chapter, I've attempted to provide a general perspective on aesthetics, defining aesthetics as an articulation of form and judgement that is not neutral, but political. We discussed the politics of aesthetics and the distribution of the sensible and went over a brief overview of affect theory. There are different ways of discussing aesthetics, which have very different definitions. These definitions nonetheless persist today in how we understand digital media. Our task here is far from complete, however. Now, we turn to a discussion of specific judgements and specific aesthetic categories, ones that range from those that have traditionally character-ized aesthetic thought to a number of emergent categories that describe the transformations digital media has provoked in creative expression, labour, and more.

NOTE

1. I should note that these arguments of James (in some ways) have again been challenged through recent work in neuroscience. See Lisa Feldman Barrett's *How Emotions are Made* (2017) for an overview of this work.

8

FORMS AND JUDGEMENTS

In the previous chapter, we reviewed definitions for aesthetics, explicitly framing aesthetic judgement as political. Likewise, we argued that aesthetics were linked with the affective, rather than with the neutral or dispassionate judgement of experience. This chapter defines specific aesthetic categories – be they historical ones, like beauty and the sublime, or recent categories that describe cultural transformations associated with digital media, such as cool, zany, cute, and interesting – and reviews specific forms often thought to characterize the aesthetics of digital culture, namely, participation, remix, bricolage, and glitch. This chapter is intended to review a basic vocabulary for describing the aesthetics of digital media, all while stressing the political aspects of these categories.

TERMS: affect; knowledge work; relational aesthetics; Web 2.0

THEORISTS: Theodor Adorno, Nicholas Bourriaud, Edmund Burke, Dick Hebdige, Patrick Jagoda, Immanuel Kant, Caroline Levine, Alan Liu, Sianne Ngai

EXAMPLES: Chris Rodley's Algorithmic Horror; Double Rainbow; 'Internet Ugly'; Journey; Miranda July's Somebody; Miranda July and Harrell Fletcher's Learning to Love You More; Pinterest; Takeshi Murata's Monster Movie and Untitled (Pink Dot); YouTube personality Bunny Meyer

Our discussion of aesthetics is incomplete. Now, we need to turn from the general to the specific, from larger theories about aesthetics to particular forms and judgements. In this chapter, I'll discuss some of the categories that have been influential throughout the history of aesthetic thought, beginning with the foundational concepts of the beautiful and the sublime, moving towards more recent categories said to characterize the present and, most significantly for us, the fact that our lives are heavily influenced by digital media. Following on from the previous chapter, I'm interested in demonstrating that aesthetic judgement is intrinsically linked to **affect** and emotion, even though aesthetics are often characterized as having a relation to dispassionate evaluation.

The cultural theorist Sianne Ngai has suggested that the aesthetic categories we use to describe and evaluate experience 'call forth not only specific subjective capacities for feeling and acting but also specific ways of relating to other subjects and the larger social arrangements these ways of relating presuppose. In doing so, they are compelling reminders of the general fact of social difference and conflict underlying the entire system of aesthetic judgement or taste ...' (Ngai 2012: 11). This returns us to some of the concerns brought up in our earlier discussion of culture. First, like Raymond Williams, Ngai argues that the way we make sense of our world happens through artistic documentation which inscribes how it feels to live at a specific place and time, which Williams referred to as 'the structure of feeling'. Second, we again see how the categories we use to describe the world and our experience of it are *political*. Our categories point to how our world has been differentiated and ordered, and thus direct us to inequalities of power and inequivalent social relationships – to the fact that culture is a field of *conflict*. Aesthetic categories are not universal concepts. Rather, a category like beauty performs political work in terms of ordering bodies, defining proper actions, and so on. At the same time, as we noted in the last chapter, this politics may not be the same thing as what we talk about when we think of governmental politics, or political intervention.

The goal of this chapter, then, is to go through a series of judgements that characterize aesthetic thought historically and in the present, moving to formal categories that commonly characterize both artistic works linked towards digital culture and the everyday experience of digital culture. We will begin with some important historical categories – the beautiful and the sublime – before moving towards categories thought to explicitly characterize digital culture. We will then delineate some specific forms that distinguish both art made with digital media and everyday digital culture, even though these forms are not limited to digital media as well. This chapter is therefore intended to review a basic vocabulary for describing the aesthetics of digital media, all the while stressing the political aspects of these categories, following both Ngai and the discussion of aesthetics in the previous chapter.

HISTORICIZING AESTHETIC CATEGORIES

The Beautiful and the Sublime

Edmund Burke's *A Philosophical Inquiry into the Origin of Our Ideas of the Sublime and Beautiful* (1823), first published in 1757, is one of the foundational writings about aesthetics in Western culture. Burke, in his *Inquiry*, was attempting to examine why the arts affect us, not in a dispassionate, rational way, but as a source of emotion, as that which provokes the imagination. In moving the human body, the arts would act like any other experience. Like sweet, salty, or bitter food inspires a bodily reaction that can be evaluated through our taste for specific sensations, the arts inspire 'Love, grief, fear, anger, joy … and they do not affect it in an arbitrary or causal manner, but upon certain, natural, and uniform principles' (1823: 22). For Burke, the arts provoke the body into specific emotional experiences which are innate to the capacities of the human body. Evaluating what these experiences are, along with how they are best produced, provides a way for gauging taste and identifying a 'good' work of art.

The two categories Burke focused on were the sublime and the beautiful. The sublime is provoked by 'Whatever is fitted in any sort to excite the ideas of pain and danger' and is 'productive of the strongest emotion which the mind is capable of feeling' (1823: 45). The sublime is a response produced by the fear of isolation, vulnerability, and death, fears generated by an overwhelming sense of the vastness of the world and one's ultimate insignificance. The sublime is not precisely a synonym for the experience of fear, however, as Burke is clear that the sublime is, in its own way, a pleasurable experience. The sublime reveals how fear is intertwined with wonder and is triggered not only by things that appear as dangerous, but by artworks that are large, or experiences that reveal some aspect of the vastness and infinitude of the world, which includes 'the infinite divisibility of matter' (1823: 98). Much of Burke's discussion of the sublime is dedicated towards formal elements, such as vastness, darkness, the uniformity of successive objects, overpowering loudness, and so on. Again, these are to provoke the experience of infinity, of a world that vastly exceeds one's own knowledge and control. Watching an assembly line, for instance, would be a sublime experience for Burke, given how it would be a large, loud, endless succession of the same object *ad infinitum*. Early representations of technology, such as Charlie Chaplin's *Modern Times* (1936) and Fritz Lang's *Metropolis* (1927), depict industrialization as sublime, in which men's bodies were literally incorporated into a vast machine over which they had no control, standardizing them and removing their individuality. I should note that these early representations were about the standardization of *men's* bodies. They regularly positioned women as technologies to be feared, as linked to the sublimity of the machine (see Doane 2004; Huyssen 1986).

Beauty, on the other hand, is about 'that quality, or those qualities in bodies, by which they cause love ...' (Burke 1823: 127). Beauty is neither, for Burke, related to mathematical proportion (as for Alberti), nor to the 'fitness' achieved by perfectly matching an ideal form. Rather, 'we must conclude that beauty is, for the greater part, some quality in bodies acting mechanically upon the human mind by the intervention of the senses' (1823: 162). Unlike the sublime, beauty characterizes small objects, smoothness, softness, delicacy, and subtle variation.

Burke's attempts to describe beauty lead him to creepy and explicitly sexist descriptions of women's bodies, such as one where he describes in detail the path his eyes take as they move across the body of a woman. 'Observe', Burke tells us, 'that part of a beautiful woman where she is perhaps the most beautiful, about the neck and breasts; the smoothness; the softness; the easy and insensible swell; the variety of the surface, which is never for the smallest space the same; the deceitful maze through which the unsteady eye slides giddily, without knowing where to fix, or whither it is carried. Is not this a demonstration of that change of surface, continual, and yet hardly perceptible at any point, which forms one of the great constituents of beauty?' (1823: 166). The woman's body becomes little more than the 'beautiful' object of Burke's gaze, not an agent possessive of its own will and desire. The body is reduced to a surface consumed by the (male) eye of another. The legacy of beauty is bound up with heterosexual, male desire, a point that's long been stressed by feminist critiques of visual culture, in which men act and women appear (Berger 1972; cf. Mulvey 2009). Burke's understanding of aesthetic judgement is intimately tied towards his specific bodily response to something – the terms sublime and beautiful are names given to how Burke is moved at a base, bodily level. They do not refer to intellectual evaluations. The sublime is a mix of wonder and dread that comes from the fear of insignificance and death. Beauty is inspired by, it seems, what Burke personally finds sexually arousing.

The point here isn't to define *what* beauty is, but to draw attention to *how* beauty is being defined. Beauty refers to Burke's subjective experience, although it supposedly points beyond his experience. Immanuel Kant, in his major work on aesthetics, the *Critique of Judgement* (1987), originally published in 1790, also attempts to define the beautiful and the sublime, but he changes the grounds upon which these judgements are to be made. Rather than an emphasis on the affective dimension of experience and sensation, for Kant, taste should be evaluated without interest, as a kind of dispassionate activity that takes an object of contemplation for itself, rather than in the terms of an individual's experience of it. Unlike Burke, this lack of interest would conceivably lead to universals that transcend the individual. It also transforms aesthetics from the experience of art to the communication of judgement to others. Rather than my own personal experience, judgement is about reason and the stripping away of my feelings, which are debated among members of a taste community (see Friedlander 2015). While the collective dimension of aesthetic judgement is apparent in Burke, it becomes explicit with Kant, although Kant, likewise, must eliminate the seemingly subjective, affective dimension of aesthetic judgement.

This dispassionate evaluation advocated by Kant is only one line in the history of aesthetic theory, although it is a significant one repeated by many others. Critical theorist Theodor Adorno, for instance, thought Kant was correct to argue that the aesthetic aspect of art should be divorced from sensual pleasure and bodily experience (an argument similar to Benjamin's distinction between aesthetics and politics). Aesthetic judgement, for Adorno, 'is free from immediate desire; [Kant] snatched art away from that avaricious philistinism that always wants to touch it and taste it' (Adorno 1997: 10). At the same time, Adorno did not feel that Kant went far enough. Adorno argued that the importance of art was in its critical function – that an artwork should be alienating, distancing itself (and the viewer) from assumptions about everyday experience. Like the glitch artists discussed in the last chapter, who saw Kanye West's 'Welcome to Heartbreak' music video as corrupting their supposedly critical interventions into the 'smooth', unblemished surface of digital information, Adorno sees any affective engagement with a

work of art as a repetition of mass consumption and advertising. Artworks should resist this affective relation, making sure that the viewer
(or consumer) cannot 'lose himself, forget himself, extinguish himself
in the artwork' (1997: 17). Art should deliver perceptual shocks, jolting
the viewer out of the 'false consciousness' of their everyday experience.
Of course, these 'shocks' can still be affective, even if they're framed in
terms of dispassionate judgement.

Should we lose ourselves in art? Or should we remain ultimately
dispassionate observers? Or, even further, should art force us into a
state in which we become alienated from daily life, critically exposing the reality of that which exists around us? The specific questions
asked of art have changed over time and inform larger questions about
art's social purpose. A number of recent works that examine the relation
between aesthetics and digital media, however, take a different perspective.
What, they ask, do the arts and the categories we use to describe experience tell us about how we make sense of our everyday lives? How do
they reveal or transform our understanding of digital media, information,
and infrastructures – things that are mostly invisible to everyday experience? We will briefly discuss two recent ways of theorizing the aesthetic
categories we use to describe digital media. Alan Liu's examination of
'cool' and Sianne Ngai's discussion of the categories 'zany', 'cute', and
'interesting'.

Cool

Throughout the 1990s, literary scholar Alan Liu, an expert on British
Romantic literature and poetry, began to wonder about the fate of 'knowledge' in the face of digital media, along with the forms of 'creative
destruction' associated with the first decades of the internet and the World
Wide Web. Digital media carry with them their own specific forms, such as
the database, the spreadsheet, and the hyperlink, which are different from
past media. When faced with the reality of new technologies, Liu wondered,
what will happen to art? And, in particular, what will happen if the dominant judgement of value is not beauty or the sublime, but 'cool'? 'Cool',
Liu explains, 'is the techno-informatic vanishing point of contemporary
aesthetics, psychology, morality, politics, spirituality, and everything.
No more beauty, sublimity, tragedy, grace, or evil: only cool or not cool'
(Liu 2004: 3).

For Liu, these aesthetic changes are associated with the emergence
of **knowledge work**, which characterizes a great deal of creative and

corporate labour since the late 1970s. Knowledge work is defined by the formation of temporary, flexible teams, in which information is the primary commodity generated, bought, and sold, often in the form of data and systems of organizing and interpreting data (also see Boltanski & Chiapello 2005; Moulier Boutang 2011). Identities, be they class, gender, sexuality, race, or something else, are subsumed into individual lifestyle choices and consumption patterns, which are understood as 'immaterial' signifying practices that have economic value. So, part of the culture of knowledge work is having and performing an identity – a personal identity rather than a collective identity (repeated with popular banalities such as 'Be yourself' and 'Be an individual', or in Apple's one-time slogan 'Think different') – which is then analyzed and calculated through data gathered about you and your consumption habits. For Liu, these changes in labour are characterized by an overwhelming emphasis on *coolness.*

Coolness emerges from a long history of transformations in industrial manufacturing, leading towards contemporary knowledge work. On the assembly line, for instance, workers were expected to manage their emotions and be dispassionate or robotic in their actions and movements. As workers came to be replaced by machines, and as labour moved from the factory floor towards corporate offices filled with computers and managers, there was an overwhelming emphasis on *coldness* and alienation carried over from the assembly line (Liu 2004: 120). The emotions became intensely managed, be they emotions people 'really felt' or ones they were supposed to perform given their job. This emotional management has become one of the key skills one now has to master in order to get or maintain a job today, linked together with the tasks of networking, connecting, and maintaining relationships (see Lazzarato 1996).

So, coolness is a kind of affective neutrality that has emerged through the history of major changes in labour, from the factory to the office. But, additionally, it carries with it its own set of forms, which, Liu argues, 'is the aporia of information … cool is *information designed to resist information.* … Cool is, and is not, an ethos, style, feeling, and politics of information' (2004: 179). Paradoxically, for Liu, cool is about a limit point, in which the massive complexity of the internet and digital media meet up with the supposed non-feeling that comes from managed affective labour. It relies heavily on the principles of modernist design, 'defined explicitly in informational terms as clean, efficient visual communication for an age drowning in media' (2004: 199), in which visual style should be minimal, clear, and unified. But, at the same time, it can also rely on a style that is cluttered and unreadable (the best examples here are 1990s tech and design magazines like *Mondo 2000* and the music magazine *Ray Gun*, although it can be seen in some examples of contemporary web design as well). It is a feeling that seems to rely on a lack of feeling and a kind of political 'attitude' that emphasizes 'interiority and everydayness. Politics is not about a noisy, collective action on the street. It is instead an action so immured within the cubicle, within one's individual work-station, and ultimately within the most interior of all cubicles, one's own head' (2004: 280). Cool, then, is about caring, but not caring too much. It is about communication, but in a styled way that is not just about the transmission of information. It is about the personal, and the expression of personal desires and interests, but to express one's individuality rather than membership in a larger group.

'Cool' is less a coherent style or judgement than a wide-ranging set of responses to the proliferation of information and data associated with digital media and, especially, the forms of work and expertise that rely on digital media. It simultaneously reduces informational complexity and expands it to the point of meaninglessness, relies on a set of informal, networked connections and is ultimately about individuals. It is a feeling that is never too intense. Coolness, like beauty, is not a clear judgement with universal characteristics. Rather, it is a judgement that reveals specific social relationships that are about changes in technology and the kinds of work we perform.

Liu's description of coolness seems to best characterize transforma-tions in aesthetics associated with the internet in the 1990s and early 2000s. It doesn't seem to characterize our present all that well, even though ele-ments of what he describes persist residually in styles that refer back to internet culture of the 1990s, found in names like 'vaporwave' or James Bridle's 'New Aesthetic'.

Zany, Cute, and Interesting

A bit closer to our present are arguments advanced by Sianne Ngai. Like Liu, Ngai understands aesthetic categories and judgements as revealing to us something about larger transformations in capitalism and labour. She identifies three categories – the zany, the cute, and the interesting – that she sees as having a specific relationship to how capitalism has changed in relation to digital media and networked information. These categories tell us something about how we make sense of our world and, like 'coolness', are ambivalent or weak, unlike beauty or the sublime. To demonstrate this point, Ngai asks of us:

> Consider, for example, the media sensation caused by *Double Rainbow*, an amateur video made to capture the beauty of a natural wonder by hiker Paul Vasquez. That natural wonder ended up becoming immediately upstaged, however, even as it was being viewed and recorded, by the emotional extremity of Vasquez's aesthetic response (which was simultaneously recorded). ... Opening with laughs and exclamations followed by moans and sobs and finally the anguished question, 'What does this mean?' there was something about the sheer intensity and duration of Vasquez's act of aesthetic appreciation that millions of people also seemed to affectionately appreciate but also want to immediately make fun of or belittle, as if such a powerful reaction to an aesthetic spectacle could not be taken seriously or simply left to stand on its own. (2012: 28)

Countless parodies of the *Double Rainbow* video appeared online, and many speculated that Vasquez's response to a rainbow was, in fact, inspired by drugs. Vasquez was experiencing something akin to Burke on the sublime. The double rainbow he saw provoked a mix of wonder and amazement that relied on the incomprehensibility of nature and the world. But, today, this response is seemingly odd, and certainly not 'cool'. The judgements we use, and the categories we apply to our world, implicitly carry with them ways of experiencing the world and acting within it that are 'proper' or 'improper'. Not only is there a politics to what can be seen and said, but also to *how* it can be seen and experienced.

For Ngai, the categories of zany, cute, and interesting are far more applicable to today's world than beautiful and sublime. Zany has its origins in the mostly improvisational sixteenth-century Italian theatre style *commedia dell'arte* and began as a specific character type (the zanni). Zany, for Ngai, is a judgement about that which fails to follow the cool, detached, managed affects that are assumed to characterize knowledge work. Someone who is zany, Ngai argues, works hard to look like they're having fun, revealing how a kind of cool detachment is an impossibility for some. Zaniness can be seen in characters from film and television, such as Lucille Ball's eponymous character in *I Love Lucy*, Jim Carrey in *The Cable Guy*, or Richard Pryor in *The Toy*. Even though zaniness is supposed to be 'fun', 'the zany's characters give the impression of needing to labor excessively hard to produce our laughter, straining themselves to the point of endangering not just themselves but also those around them' (Ngai 2012: 10).

The popular YouTube personality Bunny Meyer, whose name on YouTube is 'grav3yardgirl', is a good example of online 'zaniness'. Her videos are characterized by exaggerated facial expressions and a kind of overwhelming intensity even in low-key, 'friendly' situations. The zany, Ngai suggests, put themselves 'into an exhausting and precarious situation' (2012: 10), and, in spite of the fact that we may find their performances amusing, and we might admire 'the affective and physical virtuosity of their performances', they are 'not persons we imagine befriending' (2012: 9). Zaniness, then, is a specific kind of performance that involves the explicit violation of coolness; it relates to knowledge work and its reliance on friendship, and knowledge work's managed affectivity of friendliness, but also violates this assumed affective neutrality. While this performance can be leveraged into something of value (Bunny, for instance, relies explicitly on her zaniness for her success, as does Jim Carrey), it doesn't follow normative ways of acting and relating in a world in which friendliness and coolness are assumed to be ideal categories through which behaviours are evaluated.

Cuteness, on the other hand, seems to be almost the opposite of zaniness, evoking the need for intimacy and care. Ngai associates the aesthetic of cuteness with the legacy of a specific aesthetic in Japan – *kawaii* – popularized after the Second World War to signify a kind of non-threatening helplessness or powerlessness, or a kind of pliability in which something cute can bend to the will of another. Something that is cute simultaneously evokes the desire to protect and destroy (think about the desire to squeeze a cute animal or a baby's cheeks).

Cuteness is obviously all around us on the internet, especially in memes of cute animals and the over-abundance of kittens and puppies online. Robots, likewise, are designed to be cute. While it is clear why one would want to design a robot to be cute – to demonstrate that it isn't a threat in a world full of fears and anxieties about automation, alienation, and the absorption of jobs by technology – the proliferation of cute images isn't quite as clear. Regardless, cuteness tends to reveal a weak desire for intimacy and love, although one in which the viewer never loses or sacrifices their control to another (cf. Dale et al. 2017; Turkle 2011). Today, we often feel as if we have little to no control over the world around us, with our lives determined by technological systems far beyond our power. Cuteness, in performing subservience, exemplifies a relation in which one has control over another, in which the other is not particularly threatening and will bend to the will of the viewer.

Ngai's final category, 'interesting', refers to an indeterminate judgement, somewhere between fascinating and boring (or both at the same time), that links feeling-based judgements to conceptual ones (so, a judgement that would be between Burke and Kant – neither completely affective nor stripped of emotion). Interesting refers to something that is different, unique – but not that different. Ngai links this explicitly to the dominance of information in contemporary life. As we receive a near constant overload of information, 'interesting' is that which is different enough to be acknowledged, to stand out, but not different enough to warrant any truly passionate or strong response. It is difference in seriality. Ngai associates this to the works of artists like Ed Ruscha, Sol LeWitt, and John Baldessari, but we can link it to something like the social networking website Pinterest, which allows users to create 'boards' made up of images and links on the internet – called 'pins' – that they have found 'interesting' and, thus, worthy of note. These pin boards are usually grouped by theme, a grouping of different things that are worthy of interest but are not too surprising or notable. The name of Pinterest even demonstrates this link with the judgement of interesting. A pin signifies the judgement of interesting and directs us to look at something because it is worthy of interest. Yet a pin doesn't inherently signify anything other than this minor judgement of minimal difference, a small judgement of something that may be worthy of note and attention, but not significant enough to be placed outside a serial stream of images that one scrolls through as they look at Pinterest.

Zany, cute, and interesting, like coolness, are minor judgements that generally refer to a range of phenomena, but they are still somewhat subjective – in that they're based on individualized feelings and experiences – and collective – in that they refer to shared evaluations and terms. They refer to 'the increasingly intertwined ways in which late capitalist subjects labor, communicate, and consume ... our experiences of the zany, the interesting, and the cute are always implicit confrontations with the imaginary publics that these ways of working, communicating, and consuming assume or help bring forth' (Ngai 2012: 328). They aren't the only categories we can use to describe the present, but their very use as a form of judgement tells us something about what it feels like to live in today's world, along with the ways that we make sense of our world and define the kinds of experiences we have of it, and ways of acting in it.

These four aesthetic categories discussed here are not the only ways we have of evaluating our experience, yet they do seem to describe a great deal of how we make sense, understand, and judge the world around us. They communicate shared investments and values, and tell us about proper ways of acting, existing, and relating, although, at the same time, part of their importance as categories is their flexibility. Coolness, in particular, is deeply contradictory, and would seem to be defined more clearly by its negative (zaniness is much more clearly defined than coolness, in part because it seems to be a failure to be cool). The point here is not to suggest that these categories remain unchanged over time. Instead, they point to how judgements serve to help us know and make sense of how our world appears to our experience.

AESTHETIC FORMS OF DIGITAL MEDIA

These judgements have to be about something specific, however. Many elements associated with digital media are designed to elicit specific judgements, or provoke specific associations, or to elicit one judgement from one group of people and a completely different judgement from another group of people. In memes, fonts like Impact Bold and Comic Sans are chosen because they appear amateurish or ugly. We see examples of 'Internet Ugly' throughout social media, which relies on 'freehand mouse drawing, digital puppetry, scanned drawings, poor grammar and spelling, human-made glitches, and rough photo manipulation'; this ugliness is 'an imposition of messy humanity upon an online world of smooth gradients, blemish-correcting Photoshop, and AutoCorrect. It exploits tools meant to smooth and beautify, using them to muss and distort' (Douglas 2014: 314–315). Like the New Aesthetic, Internet Ugly is designed to disrupt the smoothness of digital media, although for different reasons, often using different means.

These techniques perform a political function, at least in Rancière's sense: they challenge or expose assumed formal limits of digital media, sketching out an aesthetic space that allows something to be seen and said, something judged as 'bad' or 'artless' in a context more typically defined by coolness. But, at the same time, there is a 'correct' use of style, at least if one wants to be part of a specific group. Take, for instance, the relatively common distinction between 'dank memes' and 'normie memes', which is, oddly enough, itself a meme, with the distinction played out in images circulated online. This distinction relies on a differentiation between a kind of meme that is supposedly cool or 'enlightened' (if sometimes in deeply problematic ways), often because of its inscrutability towards most people, and one that's far too popular and played out, for 'normal' people.

The aesthetic space of digital media is not uniform; in fact, it could be said to be inhabited by a number of radically different, competing aesthetic forms and judgements, even though these forms are ostensibly intended to perform a similar function of criticizing or unveiling the limits of digital media, more often than not pushing against or challenging the logic of 'cool', or reframing the 'cool' away from a kind of smooth uniformity. There are far too many aesthetic elements associated with digital media to simply enumerate the many forms we experience daily. In this section, I'm going to briefly review four formal elements that are common for the aesthetics of digital media: networks, participation, remix, and glitch. This is just a partial list of forms that are mostly conjoined or overlap, but these are often thought to be central for much of the art-making and creative practices associated with digital culture.

Networks

'Sprawling and spreading, networks might seem altogether formless, perhaps even the antithesis of form', claims Caroline Levine (2015: 112). *Networks* are defined by connectivity, of links that connect various points. In the language of network science and graph theory, they are about the 'edges' that connect 'nodes'. There are many different kinds of networks, and networks do not have an intrinsic link to digital media, but it's clear that many structures associated with digital culture, be it the internet in general or a specific social media platform, are organized in the form of a network. The history of the word 'network' preceded the technological; it was a word for manufactured fabric, then used to describe anatomy (in nervous and circulatory networks), the railroad and telegraph, branch banking, and social relations, much earlier than the emergence of the 'network society' of digital media and information in the 1970s (Bollmer 2016). Often, networks have been considered to be politically emancipatory, refusing a sense of bounded limits, although the historical use of network, more often than not, referred to a structure that contained and trapped. Consequentially, the politics of a network is, at best, ambivalent. And, while many argue that networks are intrinsically partial, connecting outwards infinitely, the simple fact is that any actually existing network has clear limits, be it because of technological, social, or geographic boundaries (so, networks of roads literally have to end because of bodies of water, the network that is the internet is limited by its literal infrastructure, and a social network is bounded by actual social relationships).

We imagine networks as boundless, ever-expanding entities because we, quite simply, cannot sense them in any clear way. The network model of connected nodes can seemingly be grafted onto almost anything we experience, giving us a sense that *'everything is everywhere'* (Galloway & Thacker 2007: 4), or that everything is linked in an unending, ever-unfolding totality of connectedness. Anna Munster, a theorist of digital media and art, suggests that we too easily slide into 'network *anesthesia* – a numbing of our perception that turns us away from [the] unevenness [of networks] and from the varying qualities of their relationality' (2013: 3). Rather than enable us to feel and experience our connectedness, networks are imagined as totalizing forms of connectivity that *cannot be experienced*. The assumption, more often than not, is that we may not *feel* connected, but we inevitably *are* connected. Rather than an aesthetic sensibility, this is literally an-aesthetic, in which our perception and sensation become numbed to our world.

Literary theorist Patrick Jagoda (2016) argues that we do have a way of experiencing networked forms of connectivity, however. Examples he provides from literature (such as Don Delillo's *Underworld*), film (*Babel, Syriana*), and television (*The Wire*) dramatize the various forms of networked connection that have emerged in the past few decades, with massively complex plots that demonstrate the connectedness of various different people, institutions, and histories. These fictional examples perform the intertwining of many different actors and elements in ways that seem to mirror the social interconnectedness that the internet and social media are thought to reveal, even if they are not intrinsically about network technologies.

Jagoda argues that specific videogames enable us to experience networked connectedness, not by visualizing networks themselves, but by emphasizing the relations between different individuals playing a game. For instance, Jagoda refers to Twitch Plays *Pokémon*, along with the game *Journey*, to demonstrate how these works perform the experience of connectivity. Twitch Plays *Pokémon*, as we've already discussed, does this by relying on a kind of networked actor comprised of many different people playing together. *Journey* does this by enabling players to cohabitate the world of the game with another who is playing elsewhere. While players cannot directly communicate with each other, at least through language,

Journey 'puts players in touch with many of the ways in which Internet users ... already construct the networked processes that constitute everyday life' (Jagoda 2016: 166). As an aesthetic form, then, networks reveal to us our connectedness, be it through the massive complexity of social relations depicted in numerous examples of contemporary popular culture, or in games that require collaboration and relation across an actual digital network.

Participation

These examples of networked games tend to foster or demand *participation* from those who are connected. Participation has long been regarded as one of the most foundational formal elements of digital culture (Deuze 2006). Digital media permit us to participate and contribute online, embodied in the transition from Web 1.0, which refers to the early days of the World Wide Web, made up of mostly static pages connected through hyperlinks, to **Web 2.0**, a term popularized by internet luminary Tim O'Reilly to describe the emergence of websites based around user-generated content, collaboration, and sharing. Digital culture, here, is reliant on a form of 'participatory culture' (Jenkins 2006), in which users are fundamentally in control of what gets produced and circulated on the internet.

Participation, then, is a general aspect of digital, networked media. Consequentially, participation is often a key element of art that relies on or is coordinated via the internet, whether in 'flash mobs' (which are now a dated fad), or through apps and projects that explicitly use digital media as a means for organizing the acts of different people. Miranda July and Harrell Fletcher's *Learning to Love You More* (2002–2009), for instance, was a website that provided participants with 70 different 'assignments', such as 'Make a child's outfit in an adult size', 'Make a poster of shadows', and 'Make a paper replica of your bed'. The over 8,000 people who participated in July and Fletcher's project would document their attempts at completing the assignment, which was then saved on the website, presented at an exhibition, or included as a performance at a museum. Another project of July's, *Somebody* (2014), was a messaging app for iOS that used the location services of an iPhone to deliver a message not to the intended recipient, but to another person who was physically nearby, who would then be tasked with finding the intended recipient of the message and delivering it verbally, as a stand-in for the sender. These works rely on the participation of numerous individuals in different spaces across the planet, who are networked through digital media.

The curator and art theorist Nicholas Bourriaud (2002) describes some of these forms of participation in art as embodying what he terms **relational aesthetics**, which stress the social relations formed in a specific place, at a specific time. While relational aesthetics do not inherently rely on digital media, 'the emergence of new technologies, like the Internet and multimedia systems, points to a collective desire to create new areas of conviviality' (Bourriaud 2002: 26). Bourriaud refers to artists such as Rirkrit Tiravanija, who, in his work *pad thai* (1990), literally cooked and served food to visitors of a gallery, and Carsten Höller, who has placed slides (that would seem more fitting for a playground) in galleries and museums across the world and, in his work *The Double Club* (2008–2009), opened a combined nightclub, bar, and restaurant in Islington, London. These artists, according to Bourriaud, are producing works that require the participation of the viewer. However, this is *not* because these works are reflective of an increase in participation elsewhere in daily life, but because of an *absence* of participation elsewhere, in which people do not feel like they have any genuine relationship to other people in daily life. For Bourriaud, while new technologies may give the appearance of being participatory, the general feeling that initiated these works was that there was little to no space for genuine participation elsewhere, and the gallery and museum end up serving as spaces for that which does not exist in daily life.

Remix

Another longstanding formal element of digital culture is the *remix*. A remix can be said to be a form of 'bricolage', a French word that refers to a kind of improvisational making, based on taking elements that are at hand, recombining and recontextualizing them, and creating something new. In Dick Hebdige's classic work of cultural studies, *Subculture: The Meaning of Style* (1979), the fashion practices associated with punk, in which symbols and objects from elsewhere, whether safety pins, trash bags, or Nazi imagery, are assembled together to create a new style with a new meaning. The formal elements that comprise punk's style are arranged as a kind of bricolage, which involves making something new with what's available, appropriating it to generate something else. Remixing, then, is another name for a specific kind of bricolage, one that takes various consumer products (usually songs, but also images, video clips, and other kinds of texts), recombines them, and invents something out of them.

While, like networks and participation, this isn't intrinsic to digital culture, it characterizes a great deal of art made with digital media. Software packages like Adobe Photoshop and Ableton Live make it easy to take pre-existing images or sounds, combine them, manipulate them, and create new things. Various genres of music and images from the past several decades rely on these techniques, poaching and plundering as a form of invention. Fan fiction, a practice that involves readers writing new stories with characters from their favourite books or television shows, has existed for decades, but has exploded with the internet as a means to share and access these stories.

In recent years, however, the legal status of many of these works has been challenged in court, as they often violate copyright and other intellectual property laws (Vaidhyanathan 2001). While remixing and bricolage are certainly still a central element of the aesthetics of digital culture, they have been legally restricted in recent years. At the same time, this aspect of digital media – and the internet in particular – has been noted by art theorist Boris Groys as 'Maybe the most interesting aspect of the Internet … precisely the possibility of decontextualization and recontextualization through the cut-and-paste operations that the Internet offers to its users' (2016: 187).

One of the most bizarre reinventions of remixing has been with the creation of artificial intelligence algorithms, which use software-based neural networks to simulate human thought, such as Google's Deep-Dream, which is designed to create images similar to that of a human mind dreaming while asleep. Those working on the DeepDream project would feed images into their software, and it would generate 'dreams' out of the elements of those images, creating surrealistic images of hybrid animals and landscapes. In 2015, a group of researchers from the University of Tübingen made a similar algorithm, one designed to detect a specific painting style from the images fed into it. The algorithm would then create a filter and copy the lines and brushstrokes from the original set of images onto another. The artist Chris Rodley, inspired by similar experiments with the Tübingen algorithm on Reddit, found that one could create filters out of repeated images, such as eyes, teeth, stock photography models, and cats, and develop disturbing and funny 'remixes' of works of art which he refers to as *Algorithmic Horror* (Figure 8.1). These images demonstrate how remixing is no longer just about human creativity in cutting up and recontextualizing images, sounds, and texts from elsewhere. Software is now 'remixing' in a relatively independent way, which, Rodley (2017) argues, has its own specific aesthetic form, which he labels as *algorithmish*, as it is partially shaped by the formal dimensions encoded into the algorithms used to generate these images.

Figure 8.1 Chris Rodley's *Algorithmic Horror* (2017), crossing Botticelli's *The Birth of Venus* with an image of two golden retrievers. Digital image, variable dimensions. Reproduced with permission from the artist.

The remix, traditionally, was something performed by a human combining different things, the creativity of the *bricoleur* expressed in the combinations and manipulations of materials found at hand. The 'remixes' of DeepDream and Rodley's *Algorithmic Horror*, however, suggests a move towards a different sense of agency, one in which the ultimate visual appearance of a work is, at least to some extent, determined by how a specific technology is designed or programmed. The 'form' in this case is less about visual form – or at least cannot be limited to the visual – but is instead found in how software is designed to combine things.

Glitch

This technological agency is even more clearly seen in works associated with *glitch*, which relies on contingency in the transmission of information, embracing noise in communication or errors (Krapp 2011: 54). Images or sounds become distorted because of problems in transmission, which are then shaped into a coherent style of music or visual art, although one in which the agency of the artist is, at least ideally, displaced – what makes a work of glitch art 'art' is, in fact, the contingency of the computer, not the intention of a human artist. Glitch is similar to a number of other processes in contemporary art that rely on file formats and problems in transmission. Some works rely on various techniques of 'lossy' compression, in which a file format cuts out information to make a file smaller, and, as a result, degrades the image, blurring it (see Hoelzl & Marie 2015: 63–80; Kelsey 2010: 15–22). These 'bad' images, like works associated with the New Aesthetic, are thought to reveal something about the 'reality' of digital images, breaking through the surface of information to demonstrate the operation of computers and software that guide daily life.

Takeshi Murata's works *Monster Movie* (2005) and *Untitled (Pink Dot)* (2007), for instance, rely on a technique called *datamoshing*, in which Murata manipulates digital files of films (a B-movie called *Caveman* and *Rambo: First Blood*, respectively) to create distorted, psychedelic images that transform the original films into fluid bursts of colour. Datamoshing exploits the technical limitations of digital encodings of video. To explain what's specifically happening in these videos requires a bit of knowledge about how digital video works. In a filmstrip, every frame includes an entire image. In a digital file, however, there are several types of frame, and, to reduce the size of the file, very few contain the entirety of an image. What's called an 'I-frame' (which stands for Intra-coded frame) contains the entire image, like a frame from a film strip. But many of the other frames are compressed – data is removed from them, based on what's in other frames. A 'P-frame' or a 'B-frame' (Predictive and Bi-predictive frames, respectively) only contain *differences* between the preceding or following frame of the video. Practically, this saves space in the file, as it greatly reduces the amount of data in the video. In addition, it rarely has a significant effect on our viewing, as we only really notice this encoding at work when something goes wrong and the image appears to glitch. Datamoshing forces a kind of glitch by removing, corrupting, or replacing the I-frames of the file. Thus, while the effect of watching a video like *Monster Movie* is aesthetically affecting in and of itself, it is implicitly making visible something specific about how digital video files work – something we overlook when we watch digital videos.

These four forms are certainly not the only ones associated with digital culture. They are simply some of the most notable forms, although most are not specific to digital media. Networks, participation, and remix do not inherently require digital media. However, there are different assumptions when it comes to glitch when compared to the other forms we've discussed, because glitches are believed to reveal something about digital media that are often obscured in daily life. In embracing points in which digital media literally do not function properly, some artists working with glitch, noise, and error believe that there is a critical function to their work: they are unveiling the 'reality' of digital media.

CONCLUSION

Continuing on from our previous discussion of aesthetics, this chapter addressed specific judgements and forms related to both the history of aesthetics and the categories and forms associated with digital media. Providing a final statement on our judgements and forms, however, is an impossible task. New forms are invented daily, forms that intersect with and relate to other forms, reliant as they are on the materiality of digital media, digital media's relation to ways of organizing bodies and labour, and various practices performed with digital media – practices that are central to people's daily lives online, but, most likely, have preceded our contemporary digital culture. But, again, understanding what's new requires us to look at what's old, differentiating the present from the recently past, thinking about what's emergent and what's residual today.

With the internet, there have been a number of theorists who claim that the totality of daily life can be thought of as a giant art project. Either the internet is a massive form of performance art (Heffernan 2016), or art today bleeds into the practices of documentation that characterize social media, in which the most significant work of digital art is our own identity (Groys 2016: 174–175). I'm not so sure I agree. Rather, I follow those like Caroline Levine and Eugenie Brinkema. We should pay attention to the specific forms we encounter today, and think about the way we describe these forms, along with the way that they shape the body's movements – the way they modulate affect. This demonstrates not that the whole world has been 'aestheticized', becoming a giant art project. Instead, it points us to the politics of aesthetics, of how the distribution of the sensible changes, which is also about how bodies and their acts are transformed and regulated.

In the next chapter, we'll continue with our discussion of form with an overview of the infrastructure of digital media and its politics.

9

INFRASTRUCTURES AND ECOLOGIES

Even though the materiality of infrastructure has been a theme throughout this book, it is only now that we'll go into detail about how infrastructure works in shaping culture. This chapter argues that infrastructure is not an isolated thing, but is fundamentally relational, serving to legitimate specific, often unequal, relations as 'natural' when they become sustained through the materiality of technology and media. This chapter then turns to two specific ways that digital media infrastructures shape daily life today: as logistical media and as media linked with the *Anthropocene* and the problems of climate change.

TERMS: Anthropocene; bias of communication (space-bias and time-bias); cultural techniques; e-waste; extrastatecraft; Global South; hyperobjects; infrastructuralism; lag; logistical media; net neutrality; platform capitalism; protocol; staples

THEORISTS: Harold Innis, Richard Maxwell, Toby Miller, John Durham Peters, Ned Rossiter, Sarah Sharma, Susan Leigh Star, MacKenzie Wark, Langdon Winner

EXAMPLES: Amazon; e-readers; Google's 'Water-Based Data Centers'; LiveJournal; rai stones on Yap; Robert Moses and bridges on Long Island; Uber and Airbnb in Austin, Texas; WalMart

Where is the internet? Most of us are aware that the internet is a material thing, not some vaporous other world of infinite possibility. And yet, the 'wirelessness' of digital culture – the fact that we access the internet via WiFi signals, and our computers and smartphones are connected through seemingly invisible forces in the air – may lead us to think that we're using a technology that is ubiquitous, placeless, and invisible, something seen in the metaphor of the 'cloud' to describe specific kinds of always-on, net-worked storage and connectivity (Franklin 2012; cf. Mackenzie 2010). When we talk of 'the cloud', we still envision the internet as a cyberspace that exists elsewhere, virtually rather than actually, demonstrating the per-sistence of the cybernetic imaginary discussed in Chapter 4.

Yet we're only connected through physical links, links that coincide with the development of technology throughout history (see Sterne 2006). The internet is made up of wires and servers throughout the planet, which are made sensible through cryptic markings on sidewalks or logos on manhole covers in the street. These technologies are frequently located in buildings designed to house earlier forms of communication, like tele-graph exchanges or pneumatic tubes (see Blum 2012; Burrington, 2016). Many of the global connections that make up the internet are based on buried 'submarine' cables that exist under the ocean (Starosielski 2015). Even wirelessness is material, as it is reliant on various physical waves that escape human sensation.

Throughout this book I've been emphasizing how the materiality of media shapes our daily lives and practices. Yet, I haven't really elaborated how materiality *works*. It may seem that the materiality of media simply exists, and that its mere existence means it has some power or control in shaping our world. But, as is usually the case, things are more complicated. This chapter stresses the role of *infrastructure* in daily life, examining how infrastructure shapes culture. In reviewing the function of infrastruc-ture, we'll pay particular attention to the political impact of *logistics* and the ecological role of digital media. A focus on infrastructure leads us to political issues that are not often part of how we understand the everyday effects of digital media, namely, questions about shipping, land use, min-ing, and energy.

Theorizing digital cultures requires attention to physical space and geography (see Hogan and Shepherd 2015: 8). Political debates over land ownership and the exploitation of natural resources intersect with our understanding of what digital media is and does, be they ecological con-siderations about mining and energy, ethical arguments about labour and the global supply chains of consumer electronics, national disputes about sovereignty and surveillance, or political deliberations of decolonization and indigenous land rights. The point here is to show how digital media are in no way immaterial, but, through infrastructures, produce a set of relations that exist between humans, technologies, and the planet that should be deeply troubling for each and every citizen today. Yet these relations, in part because of how our technologies are designed, are often ignored. How can we make them visible? How can we do something about them?

This chapter is divided into three parts. The first provides a general overview of several theories of infrastructure. The second turns to questions and claims about logistics, and, particularly, how infrastructure serves to organize the movement of material goods, human bodies, and labour, often at a global scale. The third part focuses on the ecological and environmental concerns that are central for any political understanding of digital media infrastructures today. By the end of this chapter you should understand why infrastructure matters, and how infrastructure leads us to a set of essential issues that are often neglected when we think about the politics of media.

WHY INFRASTRUCTURE?

Why is it important to think about infrastructure? We will begin by addressing some of the most significant ways that infrastructure transforms daily life, moving out to larger theoretical claims about what infrastructure is and does – in particular, to the power of state government and to the everyday lives of citizens. Throughout, I want to stress that infrastructure is *relational*, in that it relies on, transforms, and produces relations, and is not an isolated 'thing' that exists alone.

Infrastructures Transform Sovereignty

For theorists such as Lisa Parks, thinking about infrastructure is a necessary task and obligation for citizens in a digitally mediated world. Can we visualize our infrastructures, Parks asks, in ways 'that will encourage citizens to participate in sustained discussions and decisions about network ownership, development, and access?' (Parks 2009). These strategies should acknowledge the differences in infrastructures, along with the sheer number of infrastructures we encounter. Historically, infrastructure's power in daily life was about relations between citizens and the state, and was found in public works projects like roads, power grids, water pipes, and mass transit, which were often justified in the name of the military and national security (Mattern 2013). These governmental projects were (and still are) linked with the state, its boundaries, and its obligations to its citizenry. The failure of governments to maintain their infrastructures, such as, to use one example, the contaminated water supply in Flint, Michigan, which occurred through corroding water pipes that resulted in high levels of lead in drinking water, demonstrates a breakdown of this historical relationship between the state and citizenry when it comes to infrastructure. The specific case of Flint should also be articulated to poverty and race. The maintenance of infrastructures (or lack thereof) shows us how governments can calculate and dictate who are the citizens that 'matter' and who, seemingly, do not in the eyes of elected officials.

One of the functions of the state has long been to construct and maintain these massive projects of shared spaces, technologies, and objects – projects that are too large to be managed by individuals or small groups. They rely on the coordination of a broad range of processes, practices, and designs, and are implemented to (ideally) perpetuate and protect the safety and health of all citizens. This democratic demand is rarely fulfilled in reality, with infrastructures unevenly touching different groups of citizens. As is the case with Flint, infrastructure can serve to enforce or perpetuate inequalities through the built environment – a point we'll elaborate below.

In recent years, the relation between infrastructure and the state has been reshaped in at least two ways. First, many infrastructural projects have been privatized across the globe. Classical forms of infrastructure, such as bridges, power cables, and systems for parking management, have been purchased by private corporations in short-sighted acts that sell off government property, often far below value, to temporarily generate income to pay off government debts, a practice that ends up producing profits for corporations at the expense of the wellbeing of everyday citizens (see Taibbi 2011). This has led global corporations and foreign governments to invest in local and national infrastructures with the goal of making money, rather than with the intent of working to improve the daily lives of the citizenry (see Meek 2014). As with other forms of infrastructure, the tendency towards privatization also characterizes the internet. While, in the United States, the internet was created with federal funding, it has been largely given away or sold (again, usually below value) to private corporations (Tarnoff 2016; cf. Abbate 1999).

Second, digital media and the internet are, in many ways, global rather than national, even though the infrastructures of media are still maintained and managed by existing territorial powers (Starosielski 2015: 12). When it comes to communication, infrastructures like submarine cables both transcend the limits of geography and are ultimately managed by state governments. As the internet has globalized, these digital media infrastructures, which are now often coordinated by global corporations, exert power over individuals that exceeds national jurisdiction.

This infrastructural geography leads to questions about legal jurisdiction, along with the political control over information and the implementation of state and corporate surveillance. While the infrastructures themselves are often privatized, they are nonetheless maintained and regulated by territorial authorities. Servers are positioned within national boundaries and are subject to the laws of the physical place in which they are located. Specific countries can work to limit or otherwise control access to the internet through the management of infrastructure. Governments can work to monitor or even shut off access to the internet. As revealed by Edward Snowden, if a message is sent from someone in Thailand to someone in Canada, for instance, then the United States has the capacity to monitor and surveil that message if it is routed through cables located in the US, and one of the problems of the internet is that messages rarely take direct or short pathways to reach their destination, and it is impossible to totally control the route of a message (Groskopf and Slobin 2016).

But, at the same time, corporations can also control access to specific content online. The entire debate around **net neutrality** focuses on the ability of internet service providers (ISPs) to slow down, speed up, or limit access to specific parts of the internet – something they can do because of the corporate control over internet infrastructure, and may use to prevent or make difficult users' access to competitors. Should Verizon (in the US) or Optus (in Australia), for instance, be able to charge extra if a consumer wants access to Netflix? Should major media conglomerates, such as Comcast (which owns NBC, and is the largest ISP in the United States), be able to limit or privilege access to specific news outlets via the ISP side of their business? This is a particular problem in many markets, as only one or two ISPs exist in many locations, meaning that there are limited alternatives (if there even are alternatives) for accessing the internet in many places, producing a *de facto* monopoly on internet access. Advocates for net neutrality argue that all internet traffic should be treated equally by ISPs, positioning access as a kind of protected speech, and that governments should regulate ISPs to make sure equal access is protected.

The intersection of (globalized) corporations and governmental jurisdiction has produced odd effects. For instance, the website LiveJournal, founded in 1999, was once one of the most popular blogging websites in the world. It was initially located in the United States, and thus subject to

US law. In 2007, LiveJournal was purchased by the Russian media company SUP Media. While it was still managed in California, it gradually moved operations, and eventually its servers, to Russia. As of April 2017, LiveJournal was fully operating within Russia and under jurisdiction of Russian law. Many of those who signed up for LiveJournal before then have never deactivated their accounts, having forgotten about their blogs – and throughout its history LiveJournal, interestingly enough, was an important online location for Russian dissent. Initially, the physical location of its servers meant that LiveJournal was at least partially outside the control of the Russian government. Yet, as the physical location of LiveJournal's data moved from one place to another, so did any legal guarantees about freedom of speech or privacy, and LiveJournal has been complicit with the Russian government in censoring those who used it for journalistic or political purposes (see Vogt et al. 2017).

As another example, in 2009 Google was awarded a patent for a 'Water-Based Data Center', which appears to be a ship that can house internet infrastructure while at sea. Google's patent was legitimated by claiming it would allow infrastructure to become more fluid and mobile, faster (given how their boats were untethered by any fixed geographical location and could physically move closer to the places where they would be used, reducing **lag** generated by distance), and more efficient (as water would be used to cool servers, reducing energy use). These boats, however, could also (partially) remove some of Google's servers from governmental jurisdiction if implemented, given their physical location in the ocean.

The transformation of the state and governance through infrastructure has led to what architectural theorist Keller Easterling terms **extrastatecraft**:

> Far removed from familiar legislative processes, dynamic systems of space, information, and power generate de facto forms of polity faster than even quasi-official forms of governance can legislate them. ... As a site of multiple, overlapping, or nested forms of sovereignty, where domestic and transnational jurisdictions collide, infrastructure *space* becomes a medium of what might be called *extrastatecraft* – a portmanteau describing the often undisclosed activities outside of, in addition to, and sometimes even in partnership with statecraft. (2014: 15, original italics)

All of these examples and theories demonstrate that infrastructure transforms *sovereignty*, which is the ultimate power of governance. Often, sovereignty is associated with a ruler (in monarchy or dictatorships) or with the people (in a democracy). Within the boundaries of a state, it is the sovereign that possesses power. But infrastructure jettisons some aspects of the state to other authorities, giving corporations and, often, the infrastructures themselves at least some part of sovereign power. When, for instance, Uber or Airbnb enter a specific market, they often do so with little to no regard for existing laws regulating infrastructures of transit or lodging, instead provoking legal battles by deliberately breaking the law.

The belief is that these corporations and their business models are inevitable. Transformations in networked, digital media – and the model of crowdsourcing on which these companies rely – will force law to be remade in accordance with the demands of these companies. This has, generally, been how many places have responded to the blatant lawlessness of how these companies operate. Uber and Lyft left the city of Austin, Texas, because local citizens wanted to regulate them: citizens voted to record the fingerprints of these companies' drivers, encouraging appropriate background checks and maintaining the safety of consumers. After extensive lobbying by Uber and Lyft (over US$8 million, which was over seven times the record for a political campaign in the city) the state of Texas passed a bill that followed Uber and Lyft's desires rather than those of Austin's residents (Solomon 2017). This, in many ways, effectively cedes sovereignty from the citizens of Austin towards the corporate owners of Uber and Lyft, as the state of Texas has conceded that the rights of these corporations are more significant than those of the people living in its state. Admittedly, we're using a broad definition of infrastructure here, including social media platforms, cars, roads, and so on, but these governmental regulations are ultimately about how battles over different infrastructures shape the rights and abilities of citizens and corporations, along with who is considered a 'citizen' or granted rights associated with 'citizenship'.

Infrastructure is Relational

Many of these examples, especially those about LiveJournal and Google's boats, probably exceed our everyday awareness. But it's wrong to think of infrastructure as invisible, as something ignored, as it determines and shapes our daily lives. As the pioneering theorist of infrastructure Susan Leigh Star has put it, in an article co-authored with Karen Ruhleder:

> Common metaphors present [infrastructure] as a substrate: something upon which something else 'runs' or 'operates', such as a system of railroad tracks upon which rail cars run. Infrastructure

> in this image is something built and maintained, sinking into an invisible background. Such a metaphor is neither useful nor accurate … we hold that infrastructure is fundamentally and always a *relation*, never a thing. (1994: 253, original italics)

Most research into the social effects of technology focuses on people or technologies themselves. But, Star and Ruhleder argue, we should focus on *relations* instead. This is not just about human relations, but includes relations between humans and technologies, and between technologies and other technologies. Infrastructure is never the 'thing itself', then, but the relations produced at the intersection of technologies and bodies. A focus on relations 'inverts traditional historical explanations and reveals how choices and politics embedded in such systems become articulated components' (1994: 253). Infrastructures, then, are central for any and all questions about human interaction. As the feminist scholar Ara Wilson has suggested, we should study infrastructure with an eye on questions of *intimacy*, and vice versa. Intimacy, which usually refers to private relations surrounding sex and love, is 'inextricable from, and realized through, larger relays of power', which includes how architecture, technology, and digital media dictate who comes into contact and how (Wilson 2016: 250). For instance, the design of smartphone apps for sex and dating, such as Tinder and Grindr, produce intimate, 'private' relations between different bodies that are managed and shaped through 'public' technological means. Our technologies are built to produce and restrict specific relations.

Through attention to relation we can see how infrastructure is political. But this politics may be ambivalent, or have multiple, often contradictory, dimensions. The very term 'infrastructure', as the historian of technology Henry Petroski (2016) has suggested, was popularized after 1960 as a term to describe what was previously labelled as 'public works'. Petroski suggests that infrastructure, as a term, lacks the collective emphasis perpetuated by the phrase 'public works', and that the unlinking of the state and citizenry through the privatization of infrastructural projects is itself conjoined with how we name and imagine roads, pipes, and wires. Are they infrastructure? Or are they public works?

Even though it may obscure the collective implications of 'the public' implicit in the phrase 'public works', infrastructure, as a term, is explicitly relational (Young 2017: 231–232), and, unlike public works, our infrastructures are not inherently linked to state authorities or even to the interests of 'the people'. We can see how infrastructure shapes relations already with our examples from LiveJournal and Google, which are certainly not 'public works'. The movement of computer hardware owned by private companies transforms how governments can regulate (or not regulate) what people say and do online. These physical infrastructures are not objects to be taken in isolation, as they produce, legitimate, and make concrete specific relations between individual citizens and their rights and abilities guaranteed under law. Infrastructure shows us how the function of media is to mediate interactions and relations.

Another well-known example of how infrastructure is fundamentally relational comes from the philosopher of technology Langdon Winner. Winner argues that technological artefacts are never neutral, but often contain within them political intentions or political outcomes. His is an argument similar to that of Star and Ruhleder. He makes this claim by looking at the underpasses of highways. 'Anyone who has traveled the highways of America and has gotten used to the normal height of overpasses may well find something a little odd about some of the bridges over the parkways on Long Island, New York', Winner notes. 'Many of the overpasses are extraordinarily low, having as little as nine feet of clearance at the curb. Even those who happened to notice this structural peculiarity would not be inclined to attach any special meaning to it. In our accustomed way of looking at things such as roads and bridges, we see the details of form as innocuous and seldom give them a second thought' (1986: 22).

These bridges, Winner argues, were designed according to plans developed by Robert Moses, the 'master builder' who shaped much of the infrastructural planning and development of New York from the 1920s to the 1970s. Moses designed the bridges of Long Island's parkways so buses could not travel through them. This, Winner suggests, reflects Moses' own classism and racial prejudice. His bridges (along with many of his plans for New York) were designed to privilege cars rather than public transit – an effect which still has implications today. As the writer Ian Frazier argued in a *New Yorker* article from 2017:

> Most descriptions of New York City are from the point of view of someone who is not driving. You hear less about how the city looks to drivers for a simple reason: almost nobody wants more drivers. And, once you make the crossover [to driving], New York turns out to be a good city to drive in. Starting with what Robert Moses did to New York in the middle of the last century, the city has remade itself to favor drivers. Those past changes cannot be easily reversed, and today the driver still enjoys the substantial advantages they created. (2017: 36)

Moses' designs for bridges impacted the lives of those who did not own cars in New York, which included a large percentage of those who were not middle class and white, preventing them from moving through specific parts of the city. One consequence of the low bridges in Long Island 'was to limit access of racial minorities and low-income groups to Jones Beach, Moses' widely acclaimed public park. Moses made doubly sure of this result by vetoing a proposed extension of the Long Island Railroad to Jones Beach' (Winner 1986: 23). While the infrastructures themselves may seem invisible because of their mundane everydayness, the relations they produce certainly are not. Moses' underpasses and infrastructural planning directly shaped who could go where and who could come into contact with each other.

Some have disputed Winner's specific claims about Robert Moses and how much discriminatory intention influenced his bridge designs for Long Island (Joerges 1999). However, even if Moses did or did not consciously intend for his bridges to discriminate, the effects were the same. The built infrastructure of Long Island ended up shaping how public transit functioned, and how specific bodies could move through a specific place. The real question is not about whether Moses was truly racist. Rather, Winner's claims are about infrastructures and how they shape and produce relations. This is a question completely divorced from intention, and it moves us further away from an intrinsic privileging of human purpose. Instead, we should understand technologies as things that can act and produce effects, effects that can discriminate and maintain racist practices independently of human will and intent.

A focus on relations can be difficult when it comes to the internet and networked forms of data storage referred to as 'the cloud', in part because of the absence of human understanding and intention. According to Tung-Hui Hu, a poet, theorist, and former network engineer, 'one of the curious dilemmas that the cloud represents is that not even the engineers who have built it typically know where the cloud is, and, as a consequence, what part of the apparatus to examine' (2015: xix). When it comes to the internet, it is difficult to see the infrastructure itself, whether it is because the buildings that house digital media infrastructures are guarded, remote, and designed to be as inconspicuous as possible, or whether it is because wires and sensors are buried underground, in walls, and located elsewhere out of view (unlike roads and bridges, which are very visible).

Thus, we need a set of conceptual tools to help us to not just make the servers, cables, and technologies of digital media infrastructure visible, but to make the relations produced by these technologies visible, a perspective that theorist and historian of media and communications John Durham Peters terms **infrastructuralism**.

Infrastructuralism

Infrastructualism is, at least partly, a punning variation on *structuralism*, a perspective that has defined a broad range of research in the humanities and the social sciences throughout the twentieth century. Structuralism has been associated with numerous prominent theorists, including such figures as Claude Lévi-Strauss, Jacques Lacan, Louis Althusser, and Roland Barthes. It often focused on how *language* 'structures' our world, creating the categories through which we make sense of our reality, experience, and relations. Words create oppositions and differences; meaning and ambiguity are made through the ability of language to communicate and make sense.

There are many limits to structuralism. Language cannot be said to define all there is. Peters wants to shift attention away from language and meaning as that which structures reality towards many of the most banal and everyday things we encounter. This is not to do away with the claims of structuralism, however, but it broadens them beyond language, arguing that technologies, acts, gestures, and other techniques likewise perform the differences that make up and order the whole way of life that is culture. Infrastructuralism's 'fascination is for the basic, the boring, the mundane, and all the mischievous work done behind the scenes. ... Infrastructure in most cases is demure. Withdrawal is its modus operandi, something that seems a more general property of media, which sacrifice their own visibility in the act of making something else appear' (Peters 2015: 33–34). Infrastructuralism is attention to details, devices, and standards: how they are ignored in daily life and yet shape the very possibility for what we see and experience. Infrastructures often escape our view because they seem 'boring'. It is in their mundanity and invisibility that infrastructures secure their power.

One of the main focuses of Peters' infrastructuralism is a stress on **logistical media**. 'The job of logistical media is to organize and orient, to arrange people and property, often into grids. They both coordinate and subordinate, arranging relationships among people and things' (2015: 37). So, for Peters, technologies like clocks and calendars are infrastructures for keeping time, for organizing the day and managing biological and ecological cycles (2015: 176). They are, to return to some of our earlier terms, **cultural techniques** that help order and manage through the production of differences. Google can be thought of in a similar way: 'Google ... provides organizational services such as search, mail, maps, document storage, calendars, translation, and reference, along with a whole host of curious side projects, and it does so around the clock and on a personalized basis' (2015: 325).

These logistical standards, when it comes to digital media, are similar to what Alexander Galloway (2004) terms **protocol**. Computers can only communicate with each other through agreed-upon standards, some of which you may have heard of, such as HTTP (Hypertext Transfer Protocol), SMTP (Simple Mail Transfer Protocol), FTP (File Transfer Protocol), or TCP/IP (Transmission Control Protocol/Internet Protocol) – HTTP is used for accessing and sending data for websites, SMTP for sending email, FTP for sending files, and TCP/IP for making a connection to the internet. For Galloway, these protocol systems are the primary way the internet controls and manages not only information, but users as well. They shape what we can say and how we can act via digital media, and they create a hierarchy of control out of the management and deployment of protocol. For Galloway, protocol must be accounted for when developing political strategies that challenge or contest how power is organized online. Galloway's attention to the specific protocols used by the internet point us back to how Peters understands infrastructure and its logistical capacities.

Peters' infrastructuralism is, perhaps, a bit different from some of the other studies devoted towards tracing infrastructures and relations I've mentioned. While, like Star and Ruhleder, he focuses on how infrastructures create relations, he also expands infrastructure out towards a wide range of seemingly banal devices and tools, such as calendars and clocks, not just bridges, roads, cables, and servers. The technologies Peters directs us towards are not intrinsically invisible but are easily overlooked given just how woven into our daily lives they are. These technologies are *differential* – they work to mark and perpetuate a system of distinctions and differences – *and relational* – they develop and maintain relations between the differences they produce (this is also one of the key claims of structuralist theory about language). As is clear from the claims of Galloway, these technologies are political, as the relations they produce are marked by power and control. And, especially, Peters points to infrastructure to examine changing relations in *space and time*, a focus he takes from the work of Canadian economist and media theorist Harold Innis.

Space, Time, and Empire

'Harold Innis', states Peters, 'was one of the first to insist that infrastructure should be at the heart of media theory' (2015: 18). Innis was born in

1894 and raised on a farm in rural Ontario, eventually becoming one of the earliest Canadian intellectuals to achieve global notoriety, not as a media theorist, but as an economic historian. Innis's early work was on natural resources, or **staples**, and how their geographical distribution determines the character of a nation. Innis argued that the economic history of Canada could only be understood through a close examination of its 'dirt', meaning its environment, its flora and fauna, and its geography. Through what he termed 'dirt research', which we would today refer to as fieldwork or ethnography, Innis argued that industries built around animals such as the beaver and the cod directly shaped Canada's economic life, along with the colonial relations that existed between Canada and the United Kingdom (see Innis 1930; Watson 2006; Young 2017).

Late in his life, Innis turned to another staple – paper. But this study of paper blossomed into a much larger investigation of the history of communication, and how the material infrastructures of communication shape the larger structure of a society, just as do other natural resources. In turning to paper and media, Innis claimed that every medium has its own **bias of communication**, which, for him, was either **time-biased** or **space-biased**. These biases play directly into larger social structures:

> A medium of communication has an important influence on the dissemination of knowledge over space and over time and it becomes necessary to study its characteristics in order to appraise its influence in its cultural setting. According to its characteristics it may be better suited to the dissemination of knowledge over time than over space, particularly if the medium is heavy and durable and not suited to transportation, or to the dissemination of knowledge over space than over time, particularly if the medium is light and easily transported. The relative emphasis on time or space will imply a bias of significance to the culture in which it is embedded. (Innis 1951: 33)

Innis is talking about something like the difference between writing on paper and writing on stone. Stone endures in time and is time-biased because of its durability. What's written on stone cannot be transported quickly because of its weight, however. Paper, on the other hand, can move very easily because of its relative lightness. But paper can be easily destroyed or become brittle and decompose after a few decades. Paper is, thus, space-biased.

A similar example can be seen with money and currency – and money is certainly a medium, even if we may not think of it as 'communicative' in the same way as writing on paper. Most currencies are comprised of paper bills or coins, not because of any intrinsic value they carry, but because they can move (or 'circulate') easily. Money is generally space-biased, and currency in active circulation degrades after a decade or two. But this is not always the case. The currency of a small island in the Pacific called Yap, which is part of Micronesia, is made of giant limestone discs called rai stones – massive rocks that are as heavy as a car (Goldstein and Kestenbaum 2010). Even if a rai stone is exchanged, it doesn't move from its physical location – one of these limestone discs is even submerged underwater. Instead, local knowledge about ownership changes, because the medium itself is time-biased.

For Innis, time-biased media sustain cultural traditions and social memory, while space-biased media support control over territory and maintain imperial relations over long distances. Innis thought that, ideally, a strong society would maintain a balance between time and space (see Innis 2007; also, Chesher 2009). Innis also saw the role of spatial or temporally biased media in the production of *colonial* relations, which he defined as the relation between *centre and margin*. The Canadian media theorist Jody Berland explains this nicely in her interpretation of Innis on newspapers:

> [Innis's] analysis of newspapers focuses on their importance in the production of centers – which produce and disseminate such materials and technologies – and margins – which provide the raw material for newsprint together with local skepticism about the knowledge thereby disseminated. ... Newspapers facilitated the center's power over the margins through productive relationships (wherein manufactured goods could be exchanged for raw materials), through the dissemination and influence of a particular mode of knowledge, and through the monopolizing ideology of the freedom of the press. (2009: 79)

Berland's reading of Innis is helpful for us in a number of ways. She brings together Innis's work on staples with his work on media and communication (which are often assumed to be separate), demonstrating how media rely on raw materials, which are taken from one geographical location (a 'margin'), transported elsewhere where they become a commodity (like paper) to be sold. When it comes to a newspaper or book, that paper is printed with symbolic content that emerges from major cities ('centres'), which are then transported back to the margins to be consumed. There is, of course, never just one centre and one margin, but a hierarchy of different infrastructural relations of raw materials, manufacturing, and the creation of 'creative' symbolic content. Berland shows how Innis's understanding of infrastructure is about relations of power. She also demonstrates how his understanding of media infrastructures always brings us back to questions of natural resources, the environment, and ecology.

Innis used his framework to describe the relations between Canada and the United Kingdom, and then between Canada and the United States. Canada was, historically, a margin to the centre of other economically and culturally imperial powers. Today, we can expand these centre–margin relations to various global supply chains that bring together mining (in places like Australia and Canada), manufacturing (in places like China), the generation of content (in the 'global cities' of the United States, Europe, and Asia), and the disposal of waste (in places like China and Africa). There are multiple centres and margins, even within the same country.

These relations are spatial. Berland's discussion of newspapers is about how colonial power is managed over vast distances, and how the movement of natural resources carries with it implications that are mostly about space. The media theorist Sarah Sharma (2014) has also provided a new way of using Innis to think of the kinds of centre and margin relations produced and legitimated by media, one that focuses on the management of time. Sharma is interested in how many of those who discuss digital and networked media claim that time is speeding up. Digital media, in extending everything spatially, seem biased towards instantaneity, leading towards a time that is constantly accelerating, and requires constant, active connection. Yet, Sharma argues, this seeming acceleration only exists for some people, and is maintained with technologies designed to manage speed and its experience.

One of Sharma's most vivid examples is that of taxi drivers:

A taxi may appear to be a liminal space … that people traverse and travel through rather than live in and make meaning. But cabs are only liminal in the back; there is a living subject in the front. It is the driver whose heart rate accelerates and adrenalin increases due to the diminishing time the passenger has left to catch a flight. … Some populations, like taxi drivers, are in motion but are inexorably tied to a structural position within capital. They are treated as mechanical pieces of the technology that 'cradle' the valuable and producing subject, the frequent business traveler. (2014: 64)

The relationship produced by the taxi is one of a temporal centre and margin. One body's speed is more important than another, and the speed of the centre (here, a business traveller), is reliant on and prioritized over the speed of the margin (here, a taxi driver). When it comes to digital technologies, this relation is entrenched with ride-sharing apps like Uber and Lyft, along with countless other service-based apps like TaskRabbit or Fiverr, all of which promise on-demand workers that are measured, scored, and tracked via the possibilities of digital media.

Rather than a uniform condition of accelerating speed, there are inequalities produced through the technologies we use to manage our experience of time, and many of us have to constantly adjust our experience of time and speed to manage our bodies, or 'recalibrate' them, in relation to the various centres that determine the temporal pace of life, something Sharma terms the 'biopolitical economy of time': 'Recalibration … accounts for the multiple ways in which individuals and social groups synchronize their body clocks, their sense of the future or the present, to an exterior relation – be it another person, pace, technology, chronometer, institution, or ideology. … Such recalibration occurs differentially and unequally' (2014: 18). This is *biopolitical* because it relies on the management and transformation of the biological capacities of the human body, regulating it and directing it, often in the name of 'optimally' shaping our physical capacities. Biopolitics is a concept derived from the work of Michel Foucault, who used the term *biopower* (1978: 143) to describe how a body was managed by statistics, forms of calculation, and other medical means to direct and conduct 'proper' forms of living. Technologies that manage our sleep and the pace of our lives are biopolitical, because they exert biopower over the capacities of our bodies.

SOFTWARE AND LOGISTICS

The examples of Uber, Lyft, and other app-based platforms introduce an additional dimension to our discussion of infrastructures, returning us to the importance of Peters' emphasis on **logistical media**. 'Logistics is the science of managing things in space and time', notes the architectural historian Jesse LeCavalier (2016: 32). While the material effects of infrastructures have, throughout history, been built into the physicality of the things themselves (so, the relations produced by a bridge or a road come from how that bridge or road has been devised; the forms of organization defined by a calendar come from how that calendar literally segments time), the logistical significance of digital technologies is usually built into *software* rather than hardware.

Logistics has its origins in the military, in which seventeenth- and eighteenth-century planners would attempt to address, on the one hand, the constant movement of troops and, on the other hand, the movement of supplies to keep troops fed, hydrated, and supplied. This model eventually migrated into business after the Second World War through the influence of cybernetics and the embrace of flexible labour and production. Technology would be used to manage raw materials and human labour, to exploit price differences in real time, to predict consumption patterns, and so on, all to generate greater efficiencies in production. So, as media theorist Ned Rossiter suggests: 'Calculations of movement, productivity, efficiency, performance. These are the regimes that govern logistical labor and life as they intersect with the software and infrastructure that comprise logistical media' (2016: 6). As LeCavalier has suggested, the drive for efficiency in these areas may cause those involved in logistical planning to 'see things like national borders, labor laws, and certain trade policies as obstacles to their ambitions' (2016: 4).

Logistical media, when it comes to digital media, can be exceptionally difficult to see. Their impact is maintained through software packages used for shipping and workforce management. So, logistical software can be used to determine how hours are parcelled out at a retail job, along with making and tracking orders and shipments for products. This software may seem incredibly dull and mundane, and it is often impossible to analyze given how software is proprietary and almost always impossible to investigate – a black box rather than something accessible. Rossiter, for instance, highlights the exceptional influence of the German company SAP, which claims that their digital infrastructures – their software packages along with the hardware required to operate it – are involved with 65% of all worldwide transaction revenue (2016: 51). This is a staggering part of the world's economy, and yet I imagine that very few readers of this book (not to mention professors and lecturers of media studies) are even aware that SAP exists.

These logistical infrastructures are a key component of what Nick Srnicek terms **platform capitalism**. 'What are platforms?' he asks. 'At the most general level, platforms are digital infrastructures that enable two or more groups to interact. They therefore position themselves as intermediaries that bring together different users: customers, advertisers, service providers, producers, suppliers, and even physical objects. More often than not, these platforms also come with a series of tools that enable their users to build their own products, services, and marketplaces' (Srnicek 2017: 43).

Again, we see how these platforms are relational. A vast range of platforms characterize digital culture. The most visible ones are, like Facebook and Google, often devoted to harvesting user data and delivering targeted advertising. But another significant platform is that of Amazon. As of 2016, Amazon was the largest employer of the digital economy, in part because it has developed an elaborate logistics network for the shipping of consumer goods and the hosting of web services. With the 2017 purchase of the grocery store Whole Foods (along with other aspects of the perpetual expansion into additional global markets), Amazon has demonstrated its desire to become a world-wide company devoted not merely to the selling of books, but to the hosting of web services, the shipping and sale of food, and a general platform for the movement, management, and sale of most consumer items.

Amazon's ventures into grocery stores should be expected. Jesse LeCavalier has highlighted how many of the innovations involved in global logistics are best seen in the transformations of supermarkets throughout the past decades. Bar codes, or Uniform Product Codes (UPCs) – first used in 1974 in a supermarket in Troy, a small city in western Ohio – make objects into data that can be scanned, identified, and accounted for, allowing stores to easily identify how much of a specific product is being bought, which can then shape future purchases in accordance with consumer demand. One of the easiest places to see the influence of logistics is in a Walmart store. Using logistical data, 'Walmart designs stores to function more as valves regulating flow than as reservoirs capturing it; they are containers, but they are also conduits. And because the distribution system is so tightly coordinated, the store designs minimize areas for stock and maximize floor space for retail. Products are not the only things always on the move: Walmart's entire system is always transforming – at different scales and speeds – as new stores are built and (sometimes) existing ones are vacated or remodeled' (LeCavalier 2016: 13–14). The various technologies found in grocery stores, such as self-service checkouts and consumer rewards programmes, are places where we can most easily identify just how software and logistics are reshaping everyday practices of consumption.

The politics of logistics are fraught. These changes have clear benefits for the corporations that use them, reducing costs, accelerating and streamlining production, and creating services and platforms that are necessary for capitalism to operate in today's world. But, some of the questions brought up about citizenship and sovereignty should recur here. For Ned Rossiter, with logistics software, the 'potential for escape, invention, and refusal become severely compromised' (2016: 84–85). Our systems are programmed to determine our behaviour and practices in ways that are simply ignored and are assumed to be an intrinsic part of our everyday lives. They are almost impossible to challenge or resist, in part because they are also operating at a global scale far beyond the abilities of an individual. And, as the state has ceded some of its power to these infrastructures, Rossiter argues, the implications of infrastructural power are more worrisome than is even visible to those of us attuned to infrastructure:

> This is not just a question of a state–corporate nexus, but a kind of institutional subsumption into infrastructure. Paradoxically and perhaps even perversely, the logistical state becomes in a sense depoliticized, because at the level of infrastructure there is 'less politics'. The depoliticized logistical state is not merely an abnegation of responsibility to outsourced corporates, but rather a technical determination of governance peculiar to the administrative and executive roles of government when they become baked into the infrastructure. (Rossiter 2016: 173)

Choices and decisions that were once clearly political appear to be less so the more they become a function of our devices and software. They appear less an object of political debate than an inevitable path we must follow. Rossiter isn't completely pessimistic about this transformation, though – it doesn't mean the end of politics, for instance. It just means that the place of political conflict may now be very different from in the past, and perhaps we now have to engage with issues of industrial design, architectural construction, and software coding for many political issues, rather than law and government.

CLIMATE CHANGE AND THE ANTHROPOCENE

One of the reasons this invisibility of software and infrastructure is a pressing problem is because of the imminent threat of climate change. Since our technologies require energy and natural resources, infrastructure is, inevitably, about our care, use, and cultivation of the planet. The term **Anthropocene**, proposed to describe our current geological age, refers to the role that human beings, via their infrastructures, have had in reshaping planetary ecology. As McKenzie Wark describes it:

> The Anthropocene is a series of metabolic rifts, where one molecule after another is extracted by labor and technique to make things for humans, but the waste products don't return so that the

cycle can renew itself. The soils deplete, the seas recede, the climate alters, the gyre widens: a world on fire. (2015: xiv)

The Anthropocene names how human activity extracts raw materials from the Earth in ways that do not 'metabolize' the energy that has been taken, used up, and transformed into carbon dioxide. The Anthropocene is marked by the increase in greenhouse gases like carbon dioxide, which is produced both by the burning of fossil fuels and by a general decline in global biodiversity as species die out (often because of human intervention). The changes associated with the Anthropocene, many fear, could lead to a radical reshaping of the planet in a surprisingly short time, making the Earth mostly uninhabitable (for human beings, at least) quite soon. These changes are directly related to the development of media over time – its reliance on minerals and plastics, for instance (Taffel 2016) – along with the massive amount of energy consumed by our infrastructures, a fact that has been the case since the industrial revolution but has accelerated exponentially with the rise and popularization of digital media (Miller 2015).

Richard Maxwell and Toby Miller, in their book *Greening the Media*, have forcefully set out the stakes that climate change and the Anthropocene have for media studies:

the media are, and have been for a long time, intimate *environmental participants*. ... The prevailing myth is that the printing press, telegraph, phonograph, photograph, cinema, telephone, wireless radio, television, and internet changed the world *without* changing the Earth. In reality, each technology has emerged by despoiling ecosystems and exposing workers to harmful environments ... (2012: 9, original italics)

This happens to be difficult to imagine because we're so often sold the idea of digital media as clean or energy efficient, or that something like an e-reader is environmentally friendly because it prevents the manufacture of books (which rely on the cutting down and processing of trees). But this is a myth that relies on how we imagine digital infrastructures to be weightless and immaterial. As Maxwell and Miller outline, a single e-reader's production (and disposal) requires far more energy and raw materials than a book printed on recycled paper. An e-reader uses 33 pounds of minerals, a book uses two-thirds of a pound. An e-reader uses 79 gallons of water to make, a book uses two. An e-reader consumes 100 kilowatt hours of energy to produce, while a book requires two. Admittedly, these estimates assume an equivalence between one book and a single e-reader, which can contain many books.

But an e-reader would have to download around 100 books before it makes up any environmental savings when positioned against a print book (Maxwell and Miller 2012: 63), and it also requires additional energy to merely operate.

Let's frame the energy use of digital media in slightly different terms, to hopefully demonstrate just how much energy is consumed by digital infrastructures. How much energy would you imagine is required to simply send out spam email, most of which is not read, and is instead filtered out by automated software? Some estimates claim that spam email consumes about as much energy as two million American homes and generates the same amount of greenhouse gases as three million cars (Bratton 2015: 94). This scale is gigantic, and shows us just how difficult it can be to imagine the effects of our technologies. The implications of climate change exist far beyond individuals, and seemingly exceed our awareness and agency. It seems like change has to come from governments, legal regulation, institutions, and new technologies. But, at the same time, Maxwell and Miller claim that we need to cultivate an 'ethical regard for the intimate bond of human and nonhuman nature', an ethical vision that relates our actions with care for others and for the planet (2012: 31).

A similar view can be seen in ecologist Timothy Morton's discussion of what he terms **hyperobjects**, which are objects like Styrofoam and plutonium that exist on temporal scales that far exceed human life and experience. 'Five hundred years from now, polystyrene objects such as cups and takeout boxes will still exist. Ten thousand years ago, Stonehenge didn't exist. Ten thousand years from now, plutonium will still exist' (Morton 2010: 130). The things we produce, consume, and throw away will be with the planet for much longer than we will personally, along with numerous generations to come. How can we imagine this scale to potentially do something about it?

The waste we produce includes digital technologies disposed of as electronic waste, or **e-waste**. E-waste is generally created in the Global North, and then shipped for disposal and 'recycling' in the **Global South**. Regulations in Global North countries often forbid the disposal of e-waste, as the chemicals and materials in computers, smartphones, and other technologies are extremely toxic. As Toby Miller describes, 'Businesses that forbid dumping in local landfills as part of their corporate policies merrily mail it elsewhere. In that "elsewhere", preteen girls pick away without protection at discarded televisions and computers, looking for precious metals to sell' (2015: 142). Our devices are made from minerals and materials that come from the Earth itself and which will eventually return there as well (Parikka 2015: 35). The 'metabolic rift' mentioned by McKenzie Wark is here ever more significant. How can we maintain some continuity between what we take from the Earth and what we return to it?

Many of those discussing climate change and media argue for the importance of artwork in visualizing the connection between media and nature (e.g. Hjorth et al. 2016; Miller 2015; Parikka 2015), in part because it's so difficult to imagine the larger implications of our technologies, and even harder to think of what to do about it. Contemporary art about climate change can help us envision and imagine how we are influencing the planet, as well as suggest possibilities for action in changing our destructive habits. One of the problems of how we imagine the environmental impact of digital media, however, is that we tend to think of the role of these technologies from a privileged position. As media theorist Sean Cubitt has pointed out, 'we are not all in this together. Indigenous people have borne the brunt of the digital boom, and gained least from it. The global poor suffer far more from pollution and environmental loss than the global rich; and much the same is true for the local poor and the local wealthy. … Environmentalism is a materialism. It demands that we understand what things are made of, and their connectedness, but also their disconnections' (Cubitt 2017a: 14–15). Or, as I've been suggesting, we need to look at the *relations* produced, along with their inequalities – the relations between centre and margin created and legitimated by infrastructure, relations that suggest some bodies should be cared for and others should be exploited and even left to die via contamination by toxic e-waste.

Our technologies are produced in countries like China, with raw materials mined from lands often held by Indigenous peoples, mined often through the breaking of legal agreements since land that was once thought to be 'empty' has now been revealed to be economically valuable because of the minerals buried underground. We use an iPhone or a MacBook for a few years, but Apple computers are designed so we cannot replace specific parts when they break (because they are very 'concrete' in the language of Gilbert Simondon). Once our phone or computer stops working, or once it gets too dated and slow (something hastened by yearly software updates that make it so we continuously need to upgrade our computers), we dispose of it. It is then sent back to China, or to Africa, where it may leak toxic chemicals into the ground and into the water. It is then left to those 'jobs' where scavengers pick through toxic waste to search for minerals that still have economic value for those in the Global North, all the while being exposed to the toxic effects of digital technologies. Needless to say, the relations shaped by digital media infrastructures are vastly unequal and are global in ways left unseen by popular imaginations of the internet as a global village, or as a metaphysical sphere of immaterial knowledge.

One way out of the problem of digital media and the Anthropocene may be to look at these marginalized relations, although it's not as easy as positioning a kind of unified environmentalist and Indigenous politics against the ecological effects of digital culture. Anthropologists Eve Vincent and Timothy Neale (2016), for instance, have demonstrated how relations between environmentalists and Indigenous peoples in Australia seem like they would mesh easily – both seem like they would be interested in maintaining the sanctity of land, preventing destructive and deadly practices of mining, and so on. Yet, in fact, they have always been 'unstable' because of different definitions of 'environmentalism' and different possibilities maintained by legal regulations about mining and land ownership. While, as Sean Cubitt (2017a) rightfully notes, the environmental politics of digital media need to acknowledge Indigenous and de-colonial political movements, an equivalence between these movements and environmentalism is not so simple.

The overview here is, perhaps, overly abstract, and to answer some of these issues requires specific negotiations that may, in the end, require us to challenge the capitalist emphasis on growth over sustainability. It may be that, in order to solve the problems of climate change, we have to question larger beliefs associated with technological progress and the ability to come up with a solution that still fits in with a capitalist worldview (see Klein 2014; Smart 2010). Most likely, the solution to climate change will not be a new, technological fix, simply because digital media and technology use energy and pollute in ways that we have only begun to understand. We have to put infrastructures and relations in the foreground, rather than let them be a background in which utopian technological imaginaries take hold of how we understand digital media.

CONCLUSION

Infrastructures are, above all, *relational*. It is in stressing the relational that we can see how infrastructures, while traditionally aligned with the state and territorial authority, are political structures, serving to unite disparate groups and keep others separate, often hidden through the seeming neutrality of boring or mundane objects and processes. One of the ways that digital infrastructures produce and maintain relations is through their role as logistical media, using software to manage and control the movement of physical bodies in time and space. This chapter also provided a brief overview of how infrastructure relates to the larger ecology of the planet, and how the challenges of the Anthropocene and climate change require attention to material infrastructures. This turn to the infrastructural produces a new kind of media politics, one that is absolutely essential for many of the larger political and social issues we currently face, but a politics that, as of now, has few clear answers, especially given just how essential digital media are in our daily lives.

AFTERWORD

WHAT COMES AFTER DIGITAL CULTURES?

There are many aspects of digital culture that I haven't covered in this book, or things that I've only barely mentioned, from the Internet of Things to Bitcoin and the blockchain, from hacking and Anonymous to the rise of far-right political movements incubated on internet message boards. I haven't discussed the promises and problems of crowdsourcing and crowdfunding, be it through platforms as diverse as Patreon, Airbnb, Uber, or any of the many start-ups that have followed in their wake. I haven't talked about recent discussions of artificial intelligence, robots, and what philosopher Nick Bostrom (2014) terms 'superintelligence', even though these issues follow from many of those covered in the previous pages. I haven't given answers for problems like the intertwining of digital infrastructures and climate change, in part because we don't have clear answers right now.

To review all aspects of digital culture would be an endless task, especially since we're still in the middle of the rise and dominance of digital culture. But the point of this book was not to give you a totally comprehensive overview. Rather, I tried to review a set of important concepts, debates, and themes, beginning with how we understand 'culture' and 'digital', extending out this view to histories of cybernetics and information, discussions of identity, aesthetics, and the political power of infrastructure. This involved going places that may not have much to do with digital media, but nonetheless provide the very foundations for how we understand and talk about culture and technology – and, by extension, our digital culture.

The story of digital culture is far from over, and these themes will likely remain relevant for some time. Not only do they tell us something about our recent history, but they also show that the concerns into which digital media intervene are fairly longstanding. These are questions we'll be discussing for decades, if not centuries to come (which may depend on, for instance, the eventual impact of climate change). Yet our technologies will eventually change. Soon, our computers may no longer be digital, and our concerns may shift as our devices are reinvented. As I write this, there's a great deal of emerging discussion about 'quantum computing', which has attracted funding from Microsoft and IBM, who are working in partnership with universities across the world. Quantum computing would rely on a completely different kind of processing than digital computers, and many speculations suggest that it would have significant effects in terms of security and encryption, along with creating smaller, faster, and different computers. Would we have an emerging quantum culture that supersedes digital culture?

It is, of course, too early to tell. But the point is, as it has been throughout this book, to look at what's happening in our world and begin to think about these events, developments, and speculations with the help of a wide range of theoretical tools. We should look towards the future with an eye to the past and look to the concrete while paying attention to the abstract. Doing so will lead us to revise our theories, to invent new explanations, to come up with new ideas and new possibilities. After we work to theorize our would and our technologies, we'll return to our technologies, devices, and everyday lives, and hopefully know how we might be able to intervene, change, or remake the world with what we've learned.

Our world is constantly changing. How can we understand these changes? What can we do about them? Where can we go from here?

GLOSSARY

The following provides limited, concise definitions of key terms that may be unfamiliar for some readers. Some key terms, such as 'culture', 'digital', 'affect', 'aesthetics', 'infrastructure', and a number of others, are not included here because of their extensive treatment within the book itself.

Anthropocene is a proposed term to describe the geological age during which humans have had a significant effect on transforming the ecology of the planet. It is characterized by increasing carbon dioxide levels from the burning of fossil fuels, the extraction and consumption of natural resources from the planet, rising temperatures associated with climate change, and the possibility of a near future mass extinction event caused by human activity.

Apophenia was originally proposed by German psychiatrist Klaus Conrad to describe early stages of schizophrenia, but today it refers to a general tendency to look for meaning and patterns in what may be random information.

Associated milieu is a term used by Gilbert Simondon to describe a specific environment linked to the operation of a specific technology. Some engines, for instance, are designed to work in water or in air, but not both. Water or air would then be part of that engine's associated milieu. This concept highlights how specific technologies cannot be completely separated from their larger environment.

Autopoiesis means 'self-creating'. It is used in variations of second-order cybernetics to refer to an act of differentiation that distinguishes a system from the environment in which it exists.

Base and superstructure is a classical Marxist concept in which the 'base', or mode of production, is contrasted with the 'superstructure', or culture and arts. Traditionally, the base is thought to determine the superstructure, a view referred to as *vulgar Marxism*. Raymond Williams, among others, has rethought this distinction to make the relation between base and superstructure more complex.

Black-boxing is a concept from the history and sociology of science, and refers to how the scientific, technological, and historical work involved in the construction of a device or object is ignored or rendered invisible once the technology seems to 'work' according to cultural assumptions about its function. Black-boxing can also refer to the general fact that consumers and users often do not know how digital technologies function, and these details are obscured or hidden from view.

Collective intelligence is a concept proposed by Pierre Lévy to describe an emerging form of knowledge that is not located in any one individual but comes from the development of 'collective' and networked forms of knowledge.

Concretization is the term used by Gilbert Simondon to describe how technologies move from the 'abstract', which involve interchangeable parts and functions, to the 'concrete', in which a technology or device is less customizable and more rigid. Most Windows-based computers, given how they often can be modified or reconfigured, are more 'abstract' than the 'concrete' MacBook or iPhone, which cannot be modified by everyday users.

Cultural techniques are material means for making and communicating symbolic distinctions that serve to order 'culture' and define cultural differences.

Determinism comes in many forms, such as economic, cultural, or technological determinism. In its most extreme, determinism suggests that one factor entirely 'determines' historical outcomes. Raymond Williams (1980) has suggested that 'determine' be defined as the exertion of pressure, which is a weaker and more useful way of imagining determinism, as it embraces multiple factors that may 'determine' culture and everyday life.

Digital dualism is a term coined by sociologist Nathan Jurgenson to describe a view that separates 'online' and 'offline' as different, incompatible things that are zero-sum.

Distribution of the sensible is the term Jacques Rancière uses to describe the politics of aesthetics, and how specific forms of experience are partitioned, resulting in differences in who can see, touch, or sense something, along with who can say something about it. Part of Rancière's politics of aesthetics involves understanding changes in the distribution of the sensible.

E-Waste refers to electronic waste. Computers, phones, and other electronic devices are often difficult to dispose of because they contain toxic chemicals and rare minerals, and are consequentially shipped globally for 'recycling', usually with unsafe conditions for those labouring in their disposal.

Entropy is a concept from thermodynamics that is a quantitative measure of disorder. In cybernetics, entropy is opposed to information, where information (as a pattern) measures order.

Epiphylogenesis is a term that Bernard Stiegler uses to describe the co-evolution of humans and technologies. It refers to evolution by external means.

Epistemology is a branch of philosophy concerned with knowledge and how truth or facts come to be known and judged as true or factual. In the history of science and technology, it often investigates how technologies participate in the generation of truth claims and scientific knowledge. Stated simply, it revolves around the question, 'How do we know?'

Essentialism and **anti-essentialism**. Essentialism is the belief that there is an 'essence' common to specific categories or things. When discussing identity, essentialism would suggest that there is an essence common to a specific gender, or a specific race. When discussing an object or technology, it argues there is an essence that particularly characterizes that class of objects or technology. Questions of essence, thus, are linked with the claims of medium specificity and ontology. Anti-essentialism, on the other hand, claims that there is nothing but pure diversity, and there is no essence that unifies particular identities, or that there is no necessary, formal aspect that results from the ontological specificity of an object or thing.

Extrastatecraft is a term from architectural theorist Keller Easterling. It refers to how digital infrastructures transform sovereignty so governance is performed by non-governmental bodies in specific spaces or locations.

Global South refers to non-Western countries often located in the Southern Hemisphere, characterized by exploitative colonial relations produced as wealthier and more powerful countries exploit poorer countries or geographical zones for natural resources and labour. This does not intrinsically include Australia and New Zealand, despite their geographical location, because of their links with Western culture and economy, and can include countries (or parts of countries) in the Northern Hemisphere.

Hylomorphism is a doctrine derived from Aristotle that suggests that matter (or *hyle*) is determined by the form (*morphe*) that inheres within it. Hylomorphism privileges form over matter and suggests that form can be isolated from matter. It is thus an 'idealist' rather than 'materialist' doctrine.

Hyperobject is the name Timothy Morton has given to objects that far exceed human life, experience, or knowledge, such as Styrofoam.

Icon is a name given by Charles Sanders Pierce to signs that resemble the object to which they refer.

Idealism refers to the view that immaterial forms, ideas, or informational patterns are more significant than materiality. It is the school of philosophy that argues that matter is secondary to thoughts or ideas that occur within one's mind.

Index and indexicality are part of Charles Sanders Peirce's system of signs, referring to a kind of sign that either points to that which it refers (which is also called *deixis*) or is a literal *trace* left by an object, which points back to the object that is no longer there. Used in theories of film and photography to distinguish light-based images (which are 'indexical') from digital ones (which are not).

Liberal humanism has many definitions, but generally refers to the modern Western belief that humans are fundamentally isolated individuals who rationally work in their own self-interest, which often involves competition in a market system. It argues that humans are fundamentally free, and that social progress should work to increase kinds of freedom.

Liminality is a concept from the anthropologist Victor Turner, referring to an 'in-between' or transitional state in which traditional rules are suspended. It is often used to refer to rituals or, when discussing digital media, games and virtual worlds.

Logistical media refers to media that segments, organizes, and manages bodies in time and space, often through quantitative standards and measurements.

Materiality, in this book, refers to the physical qualities of media, especially in their infrastructural capacities of shaping experience, sensation, and relation.

Mechanology is a French science of machines that exists at the intersection of philosophy and engineering. It is represented today by the work of Gilbert Simondon and his followers.

Medium specificity has two definitions. One definition comes from Marshall McLuhan and Harold Innis. It claims that each medium has specific cultural and political effects, which are often related to how a medium transforms relations in space and time. The other definition refers to modernist aesthetics and the belief that each medium has a form of expression that characterizes it in its specificity.

Metaphysics is, most broadly, a branch of philosophy concerned with the nature of reality, and thus contains within it ontology. Metaphysics is often contrasted with scientific and empirical thought and is also linked with spiritual concerns (such as questions about the 'soul' or god) that are not intrinsically grounded in physical reality. In the context of digital media, metaphysics often refers to beliefs that attribute a spiritual or theological dimension towards technological development.

Noosphere is a 'sphere' of 'mind' (or *nous*) that exists separately from the *atmosphere* and *biosphere*. It is central for theological views that suggest that human evolution leads towards the realization of 'mind' divorced from matter and resonates with ways of understanding digital media that are seen in theories of collective intelligence and the technological Singularity.

Ontology and **ontogenesis**. 'Ontology' is a branch of philosophy concerned with defining the essences of a thing or being. 'Ontogenesis' is a term derived from Gilbert Simondon to describe how essences are continually changing, often because of changing relations between objects or individuals, and privileges becoming rather than being.

Protocol is a concept elaborated by Alexander Galloway to describe the control implemented through digital communication standards like HTTP or TCP/IP.

Relational aesthetics is a concept devised by curator and theorist Nicolas Bourriaud to refer to a specific kind of participatory art, tangentially linked with the social, networked possibilities of digital media, that makes relations between people, within a gallery space, central for the form of an artwork.

Singularity (technological) is a concept associated with Ray Kurzweil, though he did not invent the term. The singularity refers to a point in the near future (usually around 2040) at which computers will surpass the capacities of the human brain, and humans will become merged with the technological, escaping their biology.

Structure of feeling is the term Raymond Williams used to describe what it feels like to live at a specific place at a specific time. The structure of feeling includes multiple, often competing perspectives, and is rarely something coherent or even consciously experienced by those living within it. Williams believed that art and literature are often the most valuable resources for examining the structure of feeling.

Symbol is the name Charles Sanders Peirce gives to signs that are conjoined by convention with the thing to which they refer.

Web 2.0 was a term popularized by technical writer Tim O'Reilly to describe the transition of the World Wide Web towards dynamic, interactive web pages and user-generated content.

REFERENCES

Abbate, J. 1999. *Inventing the Internet.* Cambridge, MA: MIT Press.

Ackland, C. R., ed. 2006. *Residual Media.* Minneapolis, MN: University of Minnesota Press.

Adorno, T. W. 1991. *The Culture Industry: Selected Essays on Mass Culture.* J. M. Bernstein, ed. New York: Routledge.

Adorno, T. W. 1997. *Aesthetic Theory.* G. Adorno and R. Tiedemann, eds., R. Hullot-Kentor, trans. New York: Bloomsbury.

Agamben, G. 1998. *Homo Sacer: Sovereign Power and Bare Life.* D. Heller-Roazen, trans. Stanford, CA: Stanford University Press.

Ahmed, S. 2006. *Queer Phenomenology: Orientations, Objects, Others.* Durham, NC: Duke University Press.

Ahmed, S. 2010. *The Promise of Happiness.* Durham, NC: Duke University Press.

Alberti, L. B. 2011. *On Painting: A New Translation and Critical Edition.* R. Sinsgalli, ed. and trans. Cambridge: Cambridge University Press.

Althusser, L. 2001. *Lenin and Philosophy and Other Essays.* B. Brewster, trans. New York: Monthly Review Press.

Anderson, B. 2006. *Imagined Communities: Reflections on the Origin and Spread of Nationalism* (new ed.). London: Verso.

Andrejevic, M. 2004. *Reality TV: The Work of Being Watched.* Lanham, MD: Rowman & Littlefield.

Andrejevic, M. 2013. *Infoglut: How Too Much Information is Changing the Way We Think and Know.* New York: Routledge.

Andriopoulos, S. 2013. *Ghostly Apparitions: German Idealism, the Gothic Novel, and Optical Media.* New York: Zone Books.

Apple. 2017. Apple Awards Corning First Advanced Manufacturing Fund Investment. *Apple Newsroom,* 12 May. www.apple.com/newsroom/2017/05/apple-awards-corning-first-advanced-manufacturing-fund-investment/

Arnold, M. 1993. *Culture and Anarchy and Other Writings.* S. Collini, ed. Cambridge: Cambridge University Press.

Azoulay, A. 2012. *Civil Imagination: A Political Ontology of Photography.* London: Verso.

Barad, K. 2007. *Meeting the Universe Halfway: Quantum Physics and the Entanglement of Matter and Meaning.* Durham, NC: Duke University Press.

Barrett, L. F. 2017. *How Emotions are Made: The Secret Life of the Brain.* Boston, MA: Houghton Mifflin Harcourt.

Bell, D. 2001. *An Introduction to Cybercultures.* London: Routledge.

Benjamin, W. 1968. *Illuminations: Essays and Reflections*. H. Arendt, ed., H. Zohn, trans. New York: Schocken Books.

Benjamin, W. 2008. *The Work of Art in the Age of Its Technological Reproducibility and Other Writings on Media*. M. W. Jennings, B. Doherty, and T. Y. Levin, trans. Cambridge, MA: Harvard University Press.

Bennett, J. 2010. *Vibrant Matter: A Political Ecology of Things*. Durham, NC: Duke University Press.

Berger, J. 1972. *Ways of Seeing*. London: Penguin Books.

Berland, J. 2009. *North of Empire: Essays on the Cultural Technologies of Space*. Durham, NC: Duke University Press.

Berry, D. M. 2011. *The Philosophy of Software: Code and Mediation in the Digital Age*. Basingstoke: Palgrave Macmillan.

Berry, D. M. and M. Dieter, eds. 2015. *Postdigital Aesthetics: Art, Computation and Design*. Basingstoke: Palgrave Macmillan.

Blackman, L. 2012. *Immaterial Bodies: Affect, Embodiment, Mediation*. London: Sage.

Blum, A. 2012. *Tubes: A Journey to the Center of the Internet*. New York: Harper-Collins.

Boellstorff, T. 2008. *Coming of Age in Second Life: An Anthropologist Explores the Virtually Human*. Princeton, NJ: Princeton University Press.

Bogost, I. 2012. *Alien Phenomenology, or What It's Like to Be a Thing*. Minneapolis, MN: University of Minnesota Press.

Bollmer, G. 2015. Technological Materiality and Assumptions about 'Active' Human Agency. *Digital Culture & Society*, *1*(1), 95–110.

Bollmer, G. 2016. *Inhuman Networks: Social Media and the Archaeology of Connection*. New York: Bloomsbury.

Bollmer, G. and K. Guinness. 2017. Phenomenology for the Selfie. *Cultural Politics*, *13*(2), 156–176.

Bollmer, G. and C. Rodley. 2017. Speculations on the Sociality of Socialbots. In R. W. Gehl and M. Bakardjieva, eds., *Socialbots and their Friends: Digital Media and the Automation of Sociality*. New York: Routledge, pp. 147–163.

Boltanski, L. and E. Chiapello. 2005. *The New Spirit of Capitalism*. G. Elliott, trans. New York: Verso.

Bolter, J. D. and R. Grusin. 1999. *Remediation: Understanding New Media*. Cambridge, MA: MIT Press.

Borschke, M. 2017. *This is Not a Remix: Piracy, Authenticity and Popular Music*. New York: Bloomsbury.

Bostrom, N. 2014. *Superintelligence: Paths, Dangers, Strategies*. Oxford: Oxford University Press.

Bourriaud, N. 2002. *Relational Aesthetics*. S. Pleasance and F. Woods with M. Copeland, trans. Dijon: Les Presses du Réel.

Braidotti, R. 2013. *The Posthuman*. Cambridge: Polity Press.

Brand, S. 1987. *The Media Lab: Inventing the Future at MIT*. New York: Viking.

Bratton, B. 2015. *The Stack: On Software and Sovereignty*. Cambridge, MA: MIT Press.

Brinkema, E. 2014. *The Forms of the Affects*. Durham, NC: Duke University Press.

Brown, W. 2010. *Walled States, Waning Sovereignty*. New York: Zone Books.

Brunton, F. and G. Coleman. 2014. Closer to the Metal. In T. Gillespie, P. J. Boczkowski, and K. A. Foot, eds., *Media Technologies: Essays on Communication, Materiality, and Society*. Cambridge, MA: MIT Press, pp. 77–97.

Bucher, T. 2012. Want to Be on the Top? Algorithmic Power and the Threat of Invisibility on Facebook. *New Media & Society*, 14(7), 1164–1180.

Bunz, M. 2013. As You Like It: Critique in the Era of an Affirmative Discourse. In G. Lovink and M. Rasch, eds., *Unlike Us Reader: Social Media Monopolies and Their Alternatives*. Amsterdam: Institute of Network Cultures, pp. 137–145.

Burke, E. 1823. *A Philosophical Inquiry into the Origin of Our Ideas of the Sublime and Beautiful with An Introductory Discourse Concerning Taste, and Several Other Additions*. London: Thomas McLean.

Burrington, I. 2016. *Networks of New York: An Illustrated Field Guide to Urban Internet Infrastructure*. New York: Melville House.

Butler, J. 1990. *Gender Trouble: Feminism and the Subversion of Identity*. New York: Routledge.

Carey, J. 1989. *Communication as Culture: Essays on Media and Society*. New York: Routledge.

Castells, M. 2010. *The Rise of the Network Society* (2nd ed.). Malden, MA: Blackwell Publishing.

Chesher, C. 2009. Binding Time in Digital Civilisations: Re-evauluating Innis after New Media. *Global Media Journal (Australian Edition)*, 3(1). www.hca.west ernsydney.edu.au/gmjau/archive/v3_2009_1/3vi1_chris_chesher.html

Clark, A. 2003. *Natural-Born Cyborgs: Minds, Technologies, and the Future of Human Intelligence*. Oxford: Oxford University Press.

Clough, P. T. 2008. The Affective Turn: Political Economy, Biomedia and Bodies. *Theory, Culture & Society*, 25(1), 1–22.

Combes, M. 2013. *Gilbert Simondon and the Philosophy of the Transindividual*. T. LaMarre, trans. Cambridge, MA: MIT Press.

Coté, M. 2014. Data Motility: The Materiality of Big Social Data. *Cultural Studies Review*, 20(1), 121–149.

Couldry, N. 2012. *Media, Society, World: Social Theory and Digital Media Practice*. Cambridge: Polity Press.

Crary, J. 1999. *Suspensions of Perception: Attention, Spectacle, and Modern Culture*. Cambridge, MA: MIT Press.

Crary, J. 2014. *24/7: Late Capitalism and the Ends of Sleep*. London: Verso.

Crypton Future Media. 2016. Who is Hatsune Miku? www.crypton.co.jp/miku_eng

Cubitt, S. 2017a. *Finite Media: Environmental Implications of Digital Technologies*. Durham, NC: Duke University Press.

Cubitt, S. 2017b. Glitch. *Cultural Politics*, *13*(1), 19–33.

Dale, J. P., J. Goggin, J. Leyda, A. P. McIntyre, and D. Negra, eds. 2017. *The Aesthetics and Affects of Cuteness*. New York: Routledge.

Davies, L. and E. Razlogova. 2013. Framing the Contested History of Digital Culture. *Radical History Review*, *117*, 5–31.

Dean, J. 2009. *Democracy and Other Neoliberal Fantasies: Communicative Capitalism and Left Politics*. Durham, NC: Duke University Press.

Deleuze, G. 1995. *Negotiations, 1972–1990*. M. Joughin, trans. New York: Columbia University Press.

Deleuze, G. and F. Guattari. 1983. *Anti-Oedipus: Capitalism and Schizophrenia*. R. Hurley, M. Seem, and H. R. Lane, trans. Minneapolis, MN: University of Minnesota Press.

Deleuze, G. and F. Guattari. 1987. *A Thousand Plateaus: Capitalism and Schizophrenia*. B. Massumi, trans. Minneapolis, MN: University of Minnesota Press.

Derrida, J. 1997. *Of Grammatology* (corrected ed.). G. C. Spivak, trans. Baltimore, MD: Johns Hopkins University Press.

Deuze, M. 2006. Participation, Remediation, Bricolage: Considering Principal Components of a Digital Culture. *The Information Society*, *22*, 63–75.

Didi-Huberman, G. 2003. *Invention of Hysteria: Charcot and the Photographic Iconography of the Salpêtrière*. A. Hartz, trans. Cambridge, MA: MIT Press.

Doane, M. A. 2002. *The Emergence of Cinematic Time: Modernity, Contingency, the Archive*. Cambridge, MA: Harvard University Press.

Doane, M. A. 2004. Technophilia: Technology, Representation, and the Feminine. In S. Redmond, ed., *Liquid Metal: The Science Fiction Film Reader*. London: Wallflower Press, pp. 182–191.

Doane, M. A. 2007. The Indexical and the Concept of Medium Specificity. *Differences*, *18*(1), 128–152.

Dobson, A. S. 2015. *Postfeminist Digital Cultures: Femininity, Social Media, and Self-Representation*. New York: Palgrave Macmillan.

Dollar, P. 2016. Segmenting and Refining Images with SharpMask. *Facebook Code*, 25 August. https://code.facebook.com/posts/561187904071636/segmenting-and-refining-images-with-sharpmask/

Doueihi, M. 2011. *Digital Cultures*. Cambridge, MA: Harvard University Press.

Douglas, N. 2014. It's Supposed to Look Like Shit: The Internet Ugly Aesthetic. *Journal of Visual Culture*, *13*(3), 314–339.

Dyer, R. 1997. *White*. New York: Routledge.

Dyer-Witheford, N. 2015. *Cyber-Proletariat: Global Labour in the Digital Vortex*. London: Pluto Books.

Easterling, K. 2014. *Extrastatecraft: The Power of Infrastructure Space*. London: Verso.

Edelman, L. 1994. *Homographesis: Essays in Gay Literary and Cultural Theory*. New York: Routledge.

Ernst, W. 2013. *Digital Memory and the Archive*. J. Parikka, ed. Minneapolis, MN: University of Minnesota Press.

Farman, J. 2015. The Forgotten Kaleidoscope Craze in Victorian England. *Atlas Obscura*, 9 November. www.atlasobscura.com/articles/the-forgotten-kaleidoscope-craze-in-victorian-england

Flusser, V. 2014. *Gestures*. N. A. Roth, trans. Minneapolis, MN: University of Minnesota Press.

Foucault, M. 1978. *The History of Sexuality, Volume 1: An Introduction*. R. Hurley, trans. New York: Vintage Books.

Foucault, M. 1997. *'Society Must Be Defended': Lectures at the Collège de France, 1975–76*. M. Bertani and A. Fontana, eds., D. Macey, trans. New York: Picador.

Franklin, S. 2012. Cloud Control, or the Network as Medium. *Cultural Politics*, *8*(3), 443–464.

Franklin, S. 2015. *Control: Digitality as Cultural Logic*. Cambridge, MA: MIT Press.

Frazier, I. 2017. The Pleasures of New York By Car. *New Yorker*, 28 August, 34–40.

Friedlander, E. 2015. *Expressions of Judgment: An Essay on Kant's Aesthetics*. Cambridge, MA: Harvard University Press.

Fuchs, C. 2015. *Culture and Economy in the Age of Social Media*. New York: Routledge.

Fuller, G. and C. P. Jeffery. 2017. 'There is no Zyzz': The Subcultural Celebrity and Bodywork Project of Aziz Shavershian. *Celebrity Studies*, *8*(1), 20–34.

Fusco, K. 2015. Voices from beyond the Grave: Virtual Tupac's Live Performance at Coachella. *Camera Obscura*, *30*(2), 29–53.

Galison, P. 1994. The Ontology of the Enemy: Norbert Wiener and the Cybernetic Vision. *Critical Inquiry*, *21*(1), 228–266.

Galloway, A. R. 2004. *Protocol: How Control Exists after Decentralization*. Cambridge, MA: MIT Press.

Galloway, A. R. 2011. Are Some Things Unrepresentable? *Theory, Culture & Society*, *28*(7–8), 85–102.

Galloway, A. R. 2014. *Laruelle: Against the Digital*. Minneapolis, MN: University of Minnesota Press.

Galloway, A. R. and E. Thacker. 2007. *The Exploit: A Theory of Networks*. Minneapolis, MN: University of Minnesota Press.

Gates, K. 2011. *Our Biometric Future: Facial Recognition Technology and the Culture of Surveillance*. New York: New York University Press.

Gehl, R. W. 2014. *Reverse Engineering Social Media: Software, Culture, and Political Economy in New Media Capitalism*. Philadelphia, PA: Temple University Press.

Gehl, R. W. and M. Bakardjieva, eds. 2017. *Socialbots and their Friends: Digital Media and the Automation of Sociality*. New York: Routledge.

Gehl, R. W., L. Moyer-Horner, and S. K. Yeo. 2017. Training Computers to See Internet Pornography: Gender and Sexual Discrimination in Computer Vision Science. *Television & New Media*, *18*(6), 529–547.

Gere, C. 2008. *Digital Culture* (2nd ed.). London: Reaktion Books.

Gibson, W. 1984. *Neuromancer*. New York: Ace Books.

Goffman, E. 1959. *The Presentation of Self in Everyday Life*. New York: Anchor.

Goldstein, J. and D. Kestenbaum. 2010. The Island of Stone Money. *Planet Money* [podcast], 10 December. www.npr.org/sections/money/2011/02/15/131934618/the-island-of-stone-money

Golumbia, D. 2009. *The Cultural Logic of Computation*. Cambridge, MA: Harvard University Press.

Grayson, N. 2015. *Rust* Chooses Players' Race for Them, Things Get Messy. *Kotaku*, 24 March. http://steamed.kotaku.com/rust-chooses-players-race-for-them-things-get-messy-1693426299

Gregg, M. 2011. *Work's Intimacy*. Cambridge: Polity Press.

Groskopf, C. and S. Slobin. 2016. Where Your Data Flows on the Internet Matters, and You Have No Control Over It. *Quartz*, 5 October. https://qz.com/741166/where-your-data-flows-on-the-internet-matters-and-you-have-no-control-over-it/

Grosser, B. 2014. What Do Metrics Want? How Quantification Prescribes Social Interaction on Facebook. *Computational Culture: A Journal of Software Studies*, *4*. http://computationalculture.net/article/what-do-metrics-want

Groys, B. 2016. *In the Flow*. London: Verso.

Guinness, K. n.d. For All the Young, Bored Male Artists. Manuscript.

Gumbrecht, H. U. 2006. *In Praise of Athletic Beauty*. Cambridge, MA: Harvard University Press.

Halberstam, J. 1991. Automating Gender: Postmodern Feminism in the Age of the Intelligent Machine. *Feminist Studies*, *17*(3), 439–460.

Hall, S. 1980. Cultural Studies: Two Paradigms. *Media, Culture and Society*, *2*, 57–72.

Hall, S. 2003. Marx's Notes on Method: A 'Reading' of the '1857 Introduction'. *Cultural Studies*, *17*(2), 113–149.

Halpern, O. 2014. *Beautiful Data: A History of Vision and Reason Since 1945*. Durham, NC: Duke University Press.

Hansen, M. B. N. 2000. *Embodying* Technesis: *Technology beyond Writing*. Ann Arbor, MI: University of Michigan Press.

Hansen, M. B. N. 2006. *Bodies in Code: Interfaces with Digital Media*. New York: Routledge.

Hansen, M. B. N. 2015. *Feed-Forward: On the Future of Twenty-First-Century Media*. Chicago, IL: University of Chicago Press.

Haraway, D. J. 1991. *Simians, Cyborgs, and Women: The Reinvention of Nature.* New York: Routledge.

Harvey, D. 2010. *A Companion to Marx's Capital.* London: Verso.

Hayles, N. K. 1999. *How We Became Posthuman: Virtual Bodies in Cybernetics, Literature, and Informatics.* Chicago, IL: University of Chicago Press.

Hayles, N. K. 2012. *How We Think: Digital Media and Contemporary Technogenesis.* Chicago, IL: University of Chicago Press.

Hayward, M. and B. Geoghegan. 2012. Catching Up with Simondon. *SubStance,* *41,* 3–15.

Hayward, M. and G. Thubault. 2013. Machinic Milieus: Simondon, John Hart and Mechanology. *Disability History Newsletter,* *9*(2), 28–33.

Hebdige, D. 1979. *Subculture: The Meaning of Style.* New York: Routledge.

Heffernan, V. 2016. *Magic and Loss: The Internet as Art.* New York: Simon & Schuster.

Hillis, K. 1999. *Digital Sensations: Space, Identity, and Embodiment in Virtual Reality.* Minneapolis, MN: University of Minnesota Press.

Hillis, K. 2009. *Online a Lot of the Time: Ritual, Fetish, Sign.* Durham, NC: Duke University Press.

Hillis, K., S. Paasonen, and M. Petit., eds. 2015. *Networked Affect.* Cambridge, MA: MIT Press.

Hjorth, L., S. Pink, K. Sharp, and L. Williams. 2016. *Screen Ecologies: Art, Media, and the Environment in the Asia-Pacific Region.* Cambridge, MA: MIT Press.

Hoelzl, I. and R. Marie. 2015. *Softimage: Towards a New Theory of the Digital Image.* Bristol: Intellect.

Hogan, M. and T. Shepherd. 2015. Information Ownership and Materiality in an Age of Big Data Surveillance. *Journal of Information Policy,* *5,* 6–31.

Honan, M. 2014. I Liked Everything I Saw on Facebook for Two Days. Here's What It Did to Me. *Wired,* 11 August. www.wired.com/2014/08/i-liked-everything-i-saw-on-facebook-for-two-days-heres-what-it-did-to-me/

Hu, T.-H. 2015. *A Prehistory of the Cloud.* Cambridge, MA: MIT Press.

Huhtamo, E. and J. Parikka, eds. 2011. *Media Archaeology: Approaches, Applications, and Implications.* Berkeley, CA: University of California Press.

Hui, Y. 2016. *On the Existence of Digital Objects.* Minneapolis, MN: University of Minnesota Press.

Huyssen, A. 1986. *After the Great Divide: Modernism, Mass Culture, Postmodernism.* Bloomington, IN: Indiana University Press.

Innis, H. A. 1930. *The Fur Trade in Canada: An Introduction to Canadian Economic History.* New Haven, CT: Yale University Press.

Innis, H. A. 1951. *The Bias of Communication.* Toronto: University of Toronto Press.

Innis, H. A. 2007. *Empire and Communications.* Lanham, MD: Rowman & Littlefield.

Invisible Committee, The. 2015. *To Our Friends*. R. Hurley, trans. Los Angeles, CA: Semiotext(e).

Jagoda, P. 2016. *Network Aesthetics*. Chicago, IL: University of Chicago Press.

James, W. 1890. *The Principles of Psychology* (Volume 2). New York: Dover.

Jameson, F. 1981. *The Political Unconscious: Narrative as a Socially Symbolic Act*. Ithaca, NY: Cornell University Press.

Jameson, F. 2015. *The Ancients and the Postmoderns: On the Historicity of Forms*. London: Verso.

Jenkins, H. 2006. *Convergence Culture: Where Old and New Media Collide*. New York: New York University Press.

Joerges, B. 1999. Do Politics Have Artefacts? *Social Studies of Science*, *29*(3), 411–431.

Jurgenson, N. 2012. The IRL Fetish. *The New Inquiry*, 28 June. http://thenewinquiry.com/essays/the-irl-fetish/

Kane, C. L. 2014a. *Chromatic Algorithms: Synthetic Color, Computer Art, and Aesthetics after Code*. Chicago, IL: University of Chicago Press.

Kane, C. L. 2014b. Compression Aesthetics: Glitch from the Avant-Garde to Kanye West. *InVisible Culture: An Electronic Journal for Visual Culture*, *21*, http://ivc.lib.rochester.edu/compression-aesthetics-glitch-from-the-avant-garde-to-kanye-west/

Kant, I. 1987. *Critique of Judgment*. W. S. Pluhar, trans. Indianapolis, IL: Hackett Publishing Compathy.

Katz, M. 2010. *Capturing Sound: How Technology Has Changed Music* (rev. ed.). Berkeley, CA: University of California Press.

Kelsey, J. 2010. *Rich Texts: Selected Writing for Art*. Berlin: Sternberg Press.

Kittler, F. A. 1990. *Discourse Networks 1800/1900*. M. Metteer with C. Cullens, trans. Stanford, CA: Stanford University Press.

Kittler, F. A. 1999. *Gramophone, Film, Typewriter*. G. Winthrop-Young and M. Wutz, trans. Stanford, CA: Stanford University Press.

Kittler, F. A. 2013. *The Truth of the Technological World: Essays on the Genealogy of Presence*. E. Butler, trans. Stanford, CA: Stanford University Press.

Klein, N. 2014. *This Changes Everything: Capitalism vs. The Climate*. New York: Simon & Schuster.

Krämer, S. 2015. *Medium, Messenger, Transmission: An Approach to Media Philosophy*. A. Enns, trans. Amsterdam: Amsterdam University Press.

Krapp, P. 2011. *Noise Channels: Glitch and Error in Digital Culture*. Minneapolis, MN: University of Minnesota Press.

Krauss, R. E. 2010. *Perpetual Inventory*. Cambridge, MA: MIT Press.

Krysa, J. and J. Parikka, eds. 2015. *Writing and Unwriting (Media) Art History: Erkki Kurenniemi in 2048*. Cambridge, MA: MIT Press.

Kurzweil, R. 1999. *The Age of Spiritual Machines: When Computers Exceed Human Intelligence*. New York: Penguin Books.

Kurzweil, R. 2005. *The Singularity is Near: When Humans Transcend Biology.* New York: Viking.

Lazzarato, M. 1996. Immaterial Labor. In M. Hardt, ed., *Radical Thought in Italy: A Potential Politics.* Minneapolis, MN: University of Minnesota Press, pp. 133–147.

LeCavalier, J. 2016. *The Rule of Logistics: Walmart and the Architecture of Fulfillment.* Minneapolis, MN: University of Minnesota Press.

Levine, C. 2015. *Forms: Whole, Rhythm, Hierarchy, Network.* Princeton, NJ: Princeton University Press.

Lévy, P. 1997. *Collective Intelligence: Mankind's Emerging World in Cyberspace.* R. Bononno, trans. Cambridge, MA: Perseus Books.

Lister, M., J. Dovey, S. Giddings, I. Grant, and K. Kelly. 2009. *New Media: A Critical Introduction* (2nd ed.). New York: Routledge.

Liu, A. 2004. *The Laws of Cool: Knowledge Work and the Culture of Information.* Chicago, IL: University of Chicago Press.

Lotz, A. D. 2014. *The Television Will Be Revolutionized* (2nd ed.). New York: New York University Press.

Luhmann, N. 1995. *Social Systems.* J. Bednarz, Jr. with D. Baecker, trans. Stanford, CA: Stanford University Press.

Lupton, D. 2016. *The Quantified Self.* Cambridge: Polity Press.

Lyotard, J.-F. 1991. *The Inhuman: Reflections on Time.* G. Bennington and R. Bowlby, trans. Cambridge: Polity Press.

Mackenzie, A. 2010. *Wirelessness: Radical Empiricism in Network Cultures.* Cambridge, MA: MIT Press.

Magnet, S. A. 2011. *When Biometrics Fail: Gender, Race, and the Technology of Identity.* Durham, NC: Duke University Press.

Manovich, L. 2001. *The Language of New Media.* Cambridge, MA: MIT Press.

Manovich, L. 2013. *Software Takes Command.* London: Bloomsbury.

Marwick, A. E. 2013. *Status Update: Celebrity, Publicity, and Branding in the Social Media Age.* New Haven, CT: Yale University Press.

Marwick, A. and d. boyd. 2011. I Tweet Honestly, I Tweet Passionately: Twitter Users, Context Collapse, and the Imagined Audience. *New Media & Society*, *13*(1), 114–133.

Massumi, B. 2002. *Parables for the Virtual: Movement, Affect, Sensation.* Durham, NC: Duke University Press.

Mattern, S. 2013. Infrastructural Tourism. *Places Journal*, July. https://doi.org/10.22269/130701

Maturana, H. R. and F. J. Varela. 1987. *The Tree of Knowledge: The Biological Roots of Human Understanding.* Boston, MA: Shambhala.

Mauss, M. 1992. Techniques of the Body. In J. Crary and S. Kwinter, eds., *Incorporations.* New York: Zone Books, pp. 455–477.

Maxwell, R. and T. Miller. 2012. *Greening the Media.* Oxford: Oxford University Press.

McClintock, A. 1995. *Imperial Leather: Race, Gender and Sexuality in the Colonial Contest*. New York: Routledge.

McLuhan, M. 1962. *The Gutenberg Galaxy: The Making of Typographic Man*. Toronto: University of Toronto Press.

McLuhan, M. 1964. *Understanding Media: The Extensions of Man*. Cambridge, MA: MIT Press.

McLuhan, M. 1995. *Essential McLuhan*. E. McLuhan and F. Zingrone, eds. New York: Basic Books.

Meek, J. 2014. *Private Island: Why Britain Now Belongs to Someone Else*. New York: Verso.

Merleau-Ponty, M. 1962. *Phenomenology of Perception*. C. Smith, trans. London: Routledge.

Miller, T. 2015. The Art of Waste: Contemporary Culture and Unsustainable Energy Use. In L. Parks and N. Starosielski, eds., *Signal Traffic: Critical Studies of Media Infrastructures*. Urbana, IL: University of Illinois Press, pp. 137–156.

Miller, V. 2011. *Understanding Digital Culture*. London: Sage.

Montfort, N. 2003. *Twisty Little Passages: An Approach to Interactive Fiction*. Cambridge, MA: MIT Press.

Moravec, H. 1988. *Mind Children: The Future of Robot and Human Intelligence*. Cambridge, MA: Harvard University Press.

Moravec, H. 1999. *Robot: Mere Machine to Transcendent Mind*. Oxford: Oxford University Press.

Morningstar, C. and F. R. Farmer. 1991. The Lessons of Lucasfilm's Habitat. In M. Benedikt, ed., *Cyberspace: First Steps*. Cambridge, MA: MIT Press, pp. 273–302.

Morozov, E. 2013. *To Save Everything Click Here: The Folly of Technological Solutionism*. New York: PublicAffairs.

Morton, T. 2010. *The Ecological Thought*. Cambridge, MA: Harvard University Press.

Moulier Boutang, Y. 2011. *Cognitive Capitalism*. E. Emery, trans. Cambridge: Polity Press.

Mulvey, L. 2009. *Visual and Other Pleasures* (2nd ed.). New York: Palgrave Macmillan.

Munster, A. 2013. *An Aesthesia of Networks: Conjunctive Experience in Art and Technology*. Cambridge, MA: MIT Press.

Munster, A. 2014. Materiality. In M.-L. Ryan, L. Emerson, and B. J. Robertson, eds., *The Johns Hopkins Guide to Digital Media*. Baltimore, MD: Johns Hopkins University Press, pp. 327–330.

Nakamura, L. 2002. *Cybertypes: Race, Ethnicity, and Identity on the Internet*. New York: Routledge.

Nealon, J. T. and S. S. Giroux. 2012. *The Theory Toolbox: Critical Concepts for the Humanities, Arts, and Social Sciences* (2nd ed.). Lanham, MD: Rowman & Littlefield.

Ngai, S. 2012. *Our Aesthetic Categories: Zany, Cute, Interesting.* Cambridge, MA: Harvard University Press.

Ong, W. 2002. *Orality and Literacy: The Technologizing of the Word* (2nd ed.). London: Routledge.

Otis, L. 2001. *Networking: Communicating with Bodies and Machines in the Nineteenth Century.* Ann Arbor, MI: University of Michigan Press.

Parikka, J. 2012. *What is Media Archaeology?* Cambridge: Polity Press.

Parikka, J. 2015. *A Geology of Media.* Minneapolis, MN: University of Minnesota Press.

Pariser, E. 2011. *The Filter Bubble: How the New Personalized Web is Changing What We Read and How We Think.* New York: The Penguin Press.

Parks, L. 2009. Around the Antenna Tree: The Politics of Infrastructural Visibility. *Flow*, 6 March. www.flowjournal.org/2009/03/around-the-antenna-tree-the-politics-of-infrastructural-visibilitylisa-parks-uc-santa-barbara/

Peirce, C. S. 1885. On the Algebra of Logic: A Contribution to the Philosophy of Notation. *American Journal of Mathematics, 7*(2), 180–196.

Penley, C. and A. Ross, eds. 1991. *Technoculture.* Minneapolis, MN: University of Minnesota Press.

Peters, B. 2016. Digital. In B. Peters, ed., *Digital Keywords.* Princeton, NJ: Princeton University Press, pp. 93–108.

Peters, J. D. 1988. Information: Notes Toward a Critical History. *Journal of Communication Inquiry, 12*(2), 9–23.

Peters, J. D. 1999. *Speaking into the Air: A History of the Idea of Communication.* Chicago, IL: University of Chicago Press.

Peters, J. D. 2015. *The Marvelous Clouds: Toward a Philosophy of Elemental Media.* Chicago, IL: University of Chicago Press.

Petroski, H. 2016. *The Road Taken: The History and Future of America's Infrastructure.* New York: Bloomsbury.

Pickering, A. 2010. *The Cybernetic Brain: Sketches of Another Future.* Chicago, IL: University of Chicago Press.

Preciado, P. B. 2013. *Testo Junkie: Sex, Drugs, and Biopolitics in the Pharmacopornographic Era.* B. Benderson, trans. New York: The Feminist Press at the City University of New York.

Preciado, P. B. 2014. *Pornotopia: An Essay on Playboy's Architecture and Biopolics.* New York: Zone Books.

Rancière, J. 2004. *The Politics of Aesthetics: The Distribution of the Sensible.* G. Rockhill, ed. and trans. London: Bloomsbury.

Rodley, C. 2017. Deep Muppet. https://chrisrodley.com/2017/02/01/algo-horror/

Rodowick, D. N. 2007. *The Virtual Life of Film.* Cambridge, MA: Harvard University Press.

Ronell, A. 1989. *The Telephone Book: Technology–Schizophrenia–Electric Speech.* Lincoln, NB: University of Nebraska Press.

Rose, N. 1999. *Powers of Freedom: Reframing Political Thought*. Cambridge: Cambridge University Press.

Rossiter, N. 2016. *Software, Infrastructure, Labor: A Media Theory of Logistical Nightmares*. New York: Routledge.

Rotman, B. 2008. *Becoming Beside Ourselves: The Alphabet, Ghosts, and Distributed Human Being*. Durham, NC: Duke University Press.

Ryan, M.-L. 2015. *Narrative as Virtual Reality 2: Revisiting Immersion and Interactivity in Literature and Electronic Media*. Baltimore, MD: Johns Hopkins University Press.

Salazar Sutil, N. 2015. *Motion and Representation: The Language of Human Movement*. Cambridge, MA: MIT Press.

Schmidgen, H. 2014. *The Helmholtz Curves: Tracing Lost Time*. New York: Fordham University Press.

Sconce, J. 2000. *Haunted Media: Electronic Presence from Telegraphy to Television*. Durham, NC: Duke University Press.

Senft, T. M. 2013. Microcelebrity and the Branded Self. In J. Hartley, J. Burgess, and A. Bruns, eds., *A Companion to New Media Dynamics*. Hoboken, NJ: Wiley-Blackwell, pp. 346–354.

Serres, M. 1982. *The Parasite*. L. R. Schehr, trans. Minneapolis, MN: University of Minnesota Press.

Sharma, S. 2014. *In the Meantime: Temporality and Cultural Politics*. Durham, NC: Duke University Press.

Siegert, B. 2015. *Cultural Techniques: Grids, Filters, Doors, and Other Articulations of the Real*. G. Winthrop-Young, trans. New York: Fordham University Press.

Simondon, G. 1992. The Genesis of the Individual. In J. Crary and S. Kwinter, eds., *Incorporations*. New York: Zone Books, pp. 297–319.

Simondon, G. 2017. *On the Mode of Existence of Technical Objects*. C. Malaspina and J. Rogove, trans. Minneapolis, MN: Univocal.

Smart, B. 2010. *Consumer Society: Critical Issues and Environmental Consequences*. London: Sage.

Solomon, D. 2017. One Year after Fleeing Austin, Uber and Lyft Prepare a Fresh Invasion. *Wired*, 7 May. www.wired.com/2017/05/one-year-fleeing-austin-uber-lyft-prepare-fresh-invasion/

Spinoza, B. 1994. *Ethics*. E. Curley, trans. London: Penguin Books.

Srnicek, N. 2017. *Platform Capitalism*. Cambridge: Polity Press.

Standage, T. 1998. *The Victorian Internet: The Remarkable Story of the Telegraph and the Nineteenth Century's On-Line Pioneers*. New York: Bloomsbury.

Star, S. L. and K. Ruhleder. 1994. Steps Towards an Ecology of Infrastructure: Complex Problems in Design and Access for Large-Scale Collaborative Systems. In *Proceedings of the 1994 ACM Conference on Computer Supported Cooperative Work, Chapel Hill, NC, 22–26 October*. New York: ACM, pp. 253–264.

Starosielski, N. 2015. *The Undersea Network*. Durham, NC: Duke University Press.

Stephenson, N. 1992. *Snow Crash*. New York: Bantam Dell.

Sterne, J. 2006. Transportation and Communication: Together as You've Always Wanted Them. In J. Packer and C. Robertson, eds., *Thinking with James Carey: Essays on Communications, Transportation, History*. New York: Peter Lang, pp. 117–135.

Sterne, J. 2016. Analog. In B. Peters, ed., *Digital Keywords*. Princeton, NJ: Princeton University Press, pp. 31–44.

Stiegler, B. 1998. *Technics and Time, 1: The Fault of Epimetheus*. R. Beardsworth and G. Collins, trans. Stanford, CA: Stanford University Press.

Stiegler, B. 2009. *Acting Out*. D. Barison, D. Ross, and P. Crogan, trans. Stanford, CA: Stanford University Press.

Stone, A. R. 1995. *The War of Desire and Technology at the Close of the Mechanical Age*. Cambridge, MA: MIT Press.

Taffel, S. 2016. Technofossils of the Anthropocene: Media, Geology, and Plastics. *Cultural Politics*, *12*(3), 355–375.

Taibbi, M. 2011. *Griftopia: A Story of Bankers, Politicians, and the Most Audacious Power Grab in American History*. New York: Spiegel & Grau.

Tarnoff, B. 2016. The Internet Should Be a Public Good. *Jacobin*, 31 August. www.jacobinmag.com/2016/08/internet-public-dns-privatization-icann-netflix

Taussig, M. 2012. *Beauty and the Beast*. Chicago, Il: University of Chicago Press.

Taylor, A. and J. Sadowski. 2015. How Companies Turn Your Facebook Activity into a Credit Score. *The Nation*, 27 May, www.thenation.com/article/how-companies-turn-your-facebook-activity-credit-score/

Teilhard de Chardin, P. 1959. *The Phenomenon of Man*. B. Wall, trans. New York: Harper & Row.

Terranova, T. 2004. *Network Culture: Politics for the Information Age*. London: Pluto Press.

Thompson, E. P. 1961. The Long Revolution (Part 1). *New Left Review*, *I/10*, 24–33.

Tiqqun. 2011. *This is Not a Program*. J. D. Jordan, trans. Los Angeles, CA: Semiotext(e).

Tkacz, N. 2015. *Wikipedia and the Politics of Openness*. Chicago, IL: University of Chicago Press.

Trottier, D. 2012. *Social Media as Surveillance: Rethinking Visibility in a Converging World*. Burlington, VT: Ashgate.

Turing, A. M. 1992. *Mechanical Intelligence* (Collected Works of A. M. Turing). D. C. Ince, ed. Amsterdam: Elsevier Science.

Turkle, S. 1995. *Life on the Screen: Identity in the Age of the Internet*. New York: Touchstone.

Turkle, S. 2005. *The Second Self: Computers and the Human Spirit* (20th Anniversary ed.). Cambridge, MA: MIT Press.

Turkle, S. 2011. *Alone Together: Why We Expect More from Technology and Less from Each Other*. New York: Basic Books.

Turner, V. 1982. Liminal to Liminoid, in Play, Flow, and Ritual: An Essay in Comparative Symbology. *Rice University Studies, 60*(3), 53–92.

Turow, J. 2011. *The Daily You: How the New Advertising Industry is Defining Your Identity and Your Worth*. New Haven, CT: Yale University Press.

Underwood, M. 2017. Exploring the Social Lives of Image and Performance Enhancing Drugs: An Online Ethnography of the Zyzz Fandom of Recreational Bodybuilders. *International Journal of Drug Policy, 39*, 78–85.

Vaidhyanathan, S. 2001. *Copyrights and Copywrongs: The Rise of Intellectual Property and How It Threatens Creativity*. New York: New York University Press.

Vaidhyanathan, S. 2011. *The Googlization of Everything (And Why We Should Worry)*. Berkeley, CA: University of California Press.

Vincent, E. and T. Neale, eds. 2016. *Unstable Relations: Indigenous People and Environmentalism in Contemporary Australia*. Perth: University of Western Australia Publishing.

Vismann, C. 2008. *Files: Law and Media Technology*. G. Winthrop-Young, trans. Stanford, CA: Stanford University Press.

Vogt, P. J., A. Goldman, S. Pinnamaneni, P. Bennin, and D. Marchetti. 2017. Friends and Blasphemers. *Reply All* [podcast]. 29 June. https://gimletmedia.com/episode/100-friends-blasphemers/

Wark, M. 2015. *Molecular Red: Theory for the Anthropocene*. New York: Verso.

Warner, M. 2002. *Publics and Counterpublics*. New York: Zone Books.

Watson, A. J. 2006. *Marginal Man: The Dark Vision of Harold Innis*. Toronto: University of Toronto Press.

Weber, S. 1996. *Mass Mediauras: Form, Technics, Media*. Stanford, CA: Stanford University Press.

Wiener, N. 1950. *The Human Use of Human Beings: Cybernetics and Society*. Boston, MA: Houghton Mifflin.

Wiener, N. 1956. *I Am a Mathematician: The Later Life of a Prodigy*. Cambridge, MA: MIT Press.

Wiener, N. 1961. *Cybernetics, Or Control and Communication in the Animal and the Machine* (2nd ed.). Cambridge, MA: MIT Press.

Williams, R. 1974. *Television: Technology and Cultural Form*. New York: Routledge.

Williams, R. 1977. *Marxism and Literature*. Oxford: Oxford University Press.

Williams, R. 1980. *Problems in Materialism and Culture: Selected Essays*. London: Verso.

Williams, R. 1983a. *Culture & Society: 1780–1950*. New York: Columbia University Press.

Williams, R. 1983b. *Keywords: A Vocabulary of Culture and Society* (rev. ed.). New York: Oxford University Press.

Williams, R. 2001. *The Long Revolution.* Peterborough, ON: Broadview Press.

Wilson, A. 2016. The Infrastructure of Intimacy. *Signs: Journal of Women in Culture and Society, 41*(2), 247–280.

Winner, L. 1986. *The Whale and the Reactor: A Search for Limits in an Age of High Technology.* Chicago, IL: University of Chicago Press.

Winthrop-Young, G. 2014. The *Kultur* of Cultural Techniques: Conceptual Intertia and the Parasitic Materialities of Ontologization. *Cultural Politics,* 10(3), 376–388.

Wolfe, C. 2010. *What is Posthumanism?* Minneapolis, MN: University of Minnesota Press.

Young, L. C. 2017. Innis's Infrastructure: Dirt, Beavers, and Documents in Material Media Theory. *Cultural Politics, 13*(2), 227–249.

Zahavi, D. 2003. *Husserl's Phenomenology.* Stanford, CA: Stanford University Press.

Zielinski, S. 1996. Media Archaeology. *CTheory.* www.ctheory.net/articles.aspx?id=42

Zielinski, S. 2006. *Deep Time of the Media: Toward an Archaeology of Hearing and Seeing by Technical Means.* G. Custance, trans. Cambridge, MA: MIT Press.

INDEX

Note: Page numbers in **bold** refer to terms in the glossary and page numbers in *italics* refer to figures. Page numbers followed by an n indicate end-of-chapter notes.